Paint Magic

Paint Magic

The home decorator's guide to painted finishes

Jocasta Innes

VNR VAN NOSTRAND REINHOLD COMPANY
NEW YORK   CINCINNATI   TORONTO   LONDON   MELBOURNE

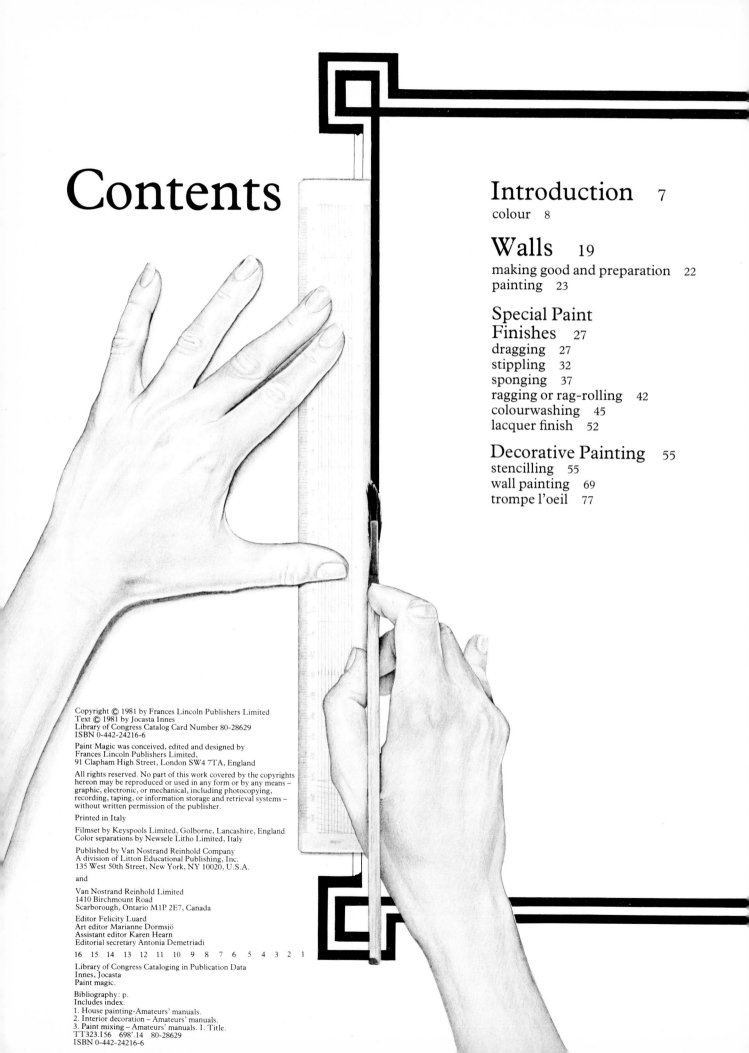

Contents

Paint Magic was conceived, edited and designed by
Frances Lincoln Publishers Limited,
91 Clapham High Street, London SW4 7TA, England

Printed in Italy

Filmset by Keyspools Limited, Golborne, Lancashire, England
Color separations by Newsele Litho Limited, Italy

Published by Van Nostrand Reinhold Company
A division of Litton Educational Publishing, Inc.
135 West 50th Street, New York, NY 10020, U.S.A.

and

Van Nostrand Reinhold Limited
1410 Birchmount Road
Scarborough, Ontario M1P 2E7, Canada

Editor Felicity Luard
Art editor Marianne Dormsjö
Assistant editor Karen Hearn
Editorial secretary Antonia Demetriadi

16   15   14   13   12   11   10   9   8   7   6   5   4   3   2   1

Library of Congress Cataloging in Publication Data
Innes, Jocasta
Paint magic.

Bibliography: p.
Includes index.
1. House painting-Amateurs' manuals.
2. Interior decoration – Amateurs' manuals.
3. Paint mixing – Amateurs' manuals. I. Title.
TT323.I56   698'.14   80-28629
ISBN 0-442-24216-6

Throughout a history reaching back to earliest times, paint has played something of a dual role. On the one hand it has had a practical application, acting both as a vehicle for pigment and a protection to the surface it covers. This is how most of us still see paint – coloured stuff bought in a can and applied with brush or roller, the important thing being to get the colour even and the surface smooth. This view is quite sound, of course, but to suppose that it sums up all the uses of paint is rather like imagining that knowing how to read and write enables one to knock off a deathless sonnet. It is less than half the story. Ever since the first shaggy hunter outlined a running deer with a stick dipped in wood ash, or puddled clay, or blood, for reasons we can only guess at, paint has served a vastly more significant and creative purpose – as a vehicle for the human imagination, a creator of illusions, the modest but endlessly pliable means of fixing a glimpse of loveliness for posterity.

The true originators in this field have always been the great artists, who plundered whatever technical resources were available to them, stretching these to new limits to suggest, on canvas, the tints of living flesh, the transparency of sunlit space, textures as different as harsh rock and fragile lace. But close behind these masters of illusion came the masters of the applied arts – designers, architects, decorators, legions of craftsmen whose vocation was to reflect contemporary standards of beauty and harmony in buildings, rooms and furniture. Naturally they borrowed freely from the techniques and materials used by the artists, developing these to suit their own ends. Thus we have the use of tinted glazes to enrich colour and give depth, of diluted water-based colours over gesso to create incomparably luminous tints, of a host of conjuring tricks with paint to suggest marble, tortoiseshell and other precious materials.

If one had to sum up the difference between this sophisticated use of paint and the more straightforward approach of the do-it-yourself painter, it would be in a phrase beloved of traditional decorators, 'broken colour', or, more succinctly still, 'distressing'. As every decorator knows, flat, uniform colour is inert and unyielding, while distressed or broken colour is suggestive, atmospheric, in a word, magical. Walls treated with distressed paint are volatilized, the brute facts of bricks and mortar dissolved in a fluent movement of transparent colour, shadows and highlights. The plainest box of a room, built yesterday, can be transformed with the right distressed paint finish into a place with a soul.

This magical, wand-waving transformation of our surroundings is in no sense beyond the reach of anyone who can read or hold a brush. Paint is cheaper than wallpaper, and distressed paint is often cheaper still, since

Opposite A dignified, masculine room, with the finishes used to stress architectural details rather than for their own sake. The upper parts of the walls, rag-rolled in thinned blue eggshell paint over a paler blue eggshell base, contrast with the marbling in the interval between chair rail and skirting and on the door panels. The cabinet is a junk-shop find stripped down to the original mahogany, the inside decorated with a tortoiseshell finish.

7

it is applied much thinned. It goes on very quickly, too, in fact there is often a race to get the room rag-rolled, dragged, stippled or sponged before the thin glaze of colour has time to dry. But does one need years of training to bring off one of these subtle and evocative effects? I can only reply that in the course of preparing material for this book, all sorts of untrained people have been moved to try their hands at unfamiliar processes. The results have been an unqualified success. Maybe a certain manual deftness, a cool head, and an appraising eye are a help toward achieving professional standards first time off. But the most exciting and instructive effects are often won by operating in blithe ignorance of all the rules. What is chiefly needed is a dash of venturesomeness, the will to get the materials together, and the curiosity to try them out.

Colour

To use colours beautifully you must *feel* them, fall a bit in love with them like that colourist of genius, Henri Matisse. 'Colours win you over more and more,' he said once. 'A certain blue enters your soul. A certain red has an effect on your blood pressure. A certain colour tones you up.' One does not have to be a painter of genius to revel in colours, but to use them resplendently one needs something of Matisse's commitment.

Colour, not necessarily bright, but always positive, is the most memorable feature of all the rooms and interiors I have enjoyed and envied, and is the first question that preoccupies me when I have a room, or several rooms, to decorate. I know that it is the one aspect of a room that will continue to affect me directly every time I walk into it. I am sure the same is true to some degree of almost everyone – after all young children react with uninhibited delight to colour, so isn't it likely that the need remains present in all of us, but that it has become diffident, or inhibited, or simply crowded out by other concerns? It merely needs to be roused and encouraged. Most people take the easy way out when choosing a colour scheme, playing safe, painting everything white or cream, getting a beige carpet because it 'goes with everything'. Colourless rooms do have their own chaste charm, but it is a pity that they should be the rule rather than the exception – think how many all-white, all-cream rooms you know – when colour is so cheap that for a modest outlay one can live surrounded by lusty reds, soulful blues and singing yellows, not to mention all the subtle mauves, and apricots and wry greenery-yallery shades between. It is rather as though, faced with a choice between a radiantly coloured Turner painting and an engraved sepia reproduction, everyone were to choose the engraving.

The most interesting discovery I have made about the use of colour in decoration is that colours that have been 'distressed' or complicated in some way are often more flattering to a room and its furnishings than flat coats of opaque colour. In other words it is not just the colour that matters, but the way it is applied. The flat, opaque colours of a conventional emulsion or latex finish tend to shrink a room, making one very much aware of its architectural defects. Brushing on a simple tinted glaze, a shade darker than the ground colour, improves the look of the place at once. Everyone knows how varnish brings up the colour of a pebble, or a bit of wood, but fewer people realize how much more impact the same trick has multiplied up to the scale of a room. By giving the illusion of depth, a coat of glaze makes the walls appear to recede, the room seem larger. I know it sounds astonishing, but it works.

The process of decoration is more like painting a picture than anything else I can think of, with the room as a blank canvas, and the colours of walls, carpet, rugs, furnishings and pictures as paints. Like painting, it is something that cannot really be taught; success depends on a sensitive eye, a readiness to experiment and to turn happy visual accidents – a vase of lilacs whose cloudy mauve lights up a corner of the room, a friend's patchwork coat left over the arm of a chair – to good use. Your eyes and your instinct are allies in the game, and these can always be made more aware and sensitive.

There is no better way of appreciating beautiful colour combinations than to look – but really *look*, with a relishing greedy eye – at the paintings of great colourists such as Bonnard, Matisse or Monet. Paintings by men like these embody more knowledge about colours and the way they work together than most of us can even guess at. But paintings are only a start – almost any arrangement of colours, formal or casual, is worth looking at in this noticing analytical way. A market stall, a line of washing, a fine Bokhara rug, a scrap of Chinese embroidery – food for the eye is to be found almost everywhere.

When it comes to turning theory into practice – painting your own room picture – the only way to find out whether particular colours really work together is to try them out, at least approximately, and to keep as many options open as possible while the place is still growing, coming together. Unless you are very rich (or very poor) your colour adventuring will probably be restricted by some expensive fixture that must be taken into account – usually a carpet. Never mind about that, it is useful to have a point of departure.

The most important colour decision to be taken in a room is nearly always about the walls. A room has a lot of wall surface and the colour must look happy with whatever fixtures you have. Tiny samples of wallpaper, or paint colour, are seldom much help in making up your mind about what you want, since any colour repeated over a large area is intensified to an unimaginable degree. Instead of using these, you could start by making up a still-life arrangement out of bits and pieces in all sorts of colours first – sweaters, book covers, anything will do. Group them near a window so you can look at them by natural light, and squint through half-closed eyes at the colours against carpet, curtains and other furnishings. This is a crude indication but it can help eliminate a few of the wilder notions that may have flashed through your mind. Next buy a tin of suitable white paint (mid-sheen for the majority of the decorative finishes, see page 214), mix up those colours you like and try them on the wall. A range of universal stainers [tinting colours or colorizers] will

A gentle room in both colour and mood, the walls lightly sponged in dark over pale umber-coloured emulsion [latex] paint. Panel lines in diluted umber emulsion add definition, while the woodwork has been discreetly dragged in matching colours. The floor shows how good hardboard can look painted and then decoratively combed in squares – here a grey-green diluted emulsion has been laid over a white emulsion base and combed with a homemade graining comb; the whole thing is finished with clear matt varnish. The Lloyd loom sofa has first been painted in a soft pink eggshell, and then striped with a thinned brownish-pink glaze.

give you most of the lighter tints. For rich, dark or strong colour, use the stainers with water only – mixing dark colours in wall paint requires a base colour near the one you are after, which could be expensive until you are sure what that is.

If the idea of experimenting straight on to the wall shocks you, use large sheets of lining paper. Mix saucers of different colours – making a note of the proportions of stainers – and slap them on to paper or wall in a position where you get a view of the wall colour juxtaposed with carpet or curtains. Then hang a picture over it, place a chair in front, and try out some different cushions. All this helps to suggest what the colour would look like as a background to the whole room. When you have whittled the possibilities down to one or two, leave these pinned up and just live with them for a few days. If after that time one colour gives you renewed pleasure every time you look at it, that's the one for you. The delight of paint is that if you still aren't entirely happy with the result after putting on the colour, it can be quickly and cheaply modified by superimposing one of the decorative finishes described in this book. Strident colours can be softened by dragging or sponging in a softer, or deeper, shade, or simply glazing with a creamy transparent oil glaze, 'thin' pastels can be made richer, drab colours given a lift, or dark ones lightened. A stencil in a second colour – either as a border, or a regularly spaced motif – would create an entirely new look. You could even lacquer the walls, or spatter them with black and white specks for a 'porphyry' effect if you don't mind the room looking somewhat monumental. If this seems a lengthy way of finding a pleasing wall colour, remind yourself that Monet was not too proud or busy to mix crushed brick into whitewash until he arrived at the precise shade he saw in his mind's eye, and that all this experimenting has cost time rather than money, and is vital training for your colour sense. Besides, living with the right, beautiful colours about you is wonderful – a constant uplift, like endless fine weather.

Having got the wall colour settled, you have blocked in the main outline of your room canvas, and the rest is merely filling in detail, and great fun. As before, go slowly, and keep an open mind. Coloured floors can look splendid. Very simply, you could stain plain wood planks dark green, or blue, as a background to old rugs. Or if you can't afford an old rug, why not paint one on the floor, in the mellowest, richest colours your imagination can supply? On the whole people tend to leave a room's woodwork white, or off-white – decorators hardly ever use pure white, they prefer it 'dirtied'. But woodwork painted a contrasting colour to the walls can look exciting, and dramatically alters the proportions of a room, tightening it up so that it feels smaller and cosier.

Furniture, decoratively painted, is another way of introducing colour – paint, used skilfully, is the best possible disguise for undistinguished furniture, or plain junk. Imagine a dull but useful little table, or cabinet, given a tortoiseshell finish. Or stencilled with a small diaper pattern for a filigree Moorish effect. Or given a sleek, pale 'lacquer' finish reminiscent of the furniture one sees in Hollywood comedies of the thirties. Picture frames are naturals for decorative treatment – marbling, tortoiseshell, sponging, spatter effects. Lamp bases, boxes, old trunks, coffee tables . . . with paint and decoration a whole mass of disparate items can be fitted into your room picture.

Colour vocabulary

The number of permutations derived from the basic primary colours is practically endless – at least if you have a sufficiently perceptive eye. And some of the semi-technical terms used in describing them can be confusing if you don't know what they mean. Hue for instance is what differentiates one colour from another – redness, blueness, and so on. It is used interchangeably with colour. The purity of a colour is its intensity, or the absence of grey in it. Pigment is what paint colours are made from, the raw material. Until the discovery of aniline dyes in the last century, pigments were made from natural substances, though these were often treated chemically to produce further colours. The oldest pigments were natural clays – ochre, sienna, umber, the brownish-reds – found in different parts of the world, and refined, and powdered. Nowadays most pigment is either wholly or partly chemical in origin.

Primaries are the colours from which all other colours can be derived – red, blue and yellow. Two primaries mixed together give a secondary colour – red and yellow make orange, yellow and blue make green, blue and red make purple. Two secondaries mixed give a tertiary colour – orange and purple make russet, purple and green make olive, green and orange give citron. A tint is the result of adding white to a colour, while a shade is the result of adding black. Tone is used to describe lighter or deeper versions of the same colour. Thus a deeper tone of red would be crimson, a much lighter tone would be pink. Value is sometimes used interchangeably with tone. Complementary colours are colours that when added together in equal proportions produce a neutral shade – for example, yellow and blue, magenta and green, red and blue-green – they are to be found at opposite points of a colour wheel. Some knowledge of all this is useful when making up paints from a limited range of stainers or acrylic colours. Mixing a little of one complementary colour with another has a softening effect – thus a little green mixed into a red will take the heat out of it, and vice versa. Any commercial paint colour that is too harsh can be softened by adding a little of the opposite shade on the colour wheel.

Qualities of colour

A common and quite useful division of colours from a decorator's point of view is into warm colours – those tending toward or containing yellow or red – and cool or cold colours – those inclining toward or containing blue. However, this division is not so straightforward as it might first appear. There are for instance warm blues (those with red or yellow in them, like indigo or duck egg blue) and cool reds (those with blue in them, like cerise), while almost every distinct colour you can think of can be given a warm or cool cast by adding a little red, yellow or blue as the case may be. Even white tends to have a blue or yellow cast, depending on its pigmentation, and this can affect any colour you mix with it. Thus the

13

A room inspired by traditional
Scandinavian and early American
interiors. Note how the combination of
strong colours shrinks the room and
makes it cosier. The walls have been
colourwashed by applying two washes of
diluted brown-red emulsion [latex] over a
white base, finishing off with another wash
in a red red. The woodwork is soft blue
grey eggshell beneath an umber antiquing
glaze. The door panels and the low chest
have been vinegar painted. For
information on the painted floorcloth, see
pages 150–51.

'brilliant white' paints sold everywhere today nearly always contain a high proportion of blue, to make the white look whiter, and are therefore to be avoided as a base for mixing other colours.

Most people know that warm colours cheer up bleak, north-facing rooms, and that light tints of the same colours make dark rooms look brighter too. The brighter warm colours are sometimes called 'advancing' colours – orange, red, yellow, magenta, emerald – as they seem to bring surfaces optically closer. The cold colours – dark green, blue, grey, purple – are 'retreating' colours, giving walls depth when they are dark, and a light, cool, airy feel in their lighter tints. Colour preferences are a highly subjective thing, but on the whole I think warm colours are easier to live with, and easier to mix together successfully. There is something high-strung and formal about many cool colours – I am thinking of some of the sharp, pale blues, greens, pinks and cerises popular with eighteenth-century designers such as Adam – which seem to demand lots of gilt and fancy plasterwork, and stiffly elegant furniture. But a clever mixture of the two is often very effective. A splash of ice blue, blue-pink or lilac can ginger up a collection of warm earth colours in the brown, russet, ochre range, while the colder blues and greens cry out for a bit of red, or a strong Chinese yellow, or rich buffs and browns. For ideas on brilliant colour mixtures, take a close look at such masterly examples of polychrome decoration as Persian and Moorish tiles, oriental rugs and batiks. The quest for the one colour that will bring a room sparklingly alive is one of the fascinations of using colours in decoration.

Colour media A very important aspect of colour is the way it changes character according to the medium, or vehicle, with which it is combined. Colours in a medium that dries flat, without shine or the slight 'fatness' given by oil or synthetic resins, look quite different from the same colours mixed in a high-gloss medium, or one that dries to a sheen. A lot of people, for example, make the mistake of trying to reproduce the colourful folk designs of old painted furniture, in today's much creamier, juicier paints. These modern paints never come across as vividly as did the originals, which were almost invariably done in a thin, flat, dry-textured medium that lets the colours speak for themselves. I have got close to these glowing folk colours by using acrylics in water, ground pigment in buttermilk, artists' oils in turpentine (which counteracts the oil), or universal stainers [tinting colours] in undercoat or flat paint.

Colour made transparent, by thinning it with water, or oil, or varnish, produces another effect again. Some colours are inherently more transparent to begin with – raw and burnt sienna, raw umber, Vandyke brown, Prussian blue, ultramarine, crimson and scarlet lake, viridian green, for example. All these are excellent for colouring transparent oil-based glazes, see pages 224–27, or for tinting varnish. One feature of colours in a transparent oil or varnish base is that they can be spread smoothly and uniformly, with few brushmarks. Colours in a water base, on the other hand, are usually purer and more vivid (oil tends to impart a

16

yellowy tinge) but they dry with a 'brushy' texture. This isn't noticeable with very pale colours, and gives darker ones an attractive and lively rustic look that makes a refreshing change from the perfectly smooth, opaque, flawless colour we are accustomed to.

In a section largely devoted to the heady effects of colour, it may seem perverse to devote a special sub-section to white, and its fashionable variant, cream. The fact is, although there is a lot of both around, they rarely seem to be handled properly. The point to be made about both white and cream walls is that the paint should be thick, pure and shadowless, and that this is arrived at only by giving the walls about twice as many coats as you might think necessary. I have known white walls given 9 coats, and very sparkling and dramatic they looked too, but 5 is just about enough according to the experts. Anything less will soon look dingy, and skimped, especially if the colour you were painting over was many shades darker, which it probably was.

White and cream

There is a strong case for choosing white, I think, where a room is of such architectural interest that introducing colour would be distracting. An example that comes to mind is the sitting room of a friend's house in the country, whose eye-catching, rugged, vaulted ceiling is believed to date back to a time when it was used as a monastic wine store. On the other hand, I have never shared the view that white is the only choice for rooms with exposed timbering. The low-ceilinged cottages that feature a lot of beams are not usually so well-proportioned that they can take such stark contrasts on walls and ceilings. So I was interested to find that in mediaeval and Tudor times these same houses very often carried bold painted designs on the interior plasterwork.

The *texture* of white and cream matters. A matt finish is most people's choice, since it makes a flattering contrast to polished furniture, gilt picture frames and so on. If you live in a town, however, you might consider using a flat oil-based paint to achieve this, rather than the usual emulsion or latex paint. It costs more and is harder to apply, but it is much more durable and washable. Unlike emulsion, which eventually becomes dingy and grubby, flat oil paint grows old gracefully, acquiring a sort of silvery patina that is rather attractive. The same goes for cream. Use emulsion for the ceiling if you like, but preferably not with a 'brilliant white' finish, as its pronounced blue cast could jibe with your walls.

Decorators, as a rule, go for off-white whites. 'I like my whites dirty, much more interesting,' one of them remarked briskly to me. If you look closely at an apparently all-white room that has been professionally decorated the point becomes clearer. Instead of a thick, uniform dazzle of white, you will probably find several minutely varied shades of off-white have been used, especially over panelled woodwork, on doors, cupboards etc. Different decorators have their favourite dirty whites. John Fowler, the late prestigious English interior decorator, used a white with a touch of raw umber, which gives a slight but perceptible pewtery tinge – pleasantly aged, and full of character.

Walls

19

alls not only define and shape the given space that is a room, they also make up the largest surface area, so that what you add to them in the way of colour, pattern or texture is bound to have a considerable effect. Too many people, however, make the mistake of thinking that treating the walls to the most lavish finish they can afford – handprinted wallpaper, adhesive-backed felt, pine cladding or panelling – will make the room come together and look good, regardless of shabby furniture and ill-assorted carpet and curtains. What happens in fact is that the room appears unbalanced and uneasy, with the favoured walls making themselves oppressively felt. Furthermore, should the lavish finish turn out to be an expensive mistake, which can happen even to old hands at the game, you are stuck with it. A wall finish should be cheap enough to let you approach decisions about colour and texture in a relaxed frame of mind, which is the state most likely to produce the right decisions. And it should be flexible, so that if the colour does turn out to be wrong for the room, or just difficult to live with, you can retrieve your mistake without too much labour. What is more, you should be able to change it all quite easily every few years – walls get a lot of wear and tear and one's tastes alter.

The short answer, as you may have guessed, is to stick with the time-tested, traditional solution to all these problems: paint. Paint is the most practical, the most flexible, and, I am increasingly convinced, the most interesting, beautiful, and, in some mysterious way, the most appropriate way to cover a wall. 'There is no limit to what you can do with paint', a master-decorator friend is fond of saying. I don't think the claim is exaggerated. By paint, you must understand, he does not mean simply the standard 3 coats of emulsion [latex] paint with which most of us are familiar. Emulsion paints are useful of course, but sticking with them exclusively does limit the range of decorative possibilities. Paint imaginatively and knowledgeably used, as it is by a professional decorator (in the manner of an artist rather than a do-it-yourself expert), can be made to produce a quite breathtaking range of effects – subtle, extraordinary colours, textures and patterns.

One advantage of not being an expert (that is, someone who has done several years' training in the painting and decorating section of the local college) is that one can approach the subject unhampered by tradition and come up with some unorthodox ideas. For instance, in the various dry and technical treatises I have read I have never seen it mentioned that most of the finishes I shall be describing go on more rapidly than a conventional paint job, that they give an elegant effect for a ridiculously small outlay, or that doing them is engrossing, even exhilarating. Nor is it mentioned that you don't need to use specialized equipment – improvised tools and materials can produce equally good results, though perhaps at some sacrifice of slickness and speed. And none of the books emphasize what to me was the most surprising discovery about these finishes – that they are not at all difficult to do. Possible exceptions are the higher flights of trompe l'oeil and mural painting, although even there you can bring off

Previous page Stencilled designs, especially ones as gutsy as these, often look most effective on walls with a distressed finish. Here, two thin gouache washes, each a vivid but slightly different orange, were slapped loosely over one another above a white emulsion [latex] base, to produce a deliberately brushy effect. The stencilling on top is a modern version of an 18th-century wallpaper pattern.

unexpected successes if you are not over-ambitious, and cheat a bit.

Learning to use these techniques has other, practical advantages. The more you know about decorating, the more powerful (in the sense of being able to control your environment) and independent you become. Take choosing a colour, for instance: knowing what to use to make your own colours opens up exciting possibilities. You can mix up colour to match or complement a favourite picture or rug, play about with different glazes to create a totally new and personal colour effect, blend woodwork colour to match walls, or add a squeeze of this and that to transform a commercial paint that turned out five shades brighter than you expected. It's a nice feeling to know that with a tin of suitable white paint – or a pot of transparent oil glaze [glazing liquid], if you can get it – and a battery of stainers [tinting colours] you can achieve just about any colour scheme.

As you go along you pick up all sorts of useful decorator's tricks. You find that some finishes make a room look larger, or sunnier, while others give the meanest little box of a place a sumptuous air. Try a rosy sponged-marble effect in a bathroom, or a tortoiseshell one in a cramped corridor. If too many cupboards and doors are the problem, 'lose' them by dragging them to match the walls. You can emphasize good proportions by stencilling an elegant border in a contrasting colour at ceiling level, above the skirting or baseboard, round doors and windows. Or, conversely, if achingly empty expanses of wall are the problem, break them up visually with stencilled borders at chair-rail height, or borders and motifs painted to suggest panelling. A fine collection of old prints, photographs – any pictures in fact – gain enormously in significance when hung on walls dragged two ways to suggest coarsely woven silk. It is a fact that 'distressed' colour finishes are more flattering than solid colour as a background to polished wood, gilt, rich colours and textures.

Versatility is the keynote to these finishes. If you are going for a cottagey freshness and simplicity, they can be as artless and understated as you like. Colourwashing – applying transparent coloured washes blurrily over white – is one of the prettiest and airiest effects I know; dragging or stippling gentle colours on a white ground looks appealing too. Alternately, by applying several layers of different coloured glazes on top of each other, you can achieve a lustrous colour which would not look out of place in a Venetian palazzo.

Most of the techniques I shall be describing are traditional, and have been used by decorators as well as artists for centuries, although as yet they seem not to have percolated through to the do-it-yourself level, remaining part of the repertoire of exclusive interior decorators. I only became aware of the more recherché uses of paint by accident when I came across a painter in the middle of dragging a room and questioned him about what he was up to. It looked simple enough, and the result was so attractive that I was fired with enthusiasm to find out more. The result – some years later and after much experiment – is this book, which I hope will leave readers better informed to tackle this most fascinating aspect of interior decoration than I was on my first attempt.

Making good and preparation

The ideal ground for paint is one that is hard, smooth, dry and clean. The nearer your walls come to this ideal the more easily paint goes on, the handsomer it looks and the longer it lasts. Dirt, grease and damp prevent paint from sticking properly, cracks and craters collect dirt and look unsightly, while flaky or crumbling plaster simply drops off the wall. It makes sense to ensure that the groundwork is in good shape if one is going to the trouble of putting on a special decorative finish. If plasterwork is rough and rugged, but sound, use a matt ground paint and a soft decorative treatment such as stippling, sponging or colourwashing, which are flattering to uneven surfaces. Most other decorative finishes need smooth, level walls to look their best, the shiny, lacquer effects especially, as these magnify surface flaws. As for stencils and wall paintings, they deserve the best foundation you can provide if posterity is to have a chance to enjoy them too!

Washing down

Walls, in cities especially, collect a lot of grime, dust and grease and should always be washed down thoroughly before repainting. Use a large cellulose sponge, warm water and a cleaning agent that cuts grease – for reasonably clean walls, a mild detergent solution plus a little household ammonia, for really grimy surfaces use a mild sugar soap solution that scours as it cleans, providing a good 'key' for subsequent painting. Sugar soap comes as an alkaline powder, to be dissolved in water. There are several commercial paint cleaners available, too, which are effective but more expensive than sugar soap or detergent. If the existing wall surface is glossy, give it the sugar soap treatment, then rub it down with fine sandpaper to remove the gloss. This helps the new paint to grip.

Brush down or vacuum over surfaces first – with wallpapered walls this is all you need do – to dislodge loose dust and cobwebs, paying particular attention to picture rails, along the tops of door frames, window frames, cornices. Brush the ceiling too, even if it is not being painted. Make up a bucket of cleaning solution. Wear rubber gloves, wrap a scarf around your head, haul out the stepladder and begin at the top right-hand corner of one wall, using enough water to shift the dirt but not so much that you soak yourself and the floor. Take one section of wall at a time and work down from top to bottom so you mop up dirty streaks as you go. After washing, rinse down with clean water to remove any traces of chemicals, alkaline substances, and so on, and wipe over with a clean rag. Let the walls dry thoroughly. In fine weather leave windows and doors open, in winter close the place up and have the room well heated – overnight should be long enough, but if in doubt give them another 24 hours.

If the walls are in reasonable shape, this is all the preliminary preparation they may need, apart from filling in the odd crack or two.

Stripping old paint and wallpaper

Small areas of flaking paint can be scraped off and sanded down until the surface is smooth. If there is still a noticeable step between the painted and scraped-off areas, mix a little all-purpose filler [spackle] with water to paint consistency, brush this over the rough surface and sand when dry.

A really badly flaking paint surface will have to be completely removed, using a chemical paint stripper and scraper. Follow the maker's instructions and remember to wear rubber gloves to protect your hands.

Similarly with wallpaper – if you are painting over this – the odd peeling corner can be stuck back with wallpaper paste, which can be bought in small quantities from do-it-yourself centres, but a paper in bad condition must be stripped off with chemical paper stripper to reach the flat paint or plaster surface beneath.

Repairs to plasterwork

Use an all-purpose filler [spackle] for filling small cracks and cavities in the plasterwork. Mix to a paste with water as directed on the packet, or buy it ready-mixed in paste form. A painter's palette knife [spackling knife] is handy for small filling jobs, being whippy and neat enough to give control, but an ordinary table knife can substitute. Wet the cracks with brush or sponge, pack in filler with your tool, leaving the surface of the filler a little raised or 'proud', then wipe off flush with the wall with a damp rag just after the paste begins to stiffen and set – 5 to 10 minutes. This is a painters' tip for getting an invisible mend without sanding down. Cavities should be scratched a little to give the filler something to cling to, and larger cracks raked out with a shave hook and slightly undercut to form a 'dovetail' with the filler for the same reason. These usually need to be filled in two, or even three, stages, allowing each layer of filler to dry hard in between. When the top layer has hardened, sand down carefully to level it off with the surrounding wall, using a medium sandpaper, followed by a finer grade.

Lining

Where plasterwork is generally a bit shabby, but not so bad as to warrant stripping it all off and replastering, papering over the walls with lining paper provides a smooth, taut surface for paint or paper. Butt join the sheets; overlapping them makes a visible 'seam'. Seal the paper with a thin coat of decorators' glue before painting or papering.

Primer and undercoat

A primer is generally used only on new surfaces, to seal the plaster before painting, but follow the advice given on your tin of paint. Apply a standard undercoat over the wall surfaces before painting with oil-based paint, to get the best finish. If you are painting out a dark or bright colour with a light one, you may need 2 coats of undercoat then 1 of the top coat, in order to get thorough coverage. Usually the first coat of undercoat is thinned a little to help it sink in and bind with the surface beneath. Dark top coats require a tinted undercoat, either bought or mixed yourself.

Painting

The best type of base paint to use for the wall finishes given in this book – with the exception of colourwashing – is a mid-sheen oil- or alkyd-based paint, although an emulsion [latex] base will still produce reasonable results. If your wall is currently covered in emulsion, the experts say that you can safely and successfully put oil- or alkyd-based paint on top, as long as the emulsion coat is at least six months old, so that any moisture retained in it has had a chance to evaporate. If you have any doubts about the compatibility of paints – it may not be easy to identify the existing wall paint – there are various sealers available that act as barriers and prevent trouble. Consult your paint supplier. *Note:* A silk or satin finish emulsion may *look* like oil-based paint to a casual eye, but it is quite different structurally, being water soluble and porous. Oil-based paint is used as a base for finishes not because of its sheen, but because of its imperviousness – non-porosity. For more information about paints, see pages 212–15.

Equipment Wide decorators' brushes – 100 or 125 mm [4 or 5 in]; dusting brush; white spirit [mineral spirits]; paint kettle or bucket; fine sandpaper; rags; sheets of plastic or newspaper; a stepladder.

Method Pile the furniture in the centre of the room, roll back carpets and remove pictures. Lay sheets of plastic or plenty of newspaper over the floor – as close to the skirting or baseboard as possible – to catch drips and spatters. Brush down the walls with a soft dusting brush before painting, especially if you have done any sanding first.

Decanting some paint into a bucket or painter's kettle is sensible. It means the bulk of the paint is not exposed to the air, so hardening and drying. Also a kettle, being light and portable, is easier to paint from than a full tin. Never dip the brush bristles deep into paint – just the first 2 or 3 cm [1 in] or so. Painters remove surplus paint from a brush by pressing gently on either side of the inside of the kettle, not drawing the bristles across the rim as most of us do, which leads to sticky deposits building up and falling back into the paint. For brushing on oil-based paint the correct hold is with the fingers gripping the stock of the brush, whereas for water-based paint one holds it round the handle. If a coat of paint doesn't flow out easily, it may need thinning with a little white spirit or water, as appropriate, but read the maker's instructions and don't overdo it, or your coats won't cover properly.

Walls are usually painted before woodwork, but after ceilings. Begin painting at the top right-hand corner of a window wall – so that your first mistakes won't show up. Paint a section about 1 metre by $\frac{1}{2}$ metre [3 by $1\frac{1}{2}$ ft] at a time, brushing out carefully to spread the paint film evenly, then 'laying off' lightly to smooth out brushmarks. Laying off is that light, final brushing over with a next-to-dry brush that makes for smoothness. On walls it is done vertically, on woodwork one follows the direction of the grain. As one patch of wall is painted move on down to the next, brushing it into the first. Painting should always be done methodically, but speedily, to keep the 'wet edge' going so that one patch doesn't begin to dry before you can get around to blending the edges in with the next. Clean up with a rag and white spirit as you go along (or a wet rag if using water-thinned paint); it takes much longer to do after the paint sets. If you have to break off before finishing a room, try to stop in a corner, so that there is no obvious join when you start painting again.

Allow the first coat ample time to dry hard – consult maker's instructions. For a superfine finish rub down each coat lightly with fine sandpaper wrapped round a block, to remove 'nibs', grit and specks of dust. Then brush down. More care is needed when painting walls with oil-based paints – being stickier and slower drying than emulsion paints they are more prone to attracting dust and grit. With some finishes – stippled, sponged, rag-rolled – this doesn't matter too much, but it would spoil a lacquered finish or a marbled one.

The application of these is dealt with under the individual wall finishes. For general information on glazes and washes, see pages 224–29.

Glazes and washes

Varnish over paint plays both a functional and an aesthetic role. Tough, hard and elastic, it creates a transparent protective film that shields soft finishes from dirt, moisture and daily handling. Hard paint finishes, such as gloss and enamel, contain their own built-in varnishes and need no further protection. However, the decorative finishes described in this book are done with softer paints – undercoat, flat or mid-sheen oil-based paint – which when thinned need to be protected with varnish to make them really washable and hard-wearing. And any water-based colour, such as a gouache, artists' acrylic or a wash of emulsion [latex] paint, will simply rub off unless sealed with several coats of varnish. The right varnish does more than protect; properly applied, it creates an immaculate, glassy surface that enlivens the colours beneath, just as water brings out the colours in a pebble.

Varnishing

Use polyurethane varnish, in a matt, semigloss or gloss finish, and keep a special brush for the purpose – either an oval varnish brush, see page 231, or a 75 mm [3 in] decorators' brush. Matt varnish dries almost invisible and so does not require a perfect surface, but a shiny one will magnify any dust or grit trapped under it, so the room should be cleaned and swept first, and after varnishing shut off until the surface is quite dry. Gloss and semigloss varnish can be applied more easily if thinned – 3 parts varnish to 1 part white spirit [mineral spirits]. See also page 120 for more information on varnish.

Tack rag However careful you are, minute particles of dust and grit have a way of settling on the 'clean' surface you are about to paint, or on wet paint or varnish as they dry. A tack rag – a rag made tacky by wringing it out in varnish – is ideal for giving walls a final wipe over before applying paint or varnish, and can be used to pick hairs and particles off a still-sticky surface. Take an old clean handkerchief, dip it in warm water and squeeze dry. Sprinkle it with white spirit [mineral spirits], pour on 2 or 3 teaspoonfuls of varnish, and twist and work the cloth to distribute the mixture evenly. Store the rag in a jamjar with a screw-on lid; if it dries out sprinkle on more water and solvent.

Special Paint Finishes

The word 'dragging' is descriptive of the technique. For a dragged finish a painted wall is covered – a narrow strip at a time – with a glaze or wash of transparent colour, which is then brushed down from top to bottom with a dry brush, 'dragging' off fine stripes of colour so that the ground coat shows through. The effect is of finely graduated lines, not regularly spaced as in pinstripes, but clumped in bands rather like a striped Indian madras cotton. It looks distinguished and a little formal, more suited to well-proportioned rooms in an urban setting than to cottage or farmhouse interiors. By layering different colours or dragging one colour over a contrasting ground coat, or by dragging first vertically and then horizontally, richly complex colour effects can be obtained, as well as a delicately textured surface. As a technique dragging is a decorative development of 'wood-graining'. John Fowler is credited with making dragged finishes fashionable in English country houses and mansions in the thirties, and it remains a popular treatment, especially flattering to fine antiques and pictures. The difference those fine stripes of thin colour make is quite extraordinary – they not only soften and enrich the basic shade, but space out the walls, so that the room immediately seems larger and less boxy.

Colours The country-house version of dragging leans toward sharp pastels on white for bedrooms, and restrained tone-on-tone combinations – always safe and handsome – of buff, blue or grey for the more important rooms. Fairly wild colour combinations can also work well – grey-blue over orange, warm brown over light blue. I am fond of dragged red walls, using a darkish tone over a warm buff. Red is a difficult, though heartlifting colour in decoration, and I think gains from 'distressing' in one form or another.

For an evenly dragged finish walls should be smooth (cracks and hollows filled, unsound plasterwork renewed, see page 23). To get the best results, dragging – and indeed all the distressed finishes described here – should be applied over a base of flat or mid-sheen oil-based paint; see pages 213–14. We are so used to matt emulsion [latex] paints for walls that it may seem strange to use finishes normally reserved for woodwork; however, these not only give a much tougher and finer finish, but also are non-absorbent, so that the coloured glaze slides on easily and doesn't sink in. Dragging a glaze over emulsion does not produce such slick, hairline stripes of colour and I wouldn't expect it to last so well, but it is a useful trick for giving a wall colour you have tired of a new lease of life.

Dragging

Preparation

Opposite Dragging makes a particularly sympathetic background to fine antiques and pictures. Here the flat dragged walls have had trompe l'oeil panel lines painted on them, to produce a recessed effect. The chair rail and skirting have been marbled, while the rest of the woodwork has been dragged in shades of white. Look carefully at the bottom two 'bookshelves' – in fact they are doors, painted in trompe l'oeil.

If you are dragging with a thin emulsion wash, the base coat must be of emulsion paint – flat or mid-sheen.

Materials for dragging

Glaze or wash For a slick, slightly shiny, washable finish, use transparent oil glaze [glazing liquid] or a mid-sheen oil-based paint thinned to transparency. For a softer, matt effect use thinned flat oil-based paint or, if British readers can't get hold of this, standard undercoat. A wash of copiously thinned emulsion [latex] paint produces a soft blurry stripe. This is harder to drag successfully because it dries quickly, especially in hot weather. See glazes and washes, pages 224–29, for more details and for instructions on thinning and tinting. Use universal stainers [tinting colours], see page 218, or artists' oil colours for tinting a glaze, and stainers, artists' gouache or acrylic colours for a wash. Mix up variously tinted mixtures and experiment with them on boards or paper or in a corner to judge their effect.

A glaze or wash must be applied very sparingly or it will run, so for a smallish room, say 3 by 4 m [10 by 12 ft], ½ litre [1 US pint] of full-strength paint or glaze should be adequate.

Brushes A proper dragging brush (with extra-long, flexible bristles that effortlessly clump the stripes of colour – see page 232) costs about three times as much as a conventional large paint brush, and is available only at specialist trade suppliers or speciality paint stores, but it does give a more expert-looking and emphatic finish. If you plan to do a lot of dragging and can find this type of brush, it is worthwhile buying one. Get the largest size you can afford, as it will speed up the work considerably. If the cost puts you off, you can also use a clean, wide, standard paintbrush for dragging, 100 or 125 mm [4 or 5 in] and get a perfectly good result. You need a second wide brush for applying the glaze.

Other equipment You need white spirit [mineral spirits] for thinning glaze; a wash is thinned with water. Liquid drier is sometimes useful for fixing a very runny glaze. Glycerine, bought from a chemist or druggist, may help to keep an emulsion wash malleable longer.

A shallow wide tin is handy for mixing and this can hold the glaze or wash while you are working. Otherwise use a paint kettle, roller tray, or bucket. Colours can be mixed with an old brush, stick or wooden spoon. Keep lots of clean rags to wipe the dragging brush with. A stepladder, stable and sturdy, is essential.

Method Dragging works best with two people, one applying the glaze or wash, the other dragging it off again. I have done it myself singlehanded, but it is pretty brisk work as you need to 'keep the edge wet', as painters say – in other words you must apply your band of colour, brush it out evenly, then run up and down the ladder dragging it, and be ready to apply another band before the first one begins to set. If the edge is *not* wet you get a build-up of colour at the overlap point, producing a rather patchy final effect. Dragging with transparent oil glaze is somewhat easier than with thinned paint in this respect, since it remains workable longer. (A wash dries very quickly.) If you are dragging on your own, or you are pushed for time, aim to complete one whole wall, ending up in the corner. It is not always possible to mix up a second batch of glaze that matches the first exactly, and while this hardly shows on two adjacent walls, a demarcation line halfway across would be noticeable.

What follows is hard work, but not difficult. Painter A, using a wide standard brush, applies a narrow vertical band of colour – about 45 cm [18 in] wide is what experts recommend – from ceiling or cornice to skirting board or baseboard. Keep the glaze or wash to a thin film or it will tend to run. Transparent oil glaze is easy to drag, but if a glaze of thinned oil-based paint is over-thinned or applied too heavily the dragged stripes may merge together again. If this happens, try putting less glaze on the wall, and if still in trouble add one teaspoon of drier to $\frac{1}{2}$ litre [1 US pint] of glaze mixture. Don't add drier to a wash; a little more emulsion may help.

As soon as the strip of colour has been applied evenly, Painter B, armed with a dragging brush, clambers up the stepladder (set at a slight angle to the wall to aid descent), touches the tips of the brush bristles to the top of the wall and then brings the brush down with as steady and even pressure as possible while simultaneously descending the stepladder. It is a good idea to start dragging where a natural vertical exists already, for example alongside a door or window, or in a corner. Dragging a plumb-straight line is a real Zen target – try too hard and your brush invariably wobbles rebelliously. Attentive but relaxed is the state to aim for. Keep the bristles touching the wall surface firmly but lightly; don't scrub at it or you will get blotches. Consciously relax your pressure on the brush at both top and bottom of the wall because this is where colour tends to build up. The same applies to natural obstacles like light switches, door and window frames, mantelpieces. Wipe the dragging brush on rags every couple of strokes or so, to prevent it from becoming so loaded with glaze that it puts colour on instead of dragging it off.

People who find dragging one continuous stroke down a whole wall beyond them physically can cheat by dragging in two movements – from top to about two-thirds down, then from bottom upwards, feathering off adroitly at the meeting place. The trick is to stagger the meeting point as you move across the walls, so you don't get a continuous belt of fluffy dragging.

Painter A should be applying a second band of colour while B is dragging the first, and so on right round the room. If A has a spare moment it can be usefully spent wiping surplus glaze off woodwork or cornice. Transparent oil glaze usually takes several days to dry hard but wipes off more readily in the first half-hour or so. Build-ups of glaze at the top and bottom of the wall should be feathered out at once with a dry brush, and hard lines, splodges or missed patches gently treated in the same way. At this stage it is a common experience to see nothing but

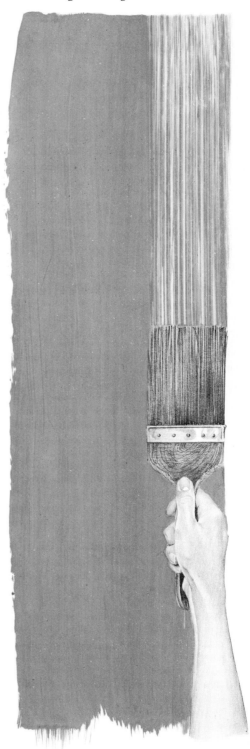

Over There is no end to the ways in which you can modify a base colour by applying a tinted glaze over it, as these examples of dragging demonstrate.

Below Hold the dragging brush in a firm but relaxed grip, and steadily draw it down through the wet glaze or wash.

29

mistakes, the slightly swerving stripes where the phone rang, or the kids rushed in. I *promise* you that once your pictures and furniture are back in place, any irregularities will be almost undetectable.

Leave transparent oil glaze to dry for a day or two. It will look shiny when freshly applied, but tones down to a subdued sheen when dry. Thinned paint dries considerably faster; although it doesn't produce quite the same crisp finish as transparent oil glaze, in some ways it is easier to handle, brushing out faster and dragging off smoothly. A wash produces a very subtle effect and dries almost immediately.

Two-directional dragging Transparent oil glaze is a good choice for two-directional dragging (that is, working horizontally as well as vertically), as the hair-fine ridges it leaves give a pronounced woven texture, remarkably similar to a handwoven Thai silk. Horizontal dragging is done in much the same way, except that it isn't necessary to glaze and drag a whole width of wall at a time. The wall surface will already be sufficiently 'busy', thanks to the previous vertical dragged coat, to make any joins invisible.

Varnish Professional decorators usually complete dragged walls (indeed most decorative finishes) with a coat of clear matt varnish, as a protection against wear and tear or washing down. It will look better longer if you do, but maybe you don't want any finish, however beautiful, to last more than a few years. Besides, if it starts looking shabby, you can always mix up another glaze or wash and drag a completely new look over the old one.

Stippling

Stippling has been practised by generations of decorators to soften colours and eliminate brushmarks from painted walls or woodwork. Using a large, fine stippling brush, the painter went over newly applied paintwork closely and quickly, to distribute the wet paint as evenly as possible, creating a matt, just perceptibly grainy texture known as 'orange peel'. A decorative stippled finish can be achieved with a stippling brush or soft wad of cloth or a roller, pressed firmly against an area of thinly applied wet glaze, so that specks of glaze are lifted off as it is removed to reveal the ground colour beneath. Depending on the tools used the effect varies from a fine freckle of colour to a soft mottling. Stippled walls make a flattering, uninsistent background to any sort of furnishings and look well in any room.

Brush and pad stippling Brush stippling gives the most delicate, even finish, like the bloom of colour on a peach. It is slow and tiring to do, however, and best reserved, I think, for small areas, woodwork or furniture. The brushes, too, are expensive as brushes go, though an ordinary painter's dusting brush makes a cheap substitute. Stippling with wads of soft cloth gives an effect halfway to rag-rolling, see pages 42–5, but tighter and more uniform.

Roller stippling Stippling with a roller goes much faster than brush or pad stippling, but requires more care to prevent skids and keep an even texture. A fluffy roller head gives a texture comparable to brush stippling, while a coarse polystyrene head leaves a slightly more granular impression and is also harder to control.

Colours

Stippling is usually done in transparent colours over a white or light-coloured base coat. Just enough of the base colour shows through to soften and lighten the glaze, so that raspberry red over white will appear as deep pink, coffee brown over cream as *café au lait*, and so on. Pastel colours are attractive and make a particularly good background for stencils.

An interesting variant of the technique, popular in the thirties, was to stipple an opaque coat (usually white or cream) over a bright and shiny base colour, such as scarlet, emerald green or cobalt blue. An opaque coat used in this way is usually called a 'scumble' (not to be confused with the transparent oil glaze sometimes sold as scumble glaze). The effect of tiny flecks of shiny colour surfacing through a matt, opaque scumble is an appealing one, but it must be done with a brush and so is probably best kept for furniture – though it is a feasible way of softening a shiny wall finish you have grown tired of. Another thirties trick was to use stippling to blend and shade bands of different wall colour into each other, creating the cloudy pastel effects that were so popular in hotel powder rooms, cinemas and cocktail bars. Overall stippling – a brush would have been used – allows one colour to merge into another gradually and almost imperceptibly, with no demarcation line.

Preparation

Wall surfaces should be sound and reasonably smooth, though bumps and cracks won't be so obvious as with a directional finish such as dragging. It is important, however, that the ground coat be a non-porous paint for the stippling to register effectively and evenly. One coat of oil-based paint with a mid-sheen finish over one of undercoat gives the right kind of base. Roller stippling, being coarser and bolder, can be done over a ground of emulsion [latex] paint, but the results will be patchier since a water-based paint will soak up the glaze unevenly.

Materials for stippling

Glaze Transparent oil glaze [glazing liquid], or a glaze of thinned oil-based flat paint, undercoat or mid-sheen finish, see pages 224–27, can all be used for the stippling coat depending on whether you want a shiny or matt finish. As for dragging, $\frac{1}{2}$ litre [1 US pint] of any of these should glaze a small room. Stippling with a wash of emulsion [latex] paint is not easy to manage because it dries so quickly – I have used a damp sponge to stipple this with quite uniform and attractive results, but whether this is stippling or sponging is open to question.

Use universal stainers [tinting colours] or artists' oil colours to tint the glaze yourself. See pages 225–26 for instructions on thinning and tinting. Note, glazes made of diluted paint tinted with stainers give a slightly

Over Stippling is a delicate, restful effect, providing just enough texture to make painted walls look interesting, and adding an air of quiet elegance to the sitting room of a house in the country.

33

different effect from tinted transparent oil glaze. They look softer, muzzier and less glowing, because of the white pigment on which most paints are based.

Tools These depend on which type of stippling you have decided upon. Stippling brushes come in various sizes, the largest being the most time-saving for wall treatments. A roller should be the textured variety, lambswool, mohair (or synthetic equivalent) or coarse polystyrene, *not* the smooth foam sort. These are so cheap that you may think it worth buying a couple of detachable roller heads to save time cleaning off the build-up of glaze. Stippling with a cloth wad offers plenty of scope for experiment. Using rags of different textures gives different effects – a soft finish with muslin, net curtains, glass curtains, or old sheeting; a crisper look with hessian, burlap, or sacking. Whichever you start with, make sure you have a plentiful supply, because the cloth pads will get hard with paint and have to be jettisoned fairly often, and changing the type of cloth halfway will give a marked change of texture to the walls. Some painters use crumpled soft paper. Try out various effects before you decide.

Other equipment You need white spirit [mineral spirits] for thinning; a little drier may be needed to correct runny paint glazes – this isn't necessary with transparent oil glaze; a paint kettle, bucket or wide flat tin to hold the glaze; a stepladder and plenty of clean rags.

Method   *Brush or pad stippling* For this sort of stippling, two people definitely get on better than one. So when you have mixed up your glaze, one member of the team brushes it evenly and finely, no thicker than a film, over a vertical strip of wall while the other follows behind stippling the surface while it is still wet and malleable. Keep the pressure on the stippling brush steady and even. Efficient teamwork is important in brush stippling because this takes quite a time, and it helps if you can be stippling the top half of a wall while your partner is brushing glaze on to the bottom. Keeping a wet edge is always important for a professional-looking wall finish. Stippling with cloth pads is less tiring than brush stippling but needs the same quick, decisive touch.

Remove surplus glaze from the brush periodically, by brushing out on waste paper or rags, to prevent it from overloading to the point where it puts on more glaze than it takes off. Change cloth pads occasionally for the same reason. Odd unevennesses can be touched out, if necessary, after you have finished a strip. Stand back for an overall impression. Darken light patches – professionals call them 'skips' or 'holidays' – by picking up a trace of glaze on pad or bristle tips and touching the colour in lightly. But go easy, colour builds up faster than you expect, and take care to clean the brush before re-using. Build-ups of glaze, where you have gone over one place twice with a loaded brush, can be toned down either by re-stippling with a clean brush or rag, or, if very stubborn, by a brush or rags moistened with a little white spirit to soften the drying glaze.

Roller stippling This is a different animal. It takes longer to brush the glaze on than to roller stipple it off again, since a roller flashes up a vertical surface in no time at all. Simply roll the roller up and down over the wet glaze, using quite firm pressure, until the colour is evenly textured. Take care not to let the roller skid over the glaze, because this wipes off streaks of colour, which then have to be patched up and re-stippled. Clean the roller head frequently by rolling vigorously on waste paper to mop up surplus colour. It is more difficult to cut in neatly at the top and bottom of a wall with a roller, and glaze may accumulate here or smudge on to the woodwork or ceiling. Keep clean rags handy for wiping off smudges, and even out built-up colour by stippling over the area with a soft rag moistened with white spirit. Clean the rollers at the end of the session by rolling on paper, then in white spirit – which has to be squeezed out by hand – then on clean paper.

Varnish If the walls are likely to need frequent washing down, varnish with clear, matt polyurethane varnish (if you have used a wash this is certainly necessary). Matt varnish dries quite flat. It will darken the colour slightly, but quite pleasingly, and gives a much tougher finish that can be wiped clean.

Over This illustrates well how a gently distressed finish in complementary colours can pull together a room with more than its fair share of structural quirks. Here, sponging in pink, beige and cream over a yellow ground discreetly suggests the opulence of marble. Note how the same finish, continued over the wall unit, focuses the eye on its contents, not the shelves themselves.

Sponging

Sponging is a really jolly decorative finish, quick and easy to do, and capable of infinitely varied effects according to the type of sponge, the way you wield it and the number of colours used.

Sponging on or off The most commonly used sponging technique differs from most of the decorative finishes described here in that the sponge is used to dab the tinted glaze or wash *on*, taking up the colour from a large flat surface, such as a palette, plate or tray. However, if you prefer, you can brush on a glaze in the usual way and then use a clean sponge to distress the wet surface – a sponge wrung out in solvent gives a very regular, prettily granulated appearance, like a close-textured stone, or knobbly knitting.

Sponging on with two colours The sponging-on method, done with two different coloured glazes or washes over a light ground, is a quick way of obtaining a marbled effect that can look opulent in a small room. For the most emphatic patterning, the wall surface should be painted first with a light-coloured, mid-sheen or flat oil-based paint. An emulsion [latex] paint ground coat is perfectly all right, but gives a softer build-up of colour. The sponged-on colours should be thinned to transparency with the appropriate diluent.

Glazes and washes For sponging on, tinted transparent oil glaze [glazing liquid] gives the most translucent marble-like effect. Otherwise use a glaze of thinned oil-based paint: mid-sheen, flat or undercoat, see pages

Materials for sponging

225–27. Flat paint and undercoat dry flat, of course, if you want a matt finish. A wash of emulsion [latex] paint thinned with water can be sponged over a matt emulsion ground, but the effect will not have the special translucency of oil-based glazes. It is important that the ground coat be clean and grease-free – brand new emulsion gives the best results.

Sponging off is more easily managed with a glaze; a wash will probably dry too quickly to be very successful.

For a small room, $\frac{1}{2}$ litre [1 US pint] of any of the above should be ample for sponging on or off. See pages 224–29 for instructions on thinning and tinting glazes and washes.

Use universal stainers [tinting colours], artists' oils, gouache or acrylic colours as appropriate for tinting. Thin transparent oil glaze and oil-based paints with white spirit [mineral spirits], if necessary adding a little drier to the thinned paints to prevent drips.

Sponges A genuine marine sponge is essential for the sponging-on technique – an old bath sponge could be pressed into service here; it doesn't have to be new. If a marine sponge is too expensive, the best substitute is a pad of soft crumpled muslin or cheesecloth, held bunched up in the hand. (Change this when it gets hard with paint.) Cellulose sponge makes hard-edged identical prints that don't flow together attractively. However, it can be used for the sponging-off method, where it will produce a regular stippled effect.

Other equipment You will need a bucket or paint kettle for mixing the glaze; a clean, flat container to use as a palette; a stepladder; and plenty of rags or waste paper for wiping up.

Method *Sponging off* For a simple, uniform, one-colour sponging, brush the thinned glaze out over a strip of wall in the usual way, then press the sponge – either dry or wrung out in white spirit [mineral spirits] – evenly over the wet glaze. This finish needs to be regular, so spend a little time working over thicker patches of colour to get the whole thing evenly distressed. You may need to wash out the sponge from time to time in white spirit if it becomes loaded with glaze.

Sponging on For two-colour sponging to produce a marbled effect, soft, transparent glazes and a light touch with the sponge help give the impression that the colour was floated on. Keep the glaze in a flat container large enough to dab the sponge into, and have waste paper handy to test the colour on before dabbing it on the wall. Thick wet prints mean the sponge is overloaded. Go on dabbing the paper until you get a soft cloudy impression; then dab over the wall surface with a light, 'pecky' hand movement, keeping the sponged prints fairly spaced out. A good bit of ground colour should show through the first sponged colour, say two-fifths of the total area. When the first glaze colour is quite dry, sponge on the second colour. Concentrate on the blank areas, but overlap with the previous prints too, to give a dappled effect that must not be allowed to become too regular and predictable. Change the position of the sponge regularly, and wipe it clean now and then on clean rags, or rinse out in solvent – but take care to squeeze it out well, or this will make the next lot of paint very diluted.

Varnish Apply varnish after 24 hours, or when the glaze is hard dry, using gloss or semigloss varnish for translucency (thinned 3 parts varnish to 1 part white spirit), or flat varnish, unthinned, for a matt look.

Above Sponge on the glaze or wash using a light 'pecky' movement, to produce a soft, cloudy impression.

Right For two-colour sponging, wait until the first colour is quite dry, then apply your second colour in the same way, for a gently marbled effect.

41

Ragging or rag-rolling

One of the most striking decorative finishes, rag-rolling or 'ragging' is a development of stippling, using bunched-up rags or a chamois leather pressed into wet glaze with a rolling movement of the hand. This creates a loose, open, fairly marked patterning with considerable surface variety. Unlike most of the other finishes described, ragging should not be regular, otherwise the markings become insistent and annoying. By varying the pressure on the bunched-up rag, rolling it this way and that, and re-arranging the rag itself from time to time, subtly varied impressions are left that create a soft but lively flow of colour over the walls. Ragging is a particularly good finish for large areas of wall, like corridors and staircases, because the non-directional movement of colour softens hard angles and enlarges confined areas, and ragging itself is quick and easy once you have acquired the knack.

Colours

Because of the relative obtrusiveness of a ragged finish, I think it is best confined to softer colours. The more 'interesting' pastels – blue-green, brownish-pink, greyish-mauve – all look attractive ragged over a slightly 'dirty' white ground – that is, a white base tinted with a little raw umber for a cool greeny-grey cast, or a little ochre and raw sienna for a warmer cream. Colour on colour looks fetching if the colours are of similar intensity or tone. One of the most attractive ragged finishes I have seen was a warm duck egg blue – a greeny blue – ragged with a transparent faded-brick colour tinted with burnt sienna. In complete contrast a parchment-tinted glaze – a little white plus raw or burnt umber – ragged over plain white gives an ultra-refined, discreetly expensive finish. The effect here is of the most delicate white marble, cool, with just enough depth to make it interesting.

Preparation

As with most of the special wall finishes, ragging with a glaze is best done over a mid-sheen oil-based paint. If you use an emulsion [latex] paint for the ground coat, again a mid-sheen finish may help, as it is more difficult to keep the wet edge going on an absorbent base. Ragging with a wash of thinned emulsion paint should be done over a flat or mid-sheen emulsion ground, preferably newly applied. Make sure the base coat is clean and dry before you start the ragged finish.

Materials for ragging

Opposite You don't need to be a professional decorator to handle colours successfully. The owner of this room, fed up with her chilly white walls, rag-rolled them on the spur of the moment with sky-blue emulsion [latex] paint. No setting could be more delicately atmospheric, or more perfectly complement the blue-green of the painted chair and the sparky pastels of the china on the table.

Glazes and washes Ragging with transparent oil glaze [glazing liquid] gives a very crisp pattern; thinned oil-based paint (mid-sheen, flat or undercoat) or a wash of thinned emulsion [latex] paint produce softer effects; see pages 212–15 for types of paint. As usual ½ litre [US pint] of full strength paint or glaze should be sufficient to rag a small room.

Thin glaze and oil-based paint with white spirit [mineral spirits], adding a little drier to thinned paint if necessary to prevent drips. Use universal stainers [tinting colours] or artists' oil colours to tint these glazes. Thin emulsion paint with water and tint with stainers or artists' gouache or acrylic colours. Thin and tint your glaze or wash in a pan,

paint kettle or bucket, following the instructions on pages 225–26. Experiment on boards, or paper, or in a corner of the room to find the effect you like.

Rags and brushes You need a wide, soft brush to apply the glaze or wash and a good supply of rags or a piece of chamois leather to distress it. Rags can be of varying texture (old sheet, gauze, net curtain or glass curtain, or even hessian or burlap), but they must be well washed and lint free, and of course the same type must be used throughout. Rags and leather can be used dry or – with a glaze – wrung out in white spirit [mineral spirits] for a softer effect.

Method Apply the glaze over a fairly large section of wall with a large soft brush. Transparent oil glaze needs to be worked over quite a lot to even out brushstrokes. The oil glaze made from the recipe on page 225 is easier to

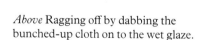

Above Ragging off by dabbing the bunched-up cloth on to the wet glaze.

Right Here the glaze or wash is being ragged *on* to the wall using a rag-rolling movement. Since it goes so quickly, ragging on is particularly suitable for applying a fast-drying wash.

brush out than a proprietary glaze, though much slower drying. There are two ways of using the rag to make a pattern. Either bunch it up in one hand and dab and push it about on the glaze with a 'loose wrist', or wrap it into a loose but compact bundle and, using both hands, *roll* this about over the wet glaze in various directions like a rolling pin. The idea is to make an irregular pattern, but one that looks fairly uniform overall. From time to time you will have to change your rag, as it will become stiffened with glaze or paint. With oil glaze or oil paint chamois leather should be used wrung out in white spirit, as this allows you to clean it now and then.

If the wet edge dries while ragging with oil-based paint, try softening it with a clean rag soaked in white spirit. A wash of emulsion paint dries very fast so if possible have two people on the job. Paint a small strip of wall at a time and fade out the wash toward the edge of the strip so that the overlap is not too thick. If the wash starts to dry before it has been ragged, dabble it with a wet sponge to make it workable. A little scouring powder on a damp cloth should cope with a recalcitrant hard edge.

Varnish For protection, a ragged finish can be covered with a coat of clear matt polyurethane varnish.

Colourwashing

Colourwashing gives a soft, delicate dapple of watery colour to a wall, perfectly suited to countrified rooms and the sort of unpretentious pine furniture, calico prints and straw matting that people today find congenial. A warm white ground colourwashed in apricot or brownish pink, gives a sunshiny look to a north-facing or underlit room, while colourwashing in pale indigo blue turns a bright sunny room into a cool underwater place, like the sea with the sun overhead.

Washes, glazes and grounds

The ideal medium for this particularly pretty finish was the old-fashioned distemper paint, which could be thinned liberally with water, was cheap, and dried to a soft, textured finish without streaking or hard edges. Unfortunately this has gone out of production, but you can make up a distemper yourself from the recipe provided below.

Homemade distemper You will need some whiting, available from builders' merchants, hardware stores and artists' suppliers; it comes in 3 kg [7 lb] bags, or in larger amounts if bought from a wholesale trader. One bag should make sufficient distemper to paint a small room. You will also need some decorators' glue size (check that it contains alum to prevent mould, which used to be a hazard with distemper). Make the glue size up according to the directions on the packet – they usually specify $\frac{1}{2}$ a kilo [1 lb] of size to 9 litres [9 US quarts] of hot water. Leave it to cool for a few hours and check that it has set to a hard jelly. Then heat it up again by placing its container in a bowl or bucket of water over a source of heat – a sort of *bain-marie* arrangement. When it is warm and runny, it will be ready for use.

Over Yellow is the sunshine colour and makes a marvellous tonic for the eye and the spirits when splashed round the walls. It does need to be a brave, positive yellow, though, not the colour of margarine. Here its sunflower brilliance enlivens the walls of a 19th-century house: a yellow glaze was slapped on over a white eggshell ground for a nice brushy texture. The rather lacquered effect comes from a finishing coat of gloss varnish.

Other requirements are cold water, a bucket, powder colour for tinting, a medium-sized spoon, and a larger bucket or tub of hot water.

To make your distemper, half fill the smaller bucket with cold water and pour in whiting until it rises to a peak about 100 mm [4 in] above the surface of the water. Leave it to soak for an hour or two and then stir. Next, dissolve some powder colour in a little cold water to make a concentrated solution and add this carefully, spoonful by spoonful, to the whiting mixture, until you achieve your desired colour. Stir the whole lot until it is evenly coloured. Now pour in your warmed glue size, mixing it thoroughly. Your distemper should be the consistency of ordinary thick paint. If it stiffens too much, as the size becomes cool, stand the bucket of distemper in a larger container of hot water to warm it up.

Do not make up more distemper than you can use at a time – it will not keep longer than a day or two. Use the distemper as it is for the ground coat. For a colour wash to go on top, thin it considerably with water to the consistency of milk.

Alternatives to distemper Other, more easily available methods give a similar effect, and they are worthwhile experimenting with. One professional decorator's substitute for the old distemper wash is to use a glaze of much thinned flat oil-based paint or undercoat over a trade eggshell base (mid-sheen oil-based paint). This gives a similar transparency of colour, dries to a matt finish, and can be manipulated so as to leave no hard edges or brushmarks.

Another method is to use a wash of emulsion [latex] paint thinned to liquidity with water, painted over a clean, flat emulsion ground. This gives visible brushmarks and plenty of texture.

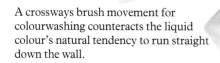

A crossways brush movement for colourwashing counteracts the liquid colour's natural tendency to run straight down the wall.

A third possibility, dear to the heart of some decorators, is to use a wash of pure colour and water, with a tiny amount of emulsion paint to give it just a little body. This gives a super-transparent colour, and lots of texture too; see the photograph on pages 18–19. The colour can be glowingly intense if richer and richer tones are used one on top of the other – working from light to dark red, for instance. Each coat of colour should be left to dry thoroughly before adding another, and slapped on fast to avoid dislodging the previous colour.

Paints and colours A wash or glaze for colourwashing is thinned a great deal more than those used for the other finishes in the book – about 9 parts water, or solvent, to 1 part paint. The usual $\frac{1}{2}$ litre [1 US pint] of paint should therefore be ample for at least two coats of colourwashing in a small room. See pages 212–15 for types of paint, and 224–29 for instructions on mixing, thinning and tinting washes and glazes.

As usual, oil paints are thinned with white spirit [mineral spirits] and tinted with universal stainers [tinting colours] or artists' oil colours; emulsion [latex] paints are thinned with water and tinted with stainers or artists' gouache or acrylic colours. Decorators prefer gouache, for the pure intensity of colour.

Other equipment You will need a bucket for the colourwash mixture – one or two (depending on how many of you there are); wide soft brushes, say 100 or 125 mm [4 or 5 in]; a stepladder; clean rags or paper for mopping up.

The application is the same whatever type of paint you use. Dip your brush into the wash, then slap the colour on loosely and irregularly in all directions, trying to avoid heavy brushmarks and hard edges. Leave a good bit of ground colour uncovered. When it is quite dry repeat the process, brushing over most of the bare patches and also over some of the first coat of colour. This gives nicely varying intensities of colour, and a dappled effect.

Thinned paint of any kind will dry very quickly, but it is probably best to leave each wash overnight to become really dry before applying the next, or you may find you are taking the colour off rather than putting it on. If this happens the bare patches can be rescued by patting on colour with a sponge. Don't be alarmed if a very watery wash runs off copiously to begin with. It may need to be gone over assiduously with a soft brush to persuade it to stick. Put lots of waterproof protection on the floor and expect the first coat to look a mess. The next coat makes a miraculous difference – the colour suddenly comes alive, and the walls knit together with the inimitable radiance that watercolour alone can give.

Varnish A matt, slightly aged and non 'finished' look is the aim with colourwashing, but if you will need to wash the walls, varnish them for protection with a clear, matt polyurethane varnish, which barely changes the colour of the paint.

Materials for colourwashing

Method

Over Red is the most inspiriting colour of all to live with but it needs careful handling – a colour of this intensity applied flat would be glaringly bright. Here a white base was rag-rolled with red-tinted glaze for a gently variegated texture. A fairly uniform spatter of off-white paint was followed by a lighter one of black (see the inset detail) and the whole thing was then given 2 coats of red-tinted polyurethane varnish for a lacquer finish.

Lacquer finish

In complete contrast to colourwashing, a rich surface gloss and depth of colour are the *lac-de-chine* characteristics that decorators are after when they suggest a 'lacquer' wall finish to their clients. I don't mean by this the sort of effect you get by simply painting everything with gloss or enamel paint. That is certainly shiny, but it looks thick and lifeless compared to more complex effects built up with matt colour and glaze or varnish. Lacquer-look finishes are a demanding background, unkind to shabby furnishings and oddly shaped rooms. Shiny colour needs a high degree of finish everywhere else – sound plasterwork, handsomely moulded cornice, well-painted woodwork, elegant furniture, velvety carpet – in short, an expensive effect. An exception to the rule might be a room where something nearer to worn old lacquer has been contrived, using dark base colours – crimson, vermilion, olive green, deep blue, chestnut – brightened with a little discreet gold stencilling and given a semigloss varnish for sheen rather than shine.

There are three ways to get a lacquer-type finish. The first, if you simply want *shine*, is to apply 1 or 2 coats of clear varnish (semigloss for sheen, gloss for a reflective high shine) over walls painted in your chosen colour. The second method, though similar, gives colour richness as well: you apply the varnish in the same way, but tint it to tone with the paint beneath. In the third method, the base coat is covered with a toning glaze, and *then* varnished. If you apply a number of coats of glaze and varnish, all tinted differently, you can get a wonderful depth of colour.

Preparation

A lacquer finish requires perfectly prepared walls. Choose the base paint colour to look good through clear varnish, or to tone with subsequent coats of glaze or tinted varnish. When it is dry, lightly sand it to remove dust, but don't grind away so hard that you cut through the paint. Dust the walls down, then wipe them over finally with a tack rag, see page 25. As for any varnishing job, the room itself should be immaculate before you begin, to prevent dust from settling on the sticky wet surface. Remove curtains or draperies and rugs, cover furniture with dust sheets, and vacuum and dust everything. Keep doors and windows closed.

Materials for lacquering

For one coat of varnish (to be thinned 3 parts varnish to 1 part white spirit [mineral spirits]) for a small room – 3 by 4 m [10 by 12 ft] – you need 1 litre [1 US quart] of clear, gloss or semigloss polyurethane varnish.

To glaze the same room you need $\frac{1}{2}$ litre [1 US pint] of mid-sheen oil-based paint *or* the same quantity of transparent oil glaze [glazing liquid]. Better still try making up the homemade oil glaze recipe described on page 225 (it is already thinned so you'll need about twice the amount). This glaze gives a beautiful glowing, transparent finish that shouldn't need varnishing, goes on very easily and doesn't leave brushmarks as the bought variety is inclined to do. However, because of the linseed oil content, it can take many days to dry really hard. Use universal stainers [tinting colours] or artists' oil colours for tinting. See pages 212–29 for information on paints and mixing and tinting glazes.

Other equipment Brushes should be fairly wide, 75 or 100 mm [3 or 4 in], and of extra-good quality. Varnish brushes should be kept for varnishing only, see page 231, as you don't want bits and pieces of old paint marring your smooth finish. White spirit [mineral spirits]; fine sandpaper; a stepladder; the usual pan, paint kettle or bucket for the thinned glaze, and plenty of clean rags are also required.

Method

Tinted varnish To tint varnish, dilute a blob of stainer [tinting colour] or artists' oil colour in a little white spirit, then add a cupful of varnish. Stir well with a stick or spoon, then add the rest of the varnish, thinning as above. Try the effect on a patch of wall. When varnishing, *flow* on the finish as evenly as possible, using a full brush; don't brush out as you would paint or glaze, since polyurethane varnishes start to dry very quickly and this will create brush tracks rather than lose them. Likewise try to avoid going over the same spot twice, as this can leave sticky deposits that dry darker. Although the varnish won't take very long to dry, allow longer than the can says if the room is not heated – ideally varnish should be applied in a mildly warm room, to help flow and drying. One coat may be enough, if you are very careful, but 2 will give greater depth of colour and shine. Let the first coat dry really hard before putting on the second – several days.

Glazing Apply glaze with a large soft brush over the entire wall surface, keeping it even and as fine as possible. Brush out well to avoid brushmarks. Leave this coat at least 24 hours until perfectly dry, then simply varnish over, thinning gloss or semigloss varnish as suggested and using a scrupulously clean brush.

Antique lacquer

For an antique lacquer effect, the colours should be softened to the patina of old japan, not used hot and strong. This can be done by painting the walls with an antique glaze, see page 207, before or after stencilling, or by adding a little of the same antiquing colours to the final varnish. Try the effect of raw and burnt umber on a patch that won't show – raw umber is particularly flattering to greens and blues, while burnt umber is richer over reds. A speck of black can be added too, to age the whole surface down even more. One coat of varnish is enough, but 2 – both thinned – are better. I think semigloss varnish gives a softer, prettier texture than gloss.

Stencils See page 68 for how to apply stencil designs in metal powder. The stencilled motif might be a simple fleur-de-lis or Tudor rose, which always looks good spaced out on a diagonal grid – see page 125. Or adapt the quaint chinoiserie figures that decorated eighteenth-century japanned pieces. You could perhaps alternate a flower-spray motif with a typical old gentleman standing on a humped-back bridge, or fishing from a sampan, and remember that the stencils can be used back to front for a slight change of emphasis. Alternatively, of course, you could limit yourself to a simple gilt border stencil.

Decorative Painting

Stencilling

The recent revival of the ancient craft of stencilling as a way of adding colour and pattern to walls, floors and furniture is one of the happiest inspirations in the field of decorating for a long time. Stencilling is art for everyone – versatile, cheap, easy and exciting to do. In an age of stereotypes and instant 'looks', a stencilled room has a handmade individuality that is rare and refreshing.

With stencils you can be as creative or as imitative as you please. Gifted pattern-makers will invent their own designs, or adapt suitable motifs from other sources. Others will find what they are looking for in the traditional stencil patterns. These have the bonus of being tried and tested, but you can still exert your creative energies in thinking up new combinations of motifs and colours. Ready-cut stencil kits are to be found, at a price: cutting your own stencils (whether originals or copies) is not difficult, and much more rewarding.

Stencils and colour

The best way to make sure a particular colour effect works – unless you are producing a traditional scheme or are very adept with colour – is to mock up a small area using a variety of colours. You can try this in crayons on a scale drawing or sketch of the room. Better still, since it takes factors like the room's proportions and lighting into account, try the effect out *in situ*. Make variously coloured 'proofs' from the stencils you have chosen, and juggle them about on the wall with masking tape until you like the result. If you have not finally decided on a ground colour, paint a large sheet of lining paper in the shade you are considering, and fix that up as a background for the proofs. Colour combinations can play odd visual tricks that are not obvious from a small-scale sketch. For instance, colours of the same tonal intensity – ones that would look identical if photographed in black and white – often seem to knock each other out visually if combined in roughly equal proportions. This could work, or it could flop. Check first.

If you decide to use traditional designs it is always worth studying the original colour combinations since their creators drew upon much practical experience in thinking them up. It would be hard, for example, to improve on some of the Early American colour schemes. They usually favoured warm, earthy colours like ochre, Venetian red and green, with black for emphasis, stencilled over pale washed grounds of light red, grey or indigo. Overly sophisticated colours look wrong for these naif designs, though a reversal of the effects can be very successful: motifs stencilled in pale colours on a richly coloured ground. Patterns in pale blue, grey or cream on a soft, dull red look very tempting.

Opposite Glowing orange colourwashed walls, stencilled in blue and cream with blue colour bands, make an attic sitting room come singingly alive. More colour and pattern have been heaped on in the form of cushions, pictures, rugs and an eclectic assortment of personal treasures, and the result is as rich and harmonious as a bunch of June flowers.

Stencils used architecturally

Since stencils are so versatile they can be arranged so as to make a feature of any attractively quirky bit of existing architecture. Odd-shaped walls, sloping ceilings, dormer windows and attractive alcoves can all be discreetly emphasized by appropriate stencils. They can also be used to divide up the surfaces of a rather characterless box of a room, to give more definition and improve its proportions. A room that feels too high for its floor space is immediately cut down to size if you run a stencilled border round at cornice level and again at chair-rail level; if the ceiling is excessively high, have the first border at picture-rail height to cut the expanse still further. Leave the expanse above white like the ceiling to fade it out, or fill in the space between ceiling and border with a wide stencilled frieze, to make it look lower. Rooms with the opposite problem – too long for their height or just too much blank wall space, as in corridors – are improved by a strongly vertical stencil treatment, or by arranging stencils in regular panels. Don't be afraid of positive colours and powerful designs. My complaint about most contemporary stencil-work is that it looks too dainty to make any architectural contribution to a room. Pretty little floral borders are lost in a fair-sized room. Study how the old stencillers skilfully balanced their designs, seeing a room as a whole, and follow their example.

Equipment for making a stencil

Quite adequate stencils can be cut from any thin cardboard with a sharp penknife, but as you get more ambitious you will probably want to buy proper tools and equipment to do the job more quickly and efficiently.

Your basic requirements for making a stencil are a pen, several sheets of acetate or oiled stencil board, a flat surface for cutting on, and a sharp knife or scalpel.

Pen Black felt-tip pen gives a neat, clear line on most surfaces. A Rapidograph is essential for acetate.

Stencil material A stencil needs to be waterproof and tough. All sorts of material – leather, lead foil, thin sheets of zinc and copper, oiled or waxed paper or oiled stencil board – have been used for the purpose historically but nowadays these have been largely supplanted by acetate sheet, which, being glass clear, has the advantage that designs and motifs can be traced directly on to it, doing away with the need to use carbon paper. This is particularly useful when you have to cut two or three separate stencils for a pattern that is to be painted in several colours. Stencil board, which is like thin cardboard, is cheaper and good for intricate, small-scale work, since unlike acetate it is not likely to split as you go round a tight corner. It is also more suitable for very large stencils, where acetate tends to curl up unmanageably.

You can get both oiled stencil board and acetate sheet from artists' suppliers. The acetate sheet is more expensive, but it can be cleaned without damage and lasts much longer – useful if you are thinking of building up a stencil library.

56

Cutting board A sheet of chipboard, blockwood or plywood makes a good surface for cutting on. Better still is thick glass with all the edges covered with masking tape for safety.

Knife For both board and acetate, use a craft or Stanley knife, with plenty of blades. A scalpel will give better control for finicky designs.

Brushes The traditional stencil brush – with a fat clump of stiff bristles cut off squarely at the end – gives by far the most attractive results because the 'pouncing' motion with which it is used leaves a soft but definite stipple of colour. This can be shaded to give a subtly variegated, handmade look that is the great charm of stencilling. Stippling colour on like this also means that there is less risk of paint seeping under the stencil. But it makes your arm and shoulder ache over large areas such as borders. For these, you could use a standard decorators' brush or large size artists' brush, to brush colour on in the usual way. In some cases colour can be applied with a sponge, cloth pad, even a roller if the cut-outs are not too detailed.

Paint The main requirement is that the paint used should dry quickly. This is especially important for a multi-colour design, where you may want to stencil over a colour which was put on only half an hour earlier.

For such designs, in particular, use signwriters' colours [bulletin colours], which dry in minutes, thinned with a little matt varnish or goldsize to make them more elastic. The colour range is limited, but they have excellent coverage – handy over large areas like floors. Japan colour, which is available to American readers, is fast-drying too and has a matt finish. The ideal stencil paint, it comes in a wide range of good, strong colours.

For instant drying and excellent colour which can be used opaque or transparent, use artists' acrylics thinned with water or acrylic medium. Or mix these with a little emulsion paint to make them go further, and give 'body'. Ordinary poster colours are fine for stencilling too.

For tough, matt, opaque colour use flat oil-based paint, or undercoat, tinted with universal stainers [tinting colours] or artists' oil colours. The paint can be thinned with white spirit [mineral spirits] and have a little drier added to make it dry still faster. Or use flat emulsion [latex] paint, tinted with stainers or acrylic colours.

The early American stencillers often made up a paint from powder colours mixed with buttermilk. I have tried this legendary mixture and it works very well, making a smooth paint. Just mix powder colour into supermarket or homemade buttermilk. No, it won't turn to cheese on the walls. But motifs stencilled in this way should be matt varnished for protection.

Spray paint, as sold for touching up car bodywork, comes in a huge colour range, and certainly saves on stencilling time and effort. It works best for large motifs without much fine detail. Fix the stencil in place very

Equipment for painting a stencil

firmly – spray paint has a wicked tendency to filter underneath – carefully masking off the surrounding wall surface. Shake the can thoroughly and, holding it level with the stencil, give a short blast from the prescribed distance. Disadvantages are that it is expensive and gives stencils a thin, shadowy look. Do not apply it over oil-based paints.

Whatever type of paint you use, it should be creamy rather than watery in consistency. Watery colour tends to seep under the stencil, and leave great smudges. Very little paint should be taken up on the brush, so the colours must be intense enough to register well when only a thin coat is applied. A beginner's fault is to mix up too much colour for the job – if the stencil design is well spaced out, a saucerful of paint will be enough to decorate the whole room.

Other equipment The appropriate solvent for the paint; rags or tissues for wiping up; jars and saucers for mixed colours; masking tape; stepladder. Optional: plumb-line; chalk; T-square; straight-edge.

Marking out the stencil

The first stage is to transfer your chosen design to the stencil material. If you are using stencil board, the easiest way is to do this with sheets of carbon. Sandwich the carbon between your original design and the board, and go round the outlines with the tip of a knitting needle. If you use clear acetate, simply lay it over the design and draw the outline onto it with a Rapidograph. Fix your design firmly with masking tape to stop it slipping while you draw.

Most stencil designs are printed small and need to be blown up considerably for use. Designs can be enlarged (or reduced) by enclosing them in a measured-out grid. Scaling this grid up to the size you want allows you to reproduce a blow-up of the original, section by section, with considerable accuracy. To reduce a design, use the same method in reverse. Simpler still, get a photographic enlargement made to the size you want. See Yellow Pages, under Photographic Services.

Multi-colour stencils Designs to be stencilled in more than one colour usually need a separate stencil cut for each colour. The problem here is registration – that is, lining up the successive stencils on top of each other during painting. This is fairly simple if you use acetate: since it is transparent, you just ink in key marks from other parts of the design on each stencil and align these when you come to paint the stencil.

If you use stencil board – which is, of course, opaque – you will need extra help in registering separate stencils accurately. Trace the separate colour areas onto different sheets of board, cut them out, then line the boards up so that the parts of the design fit together perfectly. Trim the boards off to exactly the same size with a sharp knife. Then punch a couple of holes (using a nail punch), or cut two notches, one on either side of the design, through all the boards simultaneously. Make tiny pencil marks on the wall through these holes; you can then use them for matching up each stencil in turn.

The stencilled bedroom, *above*, in the American Museum in Britain is one of the freshest, most endearing examples of the craft as practised in New England over 100 years ago. The stencils, *right*, are painted on tongue and groove boards, rather than on plaster, which may account for their arrangement in simple vertical stripes – unlike the more studied and architectural effects found in many stencilled rooms of the period.

Cutting the stencil

To cut your stencil fix the board or acetate to a flat cutting surface with masking tape. Leave a good 25 mm [1 in] margin round the design part of the stencil, for strength. Cut round the inked shapes, pressing firmly down with the point of your knife blade, and keeping your cutting movement as fluent as possible. Hold the knife firmly, but not tensely. Cut towards yourself, and when you hit a curve, move the board round rather than the knife. The idea is to keep up a smooth cutting action without jags and hesitations. Any rough edges should be trimmed off carefully, and, if you are using board, smoothed with fine sandpaper.

When cutting a border or continuous pattern make quite sure that the stencil starts at the beginning of one design unit and finishes at the end of another, so that there is no break in the design when you come to stencil it.

It takes time to cut stencils so it is worth taking care of them afterwards. Mark them clearly on the back with the name of the design and the order in which they are used, then store them in an appropriately marked envelope, which should be kept flat.

Preparation

Background surface The surface you plan to stencil should be sound, dry and already painted in your chosen base colour. Any type of paint will do for this: oil-based finishes are tougher and more durable than emulsion [latex], but the latter is easy to apply and cheap. A distressed wall finish makes stencils look richer; use a matt finish and stipple, sponge or colourwash it for a gentle contrast of texture.

Below Enclose your design in a drawn-up grid, then scale it up – or down – to the required size.

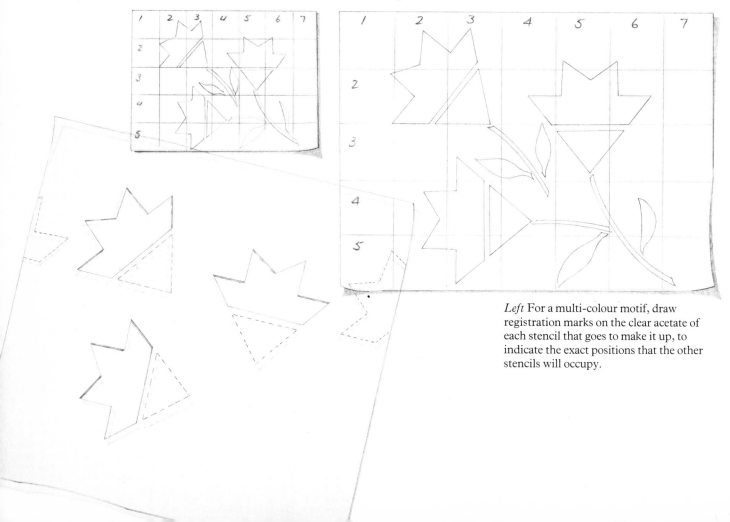

Left For a multi-colour motif, draw registration marks on the clear acetate of each stencil that goes to make it up, to indicate the exact positions that the other stencils will occupy.

Right Begin cutting a stencil with the smaller sections, working up to the larger ones, so that you don't weaken it unnecessarily. If you are using stencil board, try cutting a bevelled edge by holding the blade at an angle of 45°. This will help to prevent paint from seeping under the stencil, and give a crisper edge.

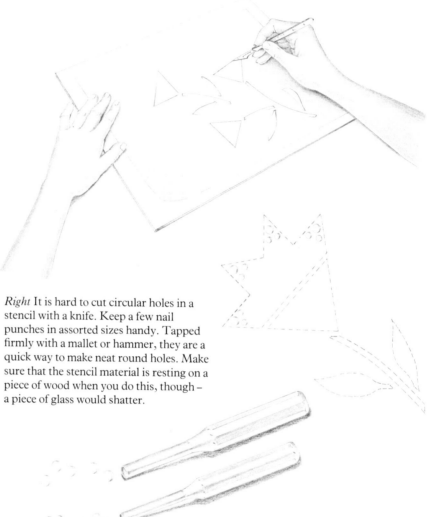

Right It is hard to cut circular holes in a stencil with a knife. Keep a few nail punches in assorted sizes handy. Tapped firmly with a mallet or hammer, they are a quick way to make neat round holes. Make sure that the stencil material is resting on a piece of wood when you do this, though – a piece of glass would shatter.

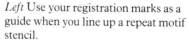

Above When you design your stencil, 'bridges' at frequent intervals help to strengthen it, as well as forming an integral part of the pattern.

Left Use your registration marks as a guide when you line up a repeat motif stencil.

A clutch of motifs of widely differing provenance – classical Greek key, 'knot' from a Cathedral floor tile, Eastern-inspired pomegranate, a 19th-century daisy-patterned border and a modern floral one – suggests the variety of effects suitable for stencilling.

Stencilled borders are the obvious and quickest way to brighten up a plainly painted room – above the skirting, at ceiling height, and defining the shapes of doors, windows and chimneybreast. They help to tie a room together without being insistent.

The Victorian daisy motif makes a charming border used on a small scale, while much enlarged, it could be used to add wide vertical stripes of pattern up pale colourwashed walls. The formal Greek motif in three colours would look handsome banding a shiny lacquered room. The pomegranate, scaled up many times, would make a splendid feature of a flat door; it could also be used at the size shown, spaced out on a diagonal grid as a repeat motif over walls. The 'knot' motif, stencilled in a dark colour, makes a crisp repeat design over a sanded wooden floor; it also looks good in a light colour, stencilled over brightly painted hardboard tiles.

Indeed, although the usual approach is a coloured stencil over a neutral ground, try a neutral stencil over bright walls for interestingly different results.

Keep a collection of old white saucers for trying out colour mixes. Train yourself to visualize stencils in different colours and different sizes, for a variety of effects. Stencils take quite a time to mark out and cut, so it's quite a challenge to see how much mileage you can get from them.

A simple but classical stencil that would look good above a doorway, or, set upright, within rectangular panels.

Positioning Small strips of masking tape (sticky tape can pull off the paintwork underneath) fixed at either side are usually enough to hold the stencil firmly in place.

Regularly spaced stencils should be positioned on a grid measured out on the surface and drawn up with chalk, see pages 128–29. Formal trellis designs and other grid patterns need accurate horizontal and vertical guidelines. To mark up a vertical line on the wall use a chalked plumb-line, or a T-square and straight-edge. For a horizontal line measure up from the floor, use your T-square and straight-edge and pencil in the line. Check along the wall that the line is still horizontal – some floors slope, walls bulge, and so on. Corners present a problem, since few walls are the right length to allow the pattern to fit neatly into the corners. Here the stencils must be bent round to fit, and the pattern grid measured on again from this point.

Putting on the paint An exciting moment this, even for old hands. Dip just the tips of the stencil brush bristles into your prepared colour, then pounce the brush, as if it were a rubber stamp, on a sheet of clean paper to distribute paint evenly through the brush and to remove excess. Using very little paint gives greater delicacy of colour and texture to your stencils, and of course prevents seepage underneath.

Holding the stencil brush firmly, pounce the colour with a rocking movement through the cuts in your stencil, working from sides to middle,

until all the gaps are filled with colour. Leave the colour for a few seconds to harden, then peel off the strips of tape and move on to the next spot. And so on round the room, until you have finished your design.

When you are doing multi-colour stencils, complete everything in one colour first and let it dry fully before doing the next. Acrylic paints and japan colours come in useful here, since they dry so fast you can finish a sequence in a day.

Cleaning up It is important to wipe the stencil off with a rag or paper tissue every so often, to prevent paint building up and clogging the detail. This happens quickly with thick paints. If you use the brush correctly it should not pick up much paint, so you will not need to rinse it during stencilling, but do clean it out thoroughly afterwards in the appropriate solvent. Transfer any leftover colour to small screwtop jars, and cap them tightly or cover with clingfilm [Saran wrap]. Clean the stencils, both sides, and dry them thoroughly.

Varnishing This is a chore but it will greatly prolong the life and good looks of a stencil scheme, especially where you have used paints that are likely to rub off such as artists' acrylics, poster colour, buttermilk paint or undercoat. A coat of clear matt varnish goes on easily and allows walls to be washed down periodically without harm to the designs. *Don't* use standard varnish over spray paint, however, only a similar spray varnish.

65

This deliciously pretty honeysuckle spray shows how a single stencil motif can be repeated, reversed, turned upside down and then combined to produce a variety of patterns. Use it in different ways to fit different situations: simply stencilled end to end it makes a delicate, casual-looking border. Back to back, it adds elegant detail to a corner. Elongated to a rectangle, it would look charming on drawer-fronts, door panels or a bedhead. Arrange it into a square to emphasize a frame or to make a repeat design on a floor. For mirror-image stencils do your original drawing on transparent paper, trace off the front on to board or acetate, then turn the sketch over and trace off the back to get a reverse motif.

Special stencil effects

A reticent use of stencils gives interestingly different results. One Italian designer, for instance, has stencilled an overall design of daisy-like flowers in flat cream paint over a gloss white ground. The contrast between matt cream and shiny white gives a subtly variegated texture, like cotton damask.

The same designer combines small-scale stencils in muted colours with thin coloured glazes brushed out patchily over the walls – walls cloudily glazed in transparently thin blue and raw umber might be stencilled over in a soft green or brown, with touches of red, producing an effect remarkably like faded antique embroidery. For glazes see pages 224–29.

Do not overdo your first stencilling stint, or you will be full of aches and pains and your enthusiasm dampened. When you have finished, treat yourself to a stiff drink. Do not be surprised if coloured spots dance before your eyes – this is a stencilling hangover, not a drink problem.

Metallic stencils

Gold or silver stencils on a dark 'lacquered' or tortoiseshelled wall look dramatic and very opulent indeed.

Spray gold paint makes tidy stencil patterns, if you are prepared to mask the wall surface out for some distance round the cut-out, but it is an expensive way of doing things. It must be finished with an aerosol varnish or fixative, since brushing over the designs with ordinary varnish smudges them hopelessly.

The gilt paint recipe given below is one used by early japanners. It can be applied on any surface but looks particularly effective over the richer painted finishes. The paint dries to a shinier, clearer finish than commercial metallic paints, and is a good deal cheaper. Silvery aluminium powder does not give as satisfactory a colour as the various bronze powders.

Materials

Metal powders; gum arabic; stencil brushes; an artists' brush for highlights; saucers for holding the powders; rags for wiping up.

Gum arabic and metal powders can be found at artists' suppliers. Metal powders come in a range of shades from pale lemon gold to antique bronzy gold and copper and silver colours too. For a richer effect use several colours, making a different stencil for each. Powder mixed into gum arabic dries hard in about 20 minutes and can then be safely varnished with a brush.

Method

Tip a little metal powder carefully, holding your breath to avoid scattering it, into a saucer – a different saucer for each powder – and add gum arabic, mixing it to a thin cream consistency. Gum arabic is water-soluble, so a little warm water can be added to thin the mixture. Test the effect on a sheet of paper.

The mixture can either be pounced or brushed through the stencil – the former producing a more shaded effect. Try them both. Highlights or thin coloured glazes can be touched in with an artists' brush afterwards, see gilding on page 194. This metal 'paint' dries quickly, so the first colour will be dry before you want to add another.

Varnishing If your gilt stencils come out too bright and shiny you can knock them back by going over them with suitable earth colours – raw or burnt sienna, raw or burnt umber, plus a speck of black – mixed in a little thinned clear varnish. Try out different effects, using a small soft artists' brush. Tinted varnish will soften and enrich the metallic ground, but do not make it so dark that it obscures it. Varnish tinted green or crimson gives the gorgeous effect found on old japanned pieces.

When the gilding is completed and any tinted varnishing quite dry, cover over the whole wall surface with semigloss or gloss clear polyurethane varnish – thinned 3 parts varnish to 1 part white spirit [mineral spirits] to enhance the old lacquer look.

Wall painting

The urge to paint pictures on walls, to turn walls into pictures, is as old as the cave paintings at Altamira. And as every parent of young children knows, the instinct is with us yet, alive, well and longing to express itself with red felt-tip pen on the nearest clean paint surface.

Wall paintings, even if it's only a modest orange tree in a tub on either side of the garden door, or a Noah's ark frieze in the nursery, have an imaginative freedom, a fantastical charm that even the most beautiful stencilling cannot match. But it must be some lingering inhibition associated with scribbling on nice clean walls and getting a good scolding for it, plus a genuine diffidence about tackling a creative job without special training, that accounts for the rarity of this form of decorative work except at the exclusive interior decorators' level. And yet, really, with a little common sense and forethought, it is not so difficult. All sorts of untrained people, from schoolchildren to Indian villagers and Mexican housepainters, quite unselfconsciously produce vigorous and charming murals. While I admire the sophisticated Italianate garden vistas and colonnaded loggias that artists like Rex Whistler, Oliver Messel and Martin Newell have conjured up for their rich patrons, I often find these less memorable and pleasing than technically more modest efforts done perhaps with greater conviction. I recall a bedroom that the owners had transformed into a fantastical plant house, inspired by botanical plates of rare and beautiful plants, which they painted round the walls casually springing up from the skirting board or baseboard, with a few butterflies and brightly coloured birds hovering above. There was no straining after 'composition' and no hurry – they just added another plant when they felt like it. But the effect was exhilarating.

The answer to the usual objection that one can't draw, can't paint and doesn't know where to start is that you don't know what you are capable of until you try. Besides, there are aids, props and cheats that make it all much easier and quicker. Copying, for instance, is perfectly honourable.

Use stencilled borders to make an architectural point, stressing good features and playing down bad ones. Test sample colour schemes on sheets of paper and fix them in place to see which works best.

Above A fragile border of morning glories and dragonflies can be trailed informally around a room at ceiling height, so that artless fronds drop across the corners. Use this effect to soften the shape of a small square room.

Below The delicately shaded border of flowers and fruit leads the eye firmly up the stone steps, and makes an ordinary stairhall memorable.

Above Orange-red on warm yellow is a powerful mix, but the delicacy of this stencilled leaf spray makes it readily acceptable.

Above right The strong diagonal created by a series of prints marching up a staircase wall is strengthened by a soft border below and balanced by a fillet of leaves at ceiling level.

Right Cut a room's height with a border a little below the ceiling. Link it with other decorations – here, a plate appears to hang from painted ribbons.

Those who cannot manage freehand copying will find that the most faithful scaled-up representations can be achieved quite mechanically by using a grid, as shown on page 60. Once you have chalked the outlines on the walls, all that remains is to reproduce the original colours, and the advice given in this book on mixing colours and producing decorative effects such as stippling or sponging should be of help here.

Designs Be realistic in your choice of subject – flat, two-dimensional treatments that rely on shape and colour rather than modelling and perspective for their effect are easiest to bring off. Look at the classical murals, Egyptian, Cretan, Etruscan and Pompeian, at tapestries, at the paintings of Uccello, Matisse, Le Douanier Rousseau, at Moghul painting and Japanese prints, lacquer screens, Delft tiles, Jacobean crewel work, at samplers and at decorative borders in children's books – these last often prove a mine of ideas. Most inspiring and helpful of all perhaps is folk art in its many manifestations – embroidery, carving, ceramics, painted furniture and, of course, murals. Folk art is living proof of how a feeling for colour and a strong decorative impulse can transcend technical limitations. Some of my favourite wall paintings are those done by the journeyman stencillers and housepainters in eighteenth- and nineteenth-century New England homes. These charming rural scenes, with little hills, winding streams, clumps of sponged-in trees, have a charm and directness that have nothing to do with technique, only a certain sensitivity to colour and design.

Preparation and paints If a mural is born of sudden impulse, by all means use whatever materials are to hand. Necessity in this sphere can be the mother of invention – odds and ends of paints left over from jobs around the house, felt-tip pens and crayons can all be pressed into use, provided the surface you are painting on is sound and reasonably smooth. Flaky, cracked plaster, overpainted lining or wallpaper that has started to peel, old, porous or greasy emulsion [latex] finish, will all reduce the life of your work. If you are planning a fairly elaborate, lengthy sort of mural, it would be worthwhile providing yourself with a durable, non-absorbent base coat such as the standard mid-sheen oil-based paint, see page 214, advocated for most of the decorative finishes, and the same paint, tinted with universal stainers [tinting colours] or artists' oils for the decorative painting. Or, if you object to a slight sheen, use flat paint or standard undercoat (which dries perfectly flat) for both ground and painting, tinted as before with stainers. On a new, sound emulsion base you could paint with emulsion paint tinted with stainers, artists' gouache, or artists' acrylic colours – these last come in an excellent colour range but are not cheap. Used neat, but extended with acrylic medium or water, they give glowing, fast-drying colours, useful perhaps for detail but too expensive for large areas. See pages 218–23 for how to tint paints.

Brushes and other materials You will need brushes in various sizes: small artists' brushes for details and ordinary 12 or 25 mm [$\frac{1}{2}$ or 1 in] decorators' brushes (or artists' oil brushes if you can afford them) for brushing in larger areas; a wider, 75 or 100 mm [3 or 4 in] brush might be helpful for filling in sweeps of background colour such as blue sky or green hills. Equipment for stippling, sponging or stencilling may be required (see appropriate sections). Chalk or charcoal for drawing in rough outlines; white spirit [mineral spirits]; jars with screwtop lids to hold surplus mixed paint colours; saucers to use as improvised palettes, one for each

Painting a make-believe door with an enticing view beyond is a witty idea for a plain interior wall. Use grisaille for the doorway itself. Painted orange trees and tubs make charming additions to a doorway, real or trompe l'oeil.

A New England stairhall, decorated in
1831 by an itinerant painter, William
Price, who used water-based paint over
plaster. It is one of those rare scenes where
everything – from the harmonious colour
of the woodwork to the briskly
perfunctory newel post and the painted
tree stump halfway up the stairs – seems as
inevitably placed as the words in a line of
great poetry.

75

colour; a paint kettle or bucket for larger amounts; stepladder; plumb-line; rags and newspapers.

Method

The design A simple project, such as painting orange trees on either side of a door, will give an idea of different ways of using materials and techniques for varying effects. In this example it is decorative shape and colour we are after, not botanical realism. So the trees should be stylized like those in a sampler, mop heads or pyramids or espalier shapes, studded with bright fruit (a stencil might be used to do these) and standing in decoratively shaped and textured containers – baskets or Versailles tubs. Sketch various shapes and arrangements first, on squared paper in coloured pens, until you find one you like. Copy this on one side of the door with chalk, scaling it up as shown on page 60, keeping to the proportions of your sketch. You can use the first tree to measure up the second.

Colour and relief Now for the colour – decide whether you want the colour simple and flat, which emphasizes shape and colour contrast, or enriched by glaze and surface treatments. If you can't immediately decide, play safe by painting different parts in flat, pale colour – grey trunk, sap-green leaves, pale orange fruit, yellow basket. The surface interest can then be added, if required, using darker tinted glazes – thinned versions of the paint you are using – brown for the trunk, bright green sponged on for foliage, vermilion stippled on the fruit, burnt umber dragged crisscross over the yellow to suggest basketwork. Glazes – see page 225 for how to thin and tint paint to make them – give depth of colour, and in this case a suggestion of relief or modelling. Stipple highlights on the fruit, by dabbing the bristle tips in off-white glaze, or paler areas of foliage, using yellow-green. Likewise, the basketwork can be given more prominence by shading and highlighting the wicker strands. But it is always as well to pause before elaborating a mural treatment too much and ask yourself whether you want your tree or whatever to stand out in greater relief. For while the eye happily accepts incongruities, like trees in tubs floating above the skirting board or baseboard when the treatment is flat and purely decorative, greater realism in the handling might make this sort of thing disturbingly surreal. Trompe l'oeil, see pages 77–81, which is a sort of visual joke, exploits such incongruities. Otherwise, it is an accepted mural convention that flat two-dimensional shapes work best unless the mural is actually intended to open up walls by suggesting landscapes seen in depth, framed by columns, perhaps, or fantastic topiary, or a vine-festooned pergola. Even here, though, keep the effects stylized, merely pinching a few tricks for suggesting distance, such as shading the sky from sky blue at the top to the merest wash of blue on the horizon, and using grey-mauve or grey-blue for distant hills.

Varnish Any mural that you are pleased with should be varnished with clear matt polyurethane varnish, because walls are inevitably subject to wear and knocks and may need occasional wiping down; it would be sad to watch your masterpiece fading like Leonardo da Vinci's *Last Supper*.

Trompe l'oeil

Trompe l'oeil means 'to deceive the eye'. In terms of decorative painting this involves using the traditional resources of a skilled artist to suggest three dimensions where there are only two, so that for just a fraction of a moment one believes a painted object to be real. Trompe l'oeil is chiefly used as a witty solution to an architectural, or perhaps a decorative, problem. For example, a room is unbalanced by having a prettily domed alcove on one side of the mantelpiece, but not on the other. Rather than knocking back walls and commissioning expensive carpentry, a trompe l'oeil artist paints in a matching alcove, achieving symmetry and a talking point all at once. The charm of trompe l'oeil, of course, is that you can conjure up just about anything your imagination can create, and your technique can cope with. So on a do-it-yourself level, for example, one could paint a trompe l'oeil carpet down the middle of a bare wooden staircase, or cover a wall with mock Delft tiles behind a basin or kitchen sink, or liven up a flat modern door with trompe l'oeil panels – see pages 93–7 for how to paint these.

Apart from its usefulness in disguising architectural defects, I like the jokiness, the element of surprise that never fails to get childish 'oohs' and 'aahs' as the deception is unmasked. One trompe l'oeil painting I found particularly appealing was a recessed alcove with shelves on a blank bathroom wall, holding a collection of the sort of thing one might not normally associate with bathrooms – some pretty old books with gilt tooled bindings, a vase of sweet-williams, some china ornaments. As well as filling up the blank wall nicely it gave this most utilitarian room a civilized air.

There is no use pretending trompe l'oeil is easy, like stencilling or even simple mural painting. On the other hand, I think it is worth mentioning in a book for amateur painters and decorators because it is not beyond the reach of anyone clever and patient enough to copy exactly. In other words it is imitative rather than creative. I would not leap in doing a full-scale trompe l'oeil bookcase surmounted by marble busts, unless you are a fairly skilled amateur artist or Sunday painter, but by sticking to something fairly simple like a frieze of trellis work, 'treillage', in a bedroom, or a make-believe window with a storybook view in an interior room, anyone would have a fair chance of success.

Techniques Architectural trompe l'oeil is done in a technique reminiscent of 'grisaille', which is a decorative development of the old art student's exercise in monochrome painting, or suggesting solid form, perspective and so on, with different shades of one colour only – lightened with white or darkened with black. A decorative cartouche, like a small bas-relief plaque, is often painted in grisaille over rather grandly panelled doorways to finish them off handsomely and balance up a collection of pictures.

Left Unexpectedness is the charm of much trompe l'oeil. In England, no scene is more tranquil and evocative than a country cricket match, but nowhere is it more unexpected than in a city kitchen. Even the shutters are painted to complete the illusion, so that people seated round the table are transported to a busy rural idyll.

Above More bravura trompe l'oeil painting, used to bring life to a plain, white-painted brick wall. Everything in this photograph, except the wall and the pools, is paint magic, right down to the champagne bottle left on the 'doorstep' by some munificent milkman.

79

The best way to paint a trompe l'oeil trellis is quite simply to get hold of a length of white painted trellis, pin it up, and sketch it under various lights. Place together these sketches so that they follow the light and shade as they fall on the surfaces you intend to paint in trompe l'oeil. Rendered with less painstaking exactness these will serve as a model. Remember that the degree of finish required to deceive the eye at ceiling level is not as great as is that required at eye level. If you want to add climbing plants entwined in the trellis, a short cut is to use stencils for leaf and flower motifs.

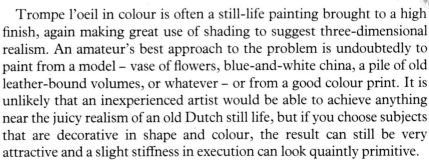

Trompe l'oeil in colour is often a still-life painting brought to a high finish, again making great use of shading to suggest three-dimensional realism. An amateur's best approach to the problem is undoubtedly to paint from a model – vase of flowers, blue-and-white china, a pile of old leather-bound volumes, or whatever – or from a good colour print. It is unlikely that an inexperienced artist would be able to achieve anything near the juicy realism of an old Dutch still life, but if you choose subjects that are decorative in shape and colour, the result can still be very attractive and a slight stiffness in execution can look quaintly primitive.

Some useful tips Here are a few suggestions you might find helpful. Don't be afraid of combining stencils with freehand work where the subject seems to admit it, for formalized forest trees, say, or sheep in a landscape, or bunches of grapes. The effect can be both pretty and witty. Using a stippled finish over any large coloured area can be effective, too, giving a pointillist effect. Sponging is always the quickest way to suggest foliage, as I have already suggested. Adding personal details is a sure way to enliven any mural – try putting familiar buildings into a landscape, or family portraits into scenes with figures, not detailed close-ups so much as characteristic outlines. Finally, over-brilliant colour effects can be toned down most easily by applying a cream glaze (white paint tinted with a little ochre and raw umber) over the whole work. Thin the glaze to make it a very fine, pale film.

Try a trompe l'oeil cartouche above a doorway: a carefully shaded sketch of a real example is the best guide, but remember that the shading should suggest even, overhead light. Formal, delicately shaded effects, like fluted pillars and pediment can be brought off using masking tape and a stippling brush to create a shaded effect. Use grey-brown glazes or paints over a creamy ground.

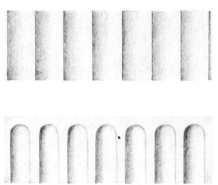

In the same way, reproduce classical stucco, plasterwork or stone by using graduated shading to suggest three-dimensional modelling, but keep the colouring simple, ranging from dirty white or cream for the highlights or prominent areas, down through buffs, greyish browns, to near-black for the most recessed and shadowed areas.

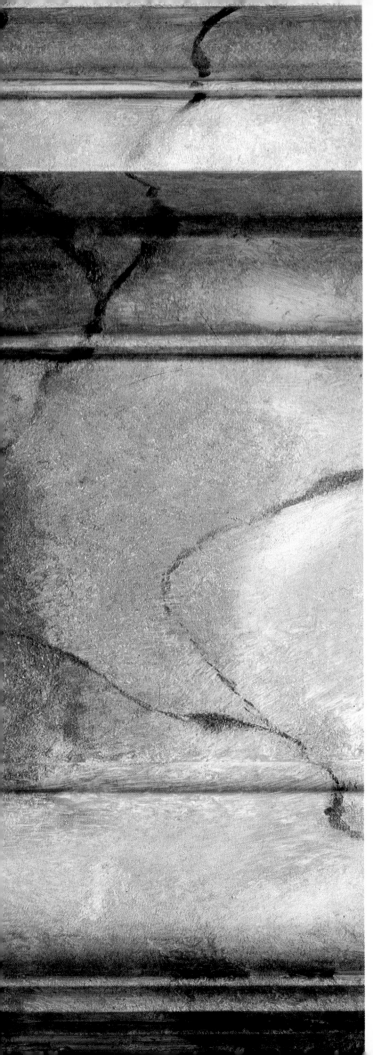

Woodwork

The woodwork in a room – doors, windows, architraves, skirting or baseboard, dado – has something of the same relationship to the walls as a frame has to a picture. It acts as a boundary, creating a useful visual break between horizontal and vertical surfaces, indoors and outdoors. Chair and picture rails, as well as serving practical functions (to protect walls from chair backs and as an anchor for pictures respectively); are also architectural devices for breaking up flat planes and improving a room's proportions. In the days when wood and labour were cheaper, all such details were generously scaled, with handsome mouldings, both solid and structural looking. Doors were panelled, architraves of a dignified width, skirtings or baseboards of a depth and thickness that balanced ceiling height and cornices. Woodwork like this adds greatly to the appearance of a room and is worth making into a decorative feature. Painting it all shiny whiter-than-white makes it compete with the wall surfaces instead of framing them. If you have well-proportioned woodwork you might consider other ways of treating it.

Making good and preparation

It always pays off to take special pains in preparing woodwork for painting. These surfaces get a lot of handling and if the paint is full of craters and cracks it will collect dirt that is hard to wipe off. The degree of making good required depends on the state of the old paintwork. If it is reasonably smooth and level it usually needs no more than washing down with weak sugar soap solution to remove grime, plus a little filling and sanding down to hide any cracks or nail holes.

Stripping down

Up to a point, badly scarred, chipped woodwork can be salvaged by extensive filling and making good. No one would needlessly undertake the job of burning off paint. But if the paintwork is really dilapidated, or if it is the sort of finish that is apt to discolour, or 'bleed' into the paint layers on top, you will save time in the long run by removing it.

Burning off with a blowlamp and combination shave hook is the quickest method: it's worth getting yourself a good-sized gas blowlamp from a builders' merchant or hardware store, which will do the job properly. Always start at the bottom of the area you are stripping – because heat rises and will soften the paint just ahead of your scraper as you work upwards – and put a metal container on the floor to catch the hot, melted fragments. Move the blowlamp to and fro, following it with the scraper. Strip mouldings first, then panels and then flat surfaces such as skirtings or baseboards; strip with the grain of the wood.

Paint stripper is a rather slower method of getting back to the wood. Follow the maker's instructions, but allow a good time for the stripper to soak into the paint and soften it before you start to scrape – and remember to wear rubber gloves to protect your hands. After stripping, wipe over the wood surface with white spirit [mineral spirits] to remove the chemical and then rub down with sandpaper. Use a flat scraper for flat areas and a shave hook for working round windows, doors and mouldings.

Previous page A wooden fire surround lavishly transformed by marbling.

To make a quick, neat job of filling extensive hairline cracks along skirting or baseboard, round door panels, or where built-in units meet walls or ceiling, mix all-purpose filler [spackle] and water to a creamy paint consistency, and brush this into the cracks with an ordinary decorators' brush. The brush will fill the cracks accurately and fast, and levels off the filler so that little or no sanding is required.

For larger cracks, use all-purpose filler mixed to a soft paste, and put a dab of undercoat or primer in the cracks first to encourage the filler to grip, and discourage it from shrinking. Fill with a table knife, or artists' palette knife, and then level off while it is still malleable by wiping with a damp rag firmly over the top. Use special wood filler [wood putty] for window frames; it is designed to expand and contract with the wood, and is applied like other fillers.

Touch in knots with patent knotting [knot sealer] – use 1 coat on stripped, seasoned old wood, 2 or 3 on new. This is important, because otherwise resin from knots will seep up as a yellow stain through subsequent paint layers.

Cracks and knots

Give new or stripped woodwork a coat of primer – the first coat in a paint system – and then an undercoat [American readers will probably use an enamel undercoater only], which you can tint to match the top finish. Rub these down lightly with fine sandpaper when dry and hard to give a superfine base for the top coat. Ideally to give body there should be 2 coats of undercoat – the first being thinned with white spirit [mineral spirits], the second used straight from the tin.

Previously painted woodwork won't need a primer, but sand down old gloss [enamel] paint after cleaning to provide tooth for the undercoat.

Always leave paint plenty of time to dry out between coats.

Primer and undercoat

Most of the woodwork finishes described here are based on a lean, matt look, achieved with a flat oil-based paint, see page 213. This is the effect most decorators prefer, as being elegantly unobtrusive. Mid-sheen oil-based paint, see page 214, can be used if you prefer a slight sheen, but don't use semigloss, gloss or enamel unless you intend to get a laquer effect. If you do want a high shine, and a greater depth of colour than gloss paint could provide, use a tinted glaze followed by gloss varnish, or just tinted varnish, as for lacquering walls, see pages 52–3.

The classic painters' routine for painting woodwork was door first, then windows, fireplace, chair rails, and finally skirting or baseboard. This is because when painting the skirting one's brush may pick up stray dust from the floor, which will get into the paint and mar the surface.

Top coat

Narrow decorators' brushes, 50 or 75 mm [2 or 3 in], plus an even smaller one 12 or 25 mm [$\frac{1}{2}$ or 1 in] for fiddly 'cutting in'; a paint kettle or tin; white spirit [mineral spirits]; fine and medium grade sandpaper; newspaper; clean rags; a stepladder. See pages 88–9 for how to paint windows and for the sequence to observe in painting panelled doors.

Equipment

Simple Decorative Treatments

Decorators often use a palette of 'dirty' or off-whites to emphasize panels on cupboards and doors, shutters, and other decorative details. This sophisticated treatment discreetly brings out their three-dimensional modelling while retaining a feeling of lightness and airiness. Equal discretion is shown in the choice of paint texture, usually flat or matt, occasionally with a sheen, never glossy. There is nothing precious or arbitrary about this, it just looks better, especially in old houses where it gives the effect of the old lead paints that changed colour with time.

Three shades of off-white are used: darkest for panels, a shade lighter for the mouldings round them, and the lightest of all for the surrounds – which would also include linking woodwork areas such as architrave, skirting or baseboard, chair rail and so forth. Some decorators reverse the sequence, using the palest shade for the panels and the darkest for surrounds. The degree of contrast between the three shades will depend on how elaborate the rest of the room scheme is, and therefore how subtle or interesting you want the woodwork to be.

Sequence of painting To paint all the woodwork in a small room you will need about $\frac{1}{2}$ a litre [1 US pint] of paint. Begin with the light areas, the surrounds. This may not be orthodox, but makes sense from the point of view of not wasting paint. Paint them in the lightest shade, just perceptibly off-white. To make it, mix a dollop of raw umber and a dot each of black and yellow ochre artists' oil colours into a flat or mid-sheen white oil-based paint. This takes the glare off the white without noticeably altering it.

Next tint some of the remaining paint a shade darker by adding a little more raw umber (very little, since the quantities are much reduced) and another speck of black and yellow. Try the effect before painting all the mouldings – it should be just perceptibly darker. Finally, repeat the tinting process again to get the darkest shade for the panels themselves. The paint by now will be a warm grey, with a slightly greenish cast, a most attractive colour that looks right with almost any wall colour or type of wall covering.

Shades of white

Opposite Built-in cupboards, while practical for storage, may overpower a room. Here, dragging in a subtle umber links the large areas of woodwork, and bridges the colour gap between the orange-tawny colourwashed walls and the flat white door panels. The dragged cupboards look less bulky and more streamlined than if they had simply been painted in plain white.

Matching colours

Colouring woodwork to match the walls is another, slightly more daring, approach effectively used in many old American houses. It looks particularly fine when there is a lot of woodwork to begin with – shutters, panelling, dado, as well as the usual doors and skirtings or baseboards. When all these are painted to match in one of the gentle but positive

Sequence for painting doors and windows

Painting the different parts of a panelled door in a specific order is not fussy pedantry, but a time-proven and logical saver of time and mess and effort.

If the door opens towards you, begin by painting (1) the rebates and (2) opening edge. If it opens away, paint the rebates and (3) hinged edge. Paint (4) the mouldings of the top panels next, then (5) the panels themselves – brush the paint well into decorative mouldings, but not so thickly that it spills over into 'runs'. Paint (6) the lower panels in the same way. Next paint (7) the central vertical section, then (8) the horizontal sections, or rails – top, middle and bottom in that order – and lastly, (9) the outer vertical sections, or stiles. Finally, paint (10) the door frame and (11) architrave. Leave the door wedged firmly ajar until dry.

For a good even surface, a large flat area, such as a flush door, is best painted in sections. Start at the top and work down, going quickly so that the paint doesn't dry before you have completed the routine of laying on, cross-brushing, smoothing out and laying off.

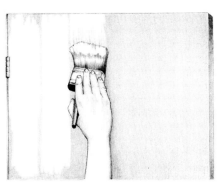

1 Lay paint on, using vertical strokes

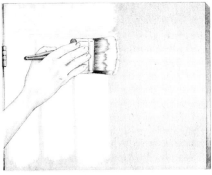

2 Without recharging bristles, cross-brush

3 Lay on and cross-brush a second section

4 Smooth out both sections

5 Lay off, moving away from the wet edge

Like doors, windows should be painted in the correct sequence, which depends upon their construction. Use a metal shield or masking tape to keep paint from getting on to the glass.

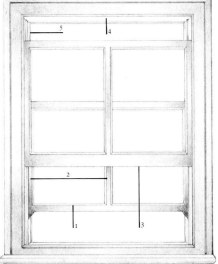 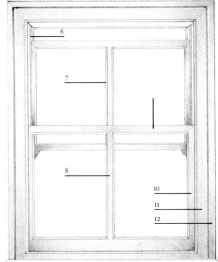

To paint a sash window, raise the lower sash and pull the upper sash down, so that you can paint (1) the meeting rail, including its rebate (where the pane meets the wood) and bottom edge. Then paint what you can of (2) the bars and stiles on the upper sash, (3) the bottom edge of the lower sash, (4) the soffit, (5) about 50mm [2in] down the outside runners.

Then close the window almost completely and paint (6) 50mm [2in] down the inside runners. Now paint all the (7) rebates, (8) the cross-bars, (9) the remaining cross-rails, (10) the stiles, (11) the window frame and (12) the architrave. Make sure you don't get paint on the sash-cords. There is no need to paint the whole length of the runners.

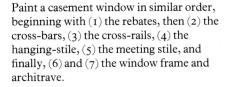

Paint a casement window in similar order, beginning with (1) the rebates, then (2) the cross-bars, (3) the cross-rails, (4) the hanging-stile, (5) the meeting stile, and finally, (6) and (7) the window frame and architrave.

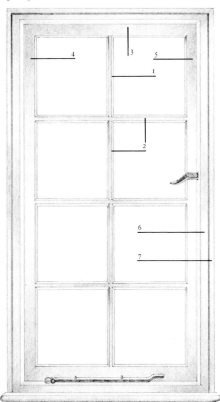

89

Opposite An exhilarating room, decorated with considerable brio and finesse, boldly using blue and off-white in a variety of textures and patterns. Study the balance between the dominant blue and the soft watery one. The former stands out in the wall and bed coverings and picks out the mouldings on the cupboard doors, while the latter is used between the door mouldings and between the cornice bands. Both have been used in the marbling of the skirting, chair rail and picture frames.

colours of the Colonial period – blueberry, cinnamon, or that especially romantic blue-green that is formed by yellowing varnish over faded blue paint – the effect is extraordinarily reposeful, with a rigorous simplicity that gives added value to rich colours in pictures, rugs and furnishings. Again, the paint should be lean-textured, flat and non-reflective. (An all-over gloss colour finish can be effective too, but in a quite different way, sleek and sophisticated, not atmospheric.) Both walls and woodwork can be dragged discreetly in a darker tone of the same colour for added texture and to soften and blend everything together.

This one-colour treatment is also useful where skirtings or baseboards and architraves are meagre and skimpy. In this case it is a mistake to call attention to them and painting them to match the walls is a good way to fade them out.

Contrasting colours

Contrasting colour in woodwork can look very rich, or very gay. I remember a room with faded red walls and grey-blue woodwork, and another, more eccentric combination of tawny orange walls and pea green woodwork, which worked very well as a background to opulent Moorish pieces and vivid embroideries and rugs. Colours usually look best when they have a similar tonal value – that is, colours that would register identically grey in a black-and-white photograph. Soft reds and blues, or greens, can look very good together. Or, if Regency sprightliness appeals to you, you could try combining pastels like pistachio green, cerise pink, wheat ear yellow. Often these contrast colour treatments on walls and woodwork are given a dragged finish, in a glaze a tone or two darker, to soften them becomingly. Or, an attractive variant of dragging is to give the tinted glaze a fanciful graining treatment, combing it to suggest some fantasy material between wood and marble.

Picking out mouldings

Picking out decorative mouldings, cornices and so on in colour is a favourite technique with decorators who want to give a crisply finished look to a room – for an example see the photograph opposite. It is also a good way to break up large expanses of woodwork, such as fitted cupboards. As the surfaces of new cupboards tend to be flat these days, you may need to add mouldings yourself first, mitring them at the corners and tacking or glueing them in place. One idea is to paint the prominent parts of the moulding or cornice in a strong colour, filling in the recessed space between them in a softer tone of the same. Choose your colour to reinforce one already in the room scheme – either a straight match or a tone lighter or darker.

Apply the colour in the form of a watery-thin glaze, made from flat or mid-sheen paint since it should look matt when dry. Try it out on a test area first, to check that it is intense enough to register. Use a soft, narrow brush – a 12 mm [$\frac{1}{2}$ in] paintbrush or artists' brush – then neaten up the edges with a fine sable one.

Dragging

Most of the decorative finishes described for use on wall surfaces – stippling, sponging, ragging – can be adapted to flatter beautiful woodwork or to make the best of the flat, usually meagre, fittings prevalent in so many modern houses. Dragging, particularly, is often employed with painted woodwork, using a thin tinted paint glaze to soften outlines and give a delicate patina of colour.

Off-white Dragging can be used very attractively in the three-shades-of-white treatment described above. To do this, first paint the woodwork surfaces with flat or mid-sheen white oil-based paint and allow to dry hard. Then mix up a thin glaze, and drag on the three shades of off-white, tinting the glaze in the same way with raw umber, black and yellow ochre oil colours.

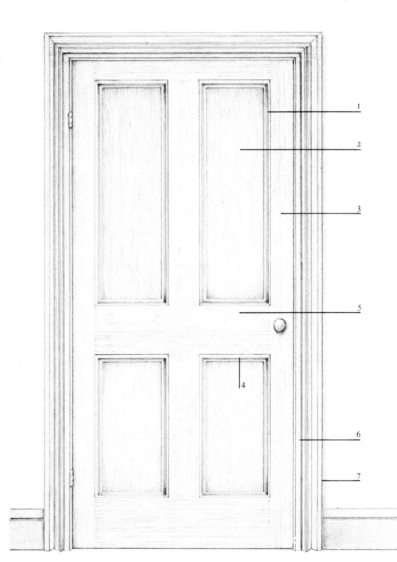

The direction in which you drag the paint on doors and other panelled woodwork usually echoes their construction – that is, the brushwork goes with the grain. Thus, dragging is vertical on (1) vertical mouldings, (2) panels and (3) stiles, and horizontal on (4) horizontal mouldings and (5) rails. Similarly, on (6) frame and (7) architrave, drag up the sides and across the top. An exception to this rule is a door with three or more crosswise panels – here the grain of the panels usually runs horizontally, and they should therefore be dragged in the same direction.

Colour Woodwork painted to match the walls, see page 87, is sometimes dragged in a darker or lighter tone of the same colour to add texture. If a wall with a distressed finish has woodwork painted in a contrasting colour, it is a useful technique to drag the latter in a darker or lighter tone, since two distressed colours provide a softer contrast than two plain ones. If the contrast between walls and woodwork is very harsh, a glaze tinted with raw umber is an ideal choice as it modifies and softens any colour attractively.

Method

Follow the instructions for dragging walls, see pages 27–32, using transparent oil glaze [glazing liquid] or thinned oil-based paint, see pages 224–27, tinted with stainers or oil colours, over a flat or mid-sheen base paint. The one difference is that dragging woodwork presents a directional problem, on panelled doors especially. I have seen these dragged entirely vertically, but the usual method is to drag in the direction of the wood grain beneath. Thus the brushstrokes are vertical on the panels, vertical timbers, and on both sides of the architrave or door frame, and horizontal on cross timbers and along the top of the frame. The same holds good for window frames and shutters. Skirting boards or baseboards, chair rails and other horizontal pieces of wood-work are dragged horizontally.

Varnish Apply 1 or 2 coats of clear, matt polyurethane varnish to protect dragged woodwork. It is especially important to varnish doors, since they do get a tremendous amount of wear, handling, slamming and so on.

Trompe l'oeil panelling

Very simple trompe l'oeil panelling does wonders for flush doors, which can look bland and dull painted plain white. The recessed panels are drawn in with a little thinned flat or mid-sheen white paint tinted to a soft greenish grey with raw umber. Slightly darkening the lines on two sides suggests shadows, giving the trompe l'oeil effect. The subtlety of the panelling is in the proportions. Most flush doors are narrow for their height. A two-panel arrangement, with the larger panel on top, helps cut the height and make the door look wider and better proportioned. French doors are traditionally panelled this way. Without seriously attempting to fool the eye, this trompe l'oeil treatment attractively breaks up the flatness of the door and helps to merge it into the overall decorative scheme. Drag the door and panels in a paler shade of the same grey, with architrave and skirting or baseboard to match.

Preparation

All surfaces should be clean, smooth and well sanded down to key them for the new paint. Gloss [enamel] paint needs extra sanding to cut the gloss. The ground colour should be white – give the door and architrave 1 coat of flat or mid-sheen white oil-based paint over 1 undercoat, or whatever white paint was already there.

The plain backs of folding shutters often look sadly blank: *left*, a trompe l'oeil scene turns them into an attractive feature. *Above*, painted detail, like the trim on door and panel and the marbled chair rail and skirting, makes all the difference to a small hallway.

Break up a large dull wall area visually by painting a decorative finish on the dado; *above*, marbling looks particularly good on hall and staircase walls. Not many rooms could take a spectacular door treatment in two tones of tortoiseshell, *right*, but here the shiny red walls hold their own.

Above Shutters look pretty painted to match the walls: here, both shutters and walls have been dragged in a gentle pink with the mouldings picked out in white for emphasis.

Left The impact here comes from the contrast between the sponged lettuce greens of the woodwork and the strawberry pink of the walls. The flat texture is important to the success of this look.

Below left and *centre* Restored graining from the Brighton Pavilion in England.

Below right Graining in conventional wood colours to imitate mahogany with oak panels.

Materials Flat or mid-sheen white oil-based paint; raw umber artists' oil colour; a 50 or 75 mm [2 or 3 in] decorators' brush; a square-ended artists' oil brush, 12 mm [½ in] wide, for painting the trompe l'oeil stripes; white spirit [mineral spirits]; clean rags or paper; pencil and ruler or straight-edge; masking tape.

Method *Panels* When the base coat is dry, mark out the panelling with a pencil and ruler or straight-edge. Draw two lines about 12 mm [½ in] apart to form each 'panel'. They should be 7 to 10 cm [3 or 4 in] inside the door edges, clearing the door handle. The space between the two panels can be a little wider – about 8 to 11 cm [3½ to 4½ in].

Having drawn in the panel lines, make about a tablespoonful of very thin medium-grey paint, by mixing 1 part white oil-based paint with 2 of white spirit, and tinting with raw umber. Fill in the lines with this, using the artists' brush. If you can do it freehand, so much the better. Stand well back and draw the brush down or across, looking at a point just beyond the brush, as for lining, pages 184–88. Otherwise stick masking tape on either side of the lines to keep the edges straight.

Add a little more raw umber to your mixture to deepen the grey and paint in the two darker lines on each panel. They will be the top and the side nearer the window; this imitates the shadows cast by real panelling. Where the light source is less direct, from a window across the room, darken the side that looks right to you. When the lines are dry, peel off the masking tape and wipe away any tacky deposit with methylated spirits [denatured alcohol].

Once mastered, the simple technique of painting trompe l'oeil 'panels' can be used on a plain flush door in many ways. The point to remember is that the two darker lines should always go where the shade would fall on genuine mouldings. Some possible combinations of panels are shown below.

Left Enliven a dull door by using a single stencil, either on the walls above the door, or, turned the other way, inside the trompe l'oeil panels themselves. For a large size version of this motif, to copy, see pages 64–5.

Dragging Now mix up further thinned white paint and raw umber, but using less umber so that you get a shade or two lighter than the original painted lines. Using the wider brush, drag this over the whole door surface and architrave for an evenly streaked effect, see pages 27–32 and 92–3. The dragging strokes should be horizontal at the top, centre and bottom, and vertical on sides and panels. Skirting or baseboard and chair rail can be painted and dragged – horizontally – with the same white base coat and pale grey thinned top coat.

Varnish When the door is quite dry, varnish over the whole surface with clear matt polyurethane varnish to protect it. Two coats are best if the door is likely to be handled a lot.

Below For an alternative flourish, try painting a trompe l'oeil fanlight in grisaille above the door.

97

Fantasy Finishes

Graining

Grainers and marblers consider themselves the elite of painters and decorators, and they are a proud body of men, who spend years learning the secrets of their craft and are apt to view with suspicion and reserve the fumbling attempts of unskilled operators in the field. Their best efforts may be seen in Victorian pubs, and in the foyers of banks and other imposing edifices. Out of deference to their feelings, let me say immediately that the sort of graining we are dealing with here is pure fantasy, a lighthearted suggestion of woodiness that makes no pretensions to botanical accuracy.

Graining need not be dark or even wood coloured. The more examples I see, the more convinced I am that this is a technique to have fun with, including using lollipop colours unknown to nature. The more realistic wood impersonations, like the rosewood graining described on pages 204–5, look distinguished where wood is appropriate, but there are places – on kitchen units, fitted cupboards or closets, bath surrounds – where fantasy graining, which is a sort of mix of distressing techniques, fits the bill neatly.

Decorators have begun to revive graining for clients who appreciate the verve of this technique, taking their inspiration from some of the more exotic traditional examples – like the doors in the Brighton Pavilion, in England, which are grained in raspberry red over buff, or shades of green, or Ham House, near London, where a quite surreal oyster walnut graining, combined with gilding, is proof that stately rooms – or even small modern ones – don't have to look frigidly well-behaved.

Opposite An example of what talent and self-confidence can achieve. A grained wall forms a corner with a trompe l'oeil bookcase, painted next to a real bookcase so cunningly that the two are almost indistinguishable. The effect is set off by a marbled skirting that echoes the shelf of genuine marble.

Preparation

A smooth ground of flat or mid-sheen oil-based paint, see pages 213–14, gives a surface over which brush or comb glides happily. The ground colour can be tinted to an approximately woody colour (buff, red-brown, dull yellow – study some pieces of grained wood and match the base shade to the lightest tone of the timber), or it could be any shade that consorts with your room decoration and would throw a fantasy-grained finish into relief. Tone on tone is the norm, like raspberry on almond pink, deep blue-green over sky blue, bottle green on pistachio green. Keep the ground colour pale, though; it has to take a lot of grained colour without looking heavy and pompous.

Materials

Glaze Transparent oil glaze [glazing liquid] or homemade glaze – see pages 224–27 – is best. Tint with universal stainers [tinting colours], or artists' oils plus a dash of drier (optional) to hurry up the time when you can safely touch it. Thinned paint glazes dry too soon to allow one to exploit the various grainers' tricks. Thin oil glaze as usual with white spirit [mineral spirits]; see pages 225–27 on thinning and tinting.

Brushes and other equipment Master grainers work with a battery of brushes designed to produce such varied effects as naturalistic knots, heart wood and oyster patterns. These brushes have Dickensian names – mottlers, overgrainers, floggers – which are a delight to con over. A flogger or dragging brush, see page 232, is particularly useful for graining, but I think beginners are likely to do just as well with a motley of improvised tools.

You need a small decorators' brush to apply the glaze and a wide, thinly bristled brush to do the graining. You could remove clumps of its bristles with a razor to give a spaced comb effect. A homemade comb with randomly notched teeth, cut from a slice of stout plastic or cardboard, will make a more dramatic grain; a large soft-bristled brush, like a painters' dusting brush, is important for softening grain patterns. You can improvise a 'knot' tool by whittling a stamp from an ordinary cork, or by coring a small stiff brush, like a stencil brush, so that it stamps a little round ring. A chamois leather is useful, as is a good supply of rags.

Method Study a cleanly figured piece of wood and memorize some of the pleasant vagaries – knots, like islands parting the flow of the grain, heart wood like mountains on contour maps, highlights that ripple like stretch marks across the graining, zigzaggy or wobbly swerves in the basically parallel grain markings. It doesn't matter too much what type of wood you are studying, though the grainier ones – oak, mahogany, walnut, pine – are obviously more stimulating. The point to keep firmly in mind is that nature, most resourceful and fertile of patternmakers, is never monotonous.

As with all the more strongly marked finishes, it makes things easier to treat your painted surface as a series of panels – abstract pictures as it were, in which the various decorative elements are differently combined each time. Some conventions should be observed. For instance, the grain should flow the way it would if you were using real wood. Too many knots, unless you want a knotty bird's-eye maple or deal effect, look spotty. A preponderance of smoothly flowing, curving grain, broken only here and there by jagged heart wood or knots, is the effect to aim at.

Begin by brushing a thin glaze of colour over your surface. Then, using the clean, dry brush with spaced bristles, draw the bristle tips over the wet glaze to make fine stripes – like dragged painting – suggesting the general grain flow. Wobble your wrist just a little in mid stroke to give a woody swerve. With the soft dusting brush or flogger, whip the stripes gently all over to blur them and give a flecked, almost hairy appearance. You now have the basic grain of the wood, a canvas with characteristic woody texture to which you can add highlights, heart wood and knots as desired. See illustrations opposite for how to do this.

When you have blocked in your graining picture – with discretion,

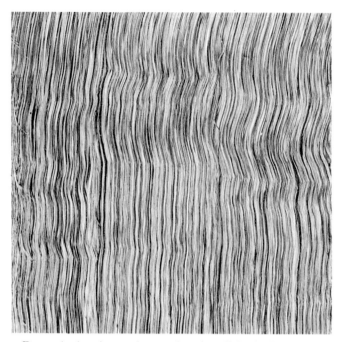

1 Drag a dry brush over the wet glaze, in a slight ripple.

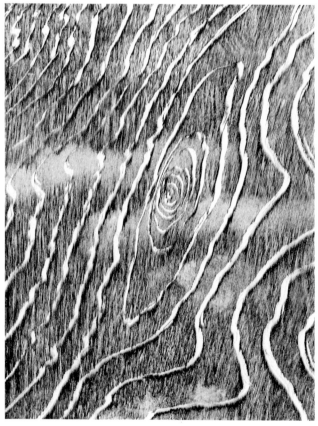

2 Blur the lines very gently with a soft, clean brush.

3 Using the sharp edge of a cork, draw heart wood lines into the wet glaze, running very roughly parallel.

4 Sketch in a knot with the cork edge, then draw in grain lines so that they part around it.

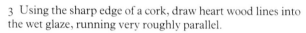

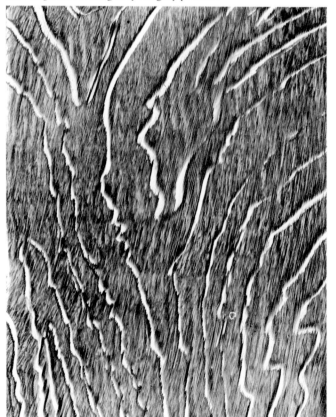

Marbling

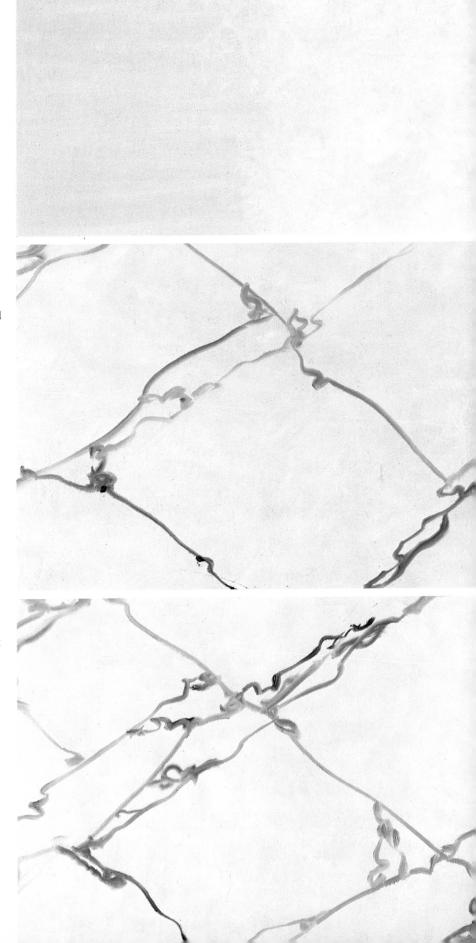

For pale, greyish marbling, start with a dry ground of white mid-sheen oil-based paint, lightly sanded. Mix up a glaze of 2 parts flat or mid-sheen white oil-based paint to 1 part white spirit [mineral spirits], tinted with a squeeze of raw umber oil colour and a dash of black. Brush this over the surface and gently sponge it.

Mix a little black oil colour into some raw umber to produce grey-brown. With a small brush and a fidgety brushstroke apply veins to the wet glazed surface. They should wander across it diagonally, branching off to left and right, and should have a beginning and end – genuine marble veining does not start or peter out in the middle of nowhere.

Sponge the veins lightly to remove excess paint. Take a dry paintbrush and gently draw it back and forth across the veining in one diagonal direction (say, bottom left to top right) and then the other, (bottom right to top left) – this softens the harsh lines. Mix up more black with less umber to get a dark grey, and take some up on your little brush. Fidget in some smaller veins, connecting them to the large ones. Like them, they should mostly run diagonally.

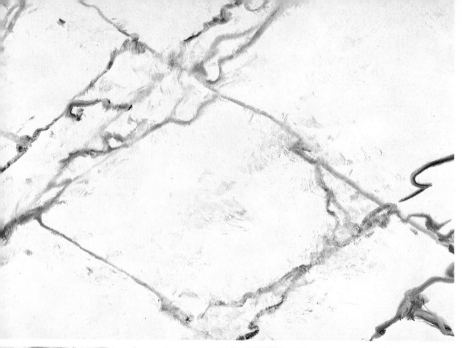

Use a sponge or paper tissue to soak up the excess paint from the little veins. You can then dab this on again in the plain areas, to imitate the variegations of real marble.

Now thoroughly soften the whole surface, drawing your dry paintbrush gently back and forth along each diagonal. Go over each diagonal at least 3 times.

When the surface is quite dry – after a few hours – fidget in extra veins in thinned white paint. Add some dabs of the same colour to form pebble shapes, for emphasis. After 24 hours, varnish with matt or semigloss polyurethane varnish – when this is almost dry, sprinkle it with French chalk or household flour, then polish it with a soft cloth. This reproduces the sheen of real marble.

don't overdo it – a very gentle softening with the soft brush, bristle tips only, in the direction of the grain usually helps to pull it all together. But do go gently – a big blur is not what you want. If you think part of the surface looks too busy, wipe it out while the glaze is still wet. Try not to smudge the rest of the work. Leave the finished graining to dry hard.

Vinegar paint Traditional grainers often preferred water-based paints, for their special transparency and speedy drying. The vinegar or stale ale mixture described on pages 201–4 is easier to manipulate than plain watercolour, as its sugar content makes it slightly sticky. So I suggest you try this if you want a more delicate look.

Varnish Oil glazes do not need varnishing, though they will be more durable if you do. Use clear matt or gloss varnish, depending on whether you want a quiet or shiny look. Vinegar or ale paint must have a final varnishing to fix and protect it.

Marbling

Marbling falls into two categories: the highly skilled, closely imitative, slow and subtle technique, based on long study of the original material and aiming to deceive the eye into accepting the painted version as real, and then a much faster, impressionistic, tongue-in-cheek technique that is content merely to suggest the rich colours and endlessly varied patterning of marble, going for a 'fantasy' effect rather than an identifiable type of stone. The latter approach, though perhaps less suited to really splendid rooms, is the one most decorators prefer, as it is lighter and less demanding, and for our purposes far more easily assimilated and successfully executed by rank amateurs. Having mastered the impressionistic style, there is nothing to prevent anyone getting hold of an example of the marble of their choice – working from life is the best training, they tell me – and experimenting with coloured glazes, brushwork and feathering to get a closer imitation of the real thing. Since there are at least eight categories of marble – brecciated, serpentine, travertine, crinoidal, variegated, unicoloured, laminated, statuary, alabaster – and endless sub-sections, the subject is not one that can be compressed into a few pages. Fantasy marbling, however, is quick and fun and allows a great deal of scope to anyone willing to try this most elegant of 'broken colour' effects.

A wooden fireplace surround looks particularly sumptuous given the fantasy-marble treatment – one might hang above it a mirror with the frame painted to match, or perhaps continue the marbling on skirting board or baseboard and dado. Alternatively, a bathroom is a good place to practise one's skills – starting with the bath surround, and extending over woodwork, walls and floors for allover splendour.

It is probably a good idea to begin on something small, but if you are marbling a large surface, it might embolden you to visualize it as lots of separate blocks, ruling these out and painting the outlines before getting down to filling them in with colour. This way you can go about the area bit by bit, and there is less chance of your marble pattern getting too fixed and unvarying, which is deadening over a large area. It is important to work quickly and firmly. Don't be afraid of making mistakes; they probably won't show, and if they do, wipe them off and start again.

The ground coat should be white mid-sheen oil-based paint, quite dry, and lightly rubbed down so that it is smooth and free from brushmarks.

Preparation

Flat or mid-sheen white oil-based paint, or undercoat; artists' oil colours in raw umber and black; a 50 mm [2 in] decorators' brush; a small, pointed artists' brush for details; a sponge (preferably marine); white spirit [mineral spirits]; jamjar; saucer; rags.

Materials

The steps described here will give you a pale, grey-green marbled finish, cool and uncompetitive. Make up a thin glaze in a jamjar by mixing roughly 2 parts paint to 1 part white spirit. Add a good squeeze of raw umber and a little black, to give a greenish-grey tint that should be pale, but strong enough to contrast with the white ground. With the decorators' brush apply the glaze over your area or 'block', then sponge it lightly all over to break up the surface.

Method

Veining Put a squirt of raw umber and a squirt of black on the saucer. Mix a little black into the umber for a darker shade of grey. With the small brush, pick up some of this colour and put in large veining across the wet glazed surface, using a fidgety brushstroke, not smooth straight lines. Marble veins tend to meander diagonally, forking off to left and right. But all veining lines should have an end and a beginning, not start in the middle of nothing and fade out again – think of them linking up like roads on a map. Gently sponge the painted veins to remove excess paint, then wipe your paintbrush dry on a rag and brush the veining lightly in one direction diagonally, and then the other, to soften and blur. Now with the small brush, take up a darker mix of black and umber, and fidget in smaller veins here and there, linking up the large ones, like secondary roads cutting across between major ones. Sponge lightly again, and soften with the dry brush. The brush softening has a magical effect – suddenly the crude squiggles begin to look like real marble. Stand back and study your handiwork. It may need a bit more veining somewhere, or perhaps a space enclosed by veining could be broken up into large and small pebble shapes, lightly drawn in with the small brush. But don't overwork it; half the battle with marbling is knowing when to stop. When the surface is dry (in a few hours), fidget some veins across the surface in plain white, to freshen, and 'lift' the marbling. Pebble shapes can be highlighted with a little white too. See the photographs on pages 102–3.

To paint veins, hold the brush loosely and apply them with a fidgety stroke.

Varnish Leave for 24 hours before varnishing with matt or semigloss polyurethane varnish. When almost dry, sprinkle the varnish with

Tortoiseshelling

The ground must be bright yellow mid-sheen oil-based paint, completely dry, and sanded. Using a large decorators' brush, cover it quickly with dark oak gloss varnish stain. Don't worry if this bubbles.

With the brush, fidget the wet varnish into diagonal stripes of zigzags about 5 cm [2 in] wide. These will begin to run into one another almost immediately. Dab walnut-sized splodges of varnish along the diagonal bands, at random but at least 6 or 7 cm [3 in] apart.

Squeeze a blob of burnt umber on to a saucer. Dip a small artists' brush in it and apply curly squiggles along the diagonals, say 2 or 3 cm [1 in] under the previous splodges.

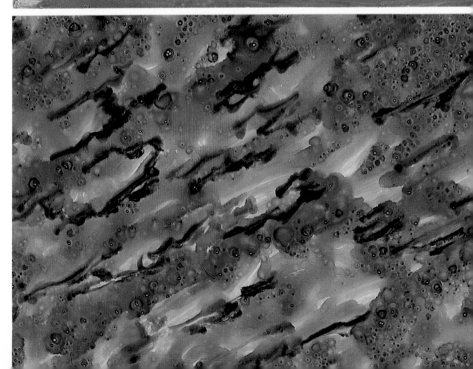

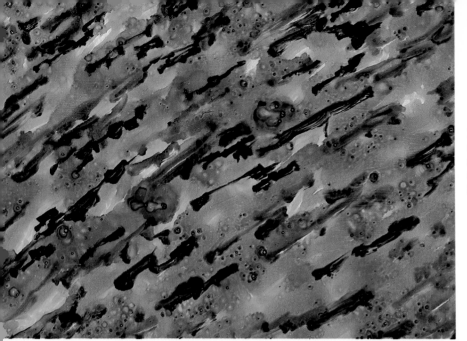

Dip another small brush into black oil colour and place small groups of tadpole shapes in the spaces between the other markings. There should be fewer black marks than umber ones.

Take a clean, dry brush and very softly stroke it across the wet varnish, following the direction of the diagonal bands – in the photograph these run from left up to right. Stroke back even more gently the other way – here, from right down to left. Now repeat this 2-way stroking on the other diagonal, from right up to left, and from left down to right.

Finally, stroke once more back and forth along the first diagonal. You will find that the individual marks have been smoothed out into the subtle patterning of genuine tortoiseshell.

French chalk or household flour and polish it with a soft cloth for a marble-like sheen.

Some tips Study examples of real marble whenever you get a chance, to see the way the surface is broken up. Don't be timid – make your veining bold, thick enough to stand out, and rhythmic. Over a large surface it should change direction fairly often, whereas on a small area it needs to be more balanced.

If you want more colour in your marble or a richer effect, you can repeat the marbling process using a different-coloured glaze – yellow, green, red-brown – on top of the first. The first layer of marbling will show through the second, creating a look of depth, as in the real stone.

Tortoiseshelling

The technique of painting woodwork, or even walls, to look like tortoiseshell is a beautiful example of the intelligent manipulation of paints and varnish to create a desired effect. Confronted by a spectacular tortoiseshell door, rippling with tawny yellow, chestnut brown and shiny black, I doubt whether anyone but an expert in paint behaviour would be able to figure out how it was achieved. Yet, once you grasp the technique, it is possible for the amateur to do, and goes fast enough to cover largish areas at a time. The whole secret is that the colours are laid into wet varnish, and the resultant 'spreading' is controlled by lightly brushing diagonally in two directions with a dry brush, creating the characteristic tortoiseshell markings almost automatically. This is not to say that you should tackle it mechanically, letting the paints do the work for you and repeating the same procedure unvaryingly across a surface. Monotony is always lifeless. Study examples of real or painted tortoiseshell before embarking on this finish, and observe the variety of figuring in the natural material or in the work of a skilled imitator. There are blonde tortoiseshells, leopard-spotted in translucent browns on an amber ground; red tortoiseshells, with a great deal of red-brown background; and darker ones inclining to black and dark browns, as the brown tortoise-shell described here. Tortoiseshell can look superb, but it takes a lot of living up to. It is a rich finish that looks best in small, confined spaces – tiny front halls, with a lot of doors leading off them, small studies, or maybe a bathroom.

Preparation The ground for brown tortoiseshell should be a smooth bright yellow, mid-sheen oil-based paint. A light, sharp yellow is best – chrome (or its lead-free substitute, arylamide) rather than ochre – because the subsequent layers of colour will darken the ground considerably.

Materials Dark oak gloss varnish stain; burnt umber and black artists' oil colours; 2 standard decorators' brushes 50 mm [2 in] wide and 2 small, flat artists' brushes about 12 mm [$\frac{1}{2}$ in] wide – one of each will do, but it means more wiping and cleaning; white spirit [mineral spirits]; clean rags.

108

Using one of the large brushes, cover the surface with the dark oak varnish stain, working speedily and not too carefully. The varnish will probably bubble, but don't worry about this. When the area is covered, use the brush to fidget the wet varnish into diagonal bands of zigzags, roughly 5 cm [2 in] wide. The varnish will go on 'moving' after you have done this, so that the bands will run into each other creating an overall impression of movement. Dab some extra splodges of varnish – about the size of a walnut – along the diagonal rows. Position these fairly quickly and randomly, but not less than about 6 or 7 cm [3 in] apart. Now take the burnt umber and squeeze a blob on to a saucer. Dip one of the small brushes in it and make lively squiggles, like Arabic writing, maybe 2 or 3 cm [1 in] under the previous splodges. Keep working on the same diagonal, and again don't join up the squiggles or make them too regular. Then dip the second small brush into the black oil colour and dab small tadpole shapes in clusters here and there in the blank spaces between the other markings. You should have fewer black squiggles than brown ones.

Stroking Now comes the exciting part. Take up the dry large brush and, following the direction of the diagonals, very gently stroke it across the wet surface to make streaky graph-like peaks as the varnish and paints flow into each other; and then stroke even more gently back in the opposite direction. Repeat this careful two-way stroking operation on the other diagonal (that is, if your paint diagonals and first stroking were top left to bottom right, now stroke from top right to bottom left, and back again). Finally stroke a second time on the original diagonal – gently in one direction and then lightly back. In all you will have brushed across the surface six times (you can soften more than this if you want), and as you do so, you'll see the blobs and streaks magically opening out into the subtle transparent markings of tortoiseshell. The colours will continue moving gently for a while after you have finished – until the varnish 'goes off' – and will dry glossy, as tortoiseshell should be. See pages 106–7.

Blonde tortoiseshell For 'blonde' tortoiseshell, use a light oak varnish stain, or dark oak thinned with white spirit [mineral spirits] over the same yellow base colour; burnt umber – which thins to a rich red-brown when stroked – for the squiggles; and a very little black, or omit it altogether.

A tortoiseshell door, mantelpiece, or whatever, has to be completed in one go so that you don't end up with demarcation lines – unless it is conveniently divided into panels and surrounds that you can treat separately. If you do have a very large area to cover – a wall for instance – you'd need at least two people on the job. Or, you could divide it into panels – say $\frac{1}{2}$ to 1 metre [2 or 3 ft] wide – mark these out with a pencil, and then paint them one by one, alternating the direction of the diagonal tortoiseshell markings to emphasize the join. Masking tape helps to keep a straight edge. Make sure a panel is completely dry before you start on the one next to it.

Floors

111

Floors always present a special problem when one is decorating. They are rarely handsome enough to leave exposed in their natural state, with just an occasional waxing to keep them in shape. Covering them, on the other hand, is expensive, especially if one has to deal with stairs, passages and landings as well as main rooms. One alternative that is becoming increasingly popular, since it is decorative as well as cheap, is to colour the bare wood with dyes, stains or paint, and then varnish for protection.

In fact, decoratively finished exposed wood floors suit many rooms, especially period ones, rather better than swathes of fitted carpet. The bone structure, so to speak, stands revealed, and greater emphasis is placed on good proportions and fine detailing of mouldings or woodwork.

Such floors do have two disadvantages. They are not draughtproof, although caulking the cracks helps, and warm rugs in strategic spots add cosiness where it is needed. They also take a fair while to do, the time being spent more on the varnishing than on the decorating itself. But, on the plus side, they offer almost limitless scope for colour and design, and are by far the cheapest method of making a floor look good whatever its condition. Properly varnished, they are easily maintained with daily sweeping and an occasional mopping, and surprisingly hard-wearing. Painted finishes last for ages, even under heavy foot traffic, providing they are given several coats of protective varnish to start off with, and a refresher coat every year or two; like many painted things, they go on getting softer, mellower and prettier all the time.

Dyeing and staining are quicker to do than painting and have the bonus that they do not obscure the natural wood grain, if that is worth calling attention to. Since most wooden boards have a yellowish cast, the stain colours also emerge attractively modified. This sort of transparent colour is a nice means of adding gentle atmosphere to a room.

However, when it comes to opportunities for colour and pattern, it is the painted finish that really scores. Professional decorators have been quick to seize on this, devising imaginative floor treatments for clients who could well afford carpeting, but are susceptible to the novelty of floors painted to simulate marble intaglio, patchwork quilts or fantastic, colourful Oriental rugs.

Stencilling is another easy way to add colour and pattern to a painted, dyed or stained floor. You can use stencils for a border, or to cover the whole floor, and they can be as lavish and intricate or geometrically simple as you choose.

Paint is a wonderful way of dealing with stairs. Try painting or stencilling a stair carpet, in a neo-Oriental or geometric design. Widthways stripes in ice-cream colours are pretty too, and make the staircase look wider. Varnish any decoration well, using a matt polyurethane varnish, and lightly rubbing down the final coat with fine steel wool to make the surface non-slippery. Another idea is to strip just the treads back to the bare wood, and paint or stencil the risers – perhaps to suggest the old tiles often used to face risers in Mediterranean

Previous page Paint the floor to pick up a theme from elsewhere in the room. This one reproduces, on a larger scale, the colours and patterns of some patchwork-printed curtains – and even continues up the skirting. It is done in flat white paint, tinted with artists' oils, and protected with polyurethane varnish. Although it is not difficult to paint such designs freehand, it is important to get the right balance of plain and patterned areas, so that the effect does not look too busy.

112

countries. Seen from the foot of the stairs the effect is really colourful – just the thing to cheer up a dark, narrow hallway. The treads can be kept bare and scrubbed, to give a safe, non-slip surface.

Neither freehand painted nor stencilled floor designs are difficult to do, but if they seem too ambitious or time-consuming consider simpler ideas. Plain paint, without trimmings, looks good when the colour is imaginative – try mixing your own. A glossy cadet blue or a greeny-yellow makes a practical and cheerful finish in a child's playroom, while matt, weathered-looking earth shades like raw sienna or Venetian red look warm and friendly on a sitting-room floor, scattered with rugs. Painting every floorboard a subtly different colour, like a faded patchwork quilt, looks pretty in a bedroom with rustic furniture. It would be ridiculous to paint fine parquet, or wide old oak boards, but as a finish for the average scarred, pitted, beat-up softwood planking, paint is hard to beat.

Making good and preparation

Unlike furniture, a floor does not need to provide an ultra-smooth foundation for a painted finish. In fact, one advantage of using paint on a floor is that it will cover a multitude of sins, provided that it is finished off with enough coats of varnish to build up a smooth, tough surface. Nevertheless, some filling and sanding down may be necessary to level the surface and disguise the worst blemishes.

Nails and tacks Nail down any loose boards and remove any protruding nails or tacks left over from previous floor coverings. Use pliers, a tack lifter or the forked end of a standard claw hammer. Obstinate nails can be punched down below the surface, using a 7 mm [$\frac{1}{4}$ in] punch.

You will often need to remove dark, gummy varnish stain, rather than paint, before you can put a finish on a floor. This tenacious substance contains black-coloured preservatives that seep into the wood beneath. Small patches can be removed by severe scrubbing with methylated spirits [denatured alcohol], but the only way to deal with large areas is by deep sanding (see below), to remove the stained layer of wood. This can be very hard work, and time-consuming. If you have a floor that has been partially or wholly finished with varnish stain, your best move is probably to sand it lightly to roughen the surface, and then paint it over completely. If you use a dye or stain you will find that the darkened areas show through.

Old paint is most efficiently and speedily removed by burning with a blowlamp and scraping off the softened paint with a straight-ended paint scraper and a shave hook for tricky corners. Hire a high-powered blowlamp fitted with a canister of liquefied gas, and follow the manufacturer's instructions. If you scorch the wood here and there while attacking stubborn deposits, this too will have to be removed by deep sanding.

Stripping down

113

Above Plain white paint, protected by varnish, makes a background to the graphically exciting lines of the furniture in this beautifully composed room. The magnificent beamed ceiling prevents the effect from being too thinly cerebral – and note how a light floor and dark ceiling reverse the customary arrangement of tones on floor and ceiling.

Right Choosing a good colour and using it generously, in expected and unexpected places, makes a room both piquant and restful. Here, the blue paint on the floor has been carried up doors, drawer fronts and bookshelves, to tie up the visual package in a refreshingly different way.

Above Stains are the simplest way to colour a modest plank floor. Using a rich orange-red takes the chilly, bare feeling off the plain boards, and makes a good foil for a collection of antique rugs.

Left Stencilled or freehand patterns rendered in wood-coloured stains give a rich marquetry effect. The shapes are lightly scored into the soft wood boards first, with a Stanley knife, to prevent the stain creeping over the edges of the design.

115

Homemade caustic stripper There are many chemical strippers available but you can make the strongest (and cheapest) kind yourself. Mix one can of caustic soda with 1 litre [1 US quart] of water, and thicken with flour or cornflour [cornstarch]. This must be used with great care, since the strong fumes could be overpowering in a confined space. Open all the windows, and wear rubber gloves, a mask and protective clothing. Caustic burns skin, hair and clothes, so if any lands on you wash it off at once with clean water. Apply it to the floor a small patch at a time, standing as far back as you safely and conveniently can. It softens paint messily but thoroughly in 10 minutes to a few hours. Do not allow it to dry out, but add more water now and then and scrub hard with a brush to loosen the softened paint. Rinse thoroughly, first with clean water then with water plus a dash of vinegar to neutralize the caustic. Caustic leaves wood roughened and whiskery so, when dry, sand the whole surface thoroughly, working from coarse to fine sandpaper. Caustic is best used for small, controllable areas like stair treads, rather than for stripping a whole floor, where you should use a blowlamp.

Levelling up A painted or stained floor will look better if larger cracks and craters in the wood are filled. With a transparent finish, such as a stain or dye, use one of the proprietary fillers designed for woodwork, since they expand and contract with the wood, and are thus less likely to shrink and drop out. Tint the filler to match the bare wood roughly, using water-based colours or universal stainers [tinting colours]. Alternatively, tint it with the dye or stain you are going to use on the floor. Do not attempt to fill every crack and knothole, just the worst scars. When the filler has dried, sand it smooth.

Under an opaque, painted surface you can use putty for filling. The crack or hole must first be roughened and given a dab of primer or undercoat, to prevent the putty from shrinking and 'lifting'.

Caulking cracks between floorboards The spaces between floorboards are a nuisance, allowing dust as well as draughts to seep up. Wide cracks can be filled successfully only by using narrow wood fillets, planed to fit and hammered in tightly with a little glue each side to hold them in place.

Narrower cracks can be stopped with a type of papier maché pulp. Shred newspaper and soak it in weak decorators' glue size or wallpaper paste until it is the consistency of porridge. Press it firmly into the cracks and level it off while it is still wet. Really widely spaced floorboards that let up a constant draught are probably best covered over altogether. Sheets of hardboard, decorated and varnished before laying, see pages 131–3, are a practical and time-saving solution.

Sanding If a floor is to be left *au naturel* and sealed, or given a transparent finish, it should first be sanded down, to remove accretions of dirt, varnish, paint or stain and to present a nice, clean blotting-paper surface. Power sanding machines do the job infinitely quicker than any small domestic sanding appliance, and can be hired from most do-it-yourself shops. The shop will advise you on how to operate them. Use a large sander for the main floor area and a small edge sander for borders and corners.

Sand down the floor before you do any other decorating. Clear the room of everything moveable and keep it sealed, since wood dust clings. Sanders produce a lot of dust, so wear a face mask or scarf over your nose and mouth. Keep the machine on the move, so that you don't scar the wood. Starting from one corner, sand the floor in diagonal strips, each strip overlapping its neighbour by about 7 cm [3 in]. When you have been over the entire floor, sand along the other diagonal in the same way. Lastly, fit a finer abrasive and sand the floor following the direction of the woodgrain. Vacuum up all the dust you can, and finish the floor off by scrubbing with water and a little bleach. Allow it to dry out thoroughly before treating it further.

Sandpaper will do to rub away the odd scar or stain. Use it wrapped round a sanding block – it is more efficient, since a wider area of the paper is kept flat on the floor, and your hand pressure is evenly distributed. Sand in the direction of the grain with long, smooth strokes, using coarse or medium, then fine, sandpaper.

Lightening

This technique for toning down natural wood colour is particularly helpful on knotty deal, or on pine, which if untreated tends to go a fiery orange colour after varnishing.

Tinted white paint is brushed on to the wood and then rubbed off again, so that a residue is deposited in the cracks and pores. Use a flat white oil-based paint softened with a squirt of raw umber and dashes of ochre and black artists' oil colours. With a stiff brush scrub this liberally over a small section of the wood, leave it for a few minutes, test to see if it is adhering, then rub it off with a rag. Rub against the grain quite firmly (enough to reveal it again), but not so hard that you remove all the paint, which should leave quite a marked veil of pallor. Repeat this treatment in sections over the entire floor.

If you want the paint to act as a grain filler as well, add a little wood filler or all-purpose filler [spackle] to thicken it up. This will need sanding with a medium sandpaper, wrapped round a cork block, to make the surface smooth again.

Leave the paint to dry hard before applying any further finishes.

Bleaching

Ordinary liquid or powdered domestic bleach, scrubbed in and rinsed off with clean water will do a lot to lighten a floor. You can also buy stronger chemical bleaches, which are applied in two stages. These should be used with care and following the manufacturer's instructions, since the concentrated fumes can be dangerous, so wear a protective mask and keep the windows open.

If you plan to varnish straight over it, bleaching is less satisfactory than lightening with paint, since varnish brings up the yellow tones inherent in the wood, however strongly you bleach them away.

117

Transparent Finishes

Dyes

Standard fabric, carpet and leather dyes work quite well on bare wood floors, provided that any wax or grease on the surface is first removed. This should be done by sanding, scrubbing and finally wiping over with rags dipped in white spirit [mineral spirits] or vinegar and water. Remember to allow for the natural tone of the wood when choosing your colour and visualizing the effect. Greens, blues and maroons look good.

Mix up a strong dye solution, following the maker's instructions, but using about half as much water. Try out a little on a patch of wood, and let it dry to gauge the effect. If you are satisfied with it, use a wad of clean, lint-free rags to swab the rest quickly, and as evenly as possible, over the entire floor. Two or three successive applications will be needed to alter the wood colour appreciably. The result is likely to be streaky, since waterborne colour permeates wood patchily according to the amount of resin the wood contains, but it looks none the less attractive for that.

The dyed floor should be left to dry, and, if necessary, sanded lightly with medium sandpaper to smooth the water-roughened grain, before being coated with polyurethane varnish. See page 120 on varnishing.

Stains

See the chart on page 217. Stains penetrate deeper into wood than dyes. They usually come in woody colours, varying from pale blonde to the darkest brown-black oak, but ranges of stains in fantasy, non-wood colours have recently become available.

The various types of stain use different media to help the pigment to penetrate the wood – water, spirit, oil and varnish. The water-based ones are the easiest to apply, but tend to dry patchily, while oil-based stains are best if you require an even colour, since they dry more slowly. Spirit stains dry very fast, so that you have to take care not to go over the same patch too often, which will make it become darker than the rest. Avoid varnish stains – you will be storing up trouble, since they leave a thick, gummy deposit.

All stains must be applied over clean, bare wood – sanded, scrubbed, and rubbed with white spirit [mineral spirits]. Follow the manufacturer's instructions. The one exception is wax stain, which needs a coat of floor seal beneath it. Make the stain by melting beeswax or paraffin wax with artists' oils in a double boiler. Let it cool to a soft paste, rub it hard into the boards with a brush or cloth, then polish for a rich shine. The surface will need frequent rubbing, however, to keep it burnished, and the wax stain must be removed completely before another finish is applied.

Opposite Staining or painting each board a different colour is an easy floor treatment – change colours wherever the planks join. Here, warm shades of orange and red produce an effect of richness, despite the fact that there are just three small rugs on a large, bare floor.

Stains and stencils

One interesting decorative possibility is to use wood stains to stencil an overall floor design. A floor stained a light, golden brown can be stencilled over in one or even two darker stains. This gives a warm, pretty marquetry effect that allows the grain of the wood to show through.

Method

Apply the first stain over the entire floor, and leave it to dry completely. See pages 125–31 for stencilling techniques. Use large, simple stencils. Dab the darker stain through the stencil holes with a lint-free rag rather than a brush, which will get too overloaded. Do not take up too much stain at a time, or it may creep under the stencil and ruin the outline. This can be prevented by coating the adjacent areas beforehand with a fast-drying shellac. When the stain is dry, wipe away the shellac with a cloth dipped in methylated spirits [denatured alcohol] – it will take any spills or seepage with it.

The marquetry effect may be heightened further by carefully scoring round the designs with a Stanley knife, or by discreetly outlining them with black felt-tip pen or paint, to imitate ebony inlay.

Finish off with between 3 and 5 coats of polyurethane varnish – see below on varnishing.

Varnish

Polyurethane varnish is tough, stain- and heat-resistant and easy to apply. It can be applied straight over a sanded wooden floor, as long as the wood is a few years old. If you do this, any filling beforehand should be done with a special polyurethane filler.

Choose matt, semigloss or gloss varnish, depending on the degree of shine you want. Gloss varnish is slower-drying and harder. It is easier to apply smoothly when thinned. If the gloss surface is too shiny (although this will wear off with use), it can be toned down by rubbing gently when quite dry and hard with medium steel wool. Varnish comes in wood-tinted, coloured and clear finishes, but even the clear ones darken and yellow colours a little, so allow for this.

Method

The room should be as clean and dust-free as possible. Keep a tack rag handy to pick up bits and pieces that settle on sticky varnish; see page 25. Apply varnish with a clean brush reserved for the purpose, laying the first coat across the grain, then levelling it off with the grain. When dry, sand it down before applying the next coat. Polyurethane varnish is touch-dry in 6 to 8 hours, but is best left overnight before recoating. From the second coat on, it can be thinned with a little white spirit [mineral spirits]: 3 parts varnish to 1 part solvent. The thinned varnish can be poured into a saucer, and if preferred, swabbed on with a soft pad made from a wad of cotton wool [absorbent cotton] wrapped in a clean, lint-free cloth.

The more coats of varnish you give the floor, the better it will wear – 3 is the minimum, but allow for 5 on a floor that takes a fair amount of traffic. It will need renewing every year or two. Before recoating it, make sure that the surface is clean, dry and free from grease.

A final thin coat of wax improves the look and durability of the varnish. But bear in mind that it will have to come off again before revarnishing.

Floor seal

Floor seal is a conveniently easy finish to apply, thin enough to be swabbed on with a soft cloth. Not as tough as polyurethane varnish, and slower-drying, it requires 4 or 5 coats to build up a surface that will withstand much wear.

The first coat should be rubbed into the wood across the grain, and the succeeding ones rubbed with the grain. Sand lightly between each coat.

Like varnish, floor seal can be re-applied if it is wearing thin, but all wax and grease must be removed first, either by scraping off, or by scrubbing with a mild sugar soap solution; see page 22.

Wax

Wax smells agreeable, gives an incomparable shine (assisted by elbow-grease) and enriches the natural wood colour in a particularly sympathetic way. But there is no getting away from the fact that it involves much hard work.

Do not apply wax directly onto bare wood, particularly a soft wood like pine, since it may allow dirt to become embedded in the fibres of the wood. Coat the surface first with floor seal. This will prevent the wax sinking in too far and will make raising a shine much easier. Swab the seal well into the woodgrain, and sand it down with fine sandpaper in the direction of the grain.

The oldest, simplest form of waxing, using nothing more than beeswax and turpentine, is still to my mind the most pleasing, because of its delicious smell and its beautifully rich honey colour. It is now too expensive to use on a large scale, and has always been a devil to apply and burnish, but for people who would like to try it out – especially on stripped pine for which it is ideal – here is the formula. Beeswax can be bought from chemists [druggists] or craft shops.

Beeswax polish To make beeswax polish, melt a chunk of wax with some pure turpentine in roughly equal proportions, in a double boiler or an old can placed in a saucepan of water. Take care that neither the wax nor the turpentine comes near direct heat, since both are highly inflammable. Leave the mixture to cool a little, and while it is still soft (but not liquid), scrub it thinly but thoroughly into the surface with an old soft brush or a lint-free cloth pad. Leave it for several hours to harden completely, then rub it up to a shine with a clean soft brush – a shoe-cleaning brush will do. This is harder and slower than it sounds, and you will need to clean the brush often or swap it for another as it clogs up. The reward is a sweet-smelling finish with a soft depth of colour and a rich gleam.

Modern waxes are considerably easier to apply, and contain silicones to make them tougher, and driers to speed hardening. Use a soft cloth to spread the wax thinly, and after a few hours' drying, a soft brush to buff up the surface. End by polishing with a soft cloth.

121

Painted Finishes

A priming coat helps paint to go over wood smoothly, to cover better and to last longer. On raw or new wood use a coat of pink primer, see page 161, and then one of undercoat. On old, well-seasoned wooden floors, brush on one or two coats of undercoat thinly and leave to dry hard. If the top coat is to be a rich or a dark colour, tint the undercoat to match – easy if you are mixing your own colour anyway. It will make any skips in the final coat less obvious. One coat of the top colour should be enough for a plain paint finish, or as a ground for further decoration.

Paint Most types of paint can be used successfully on floors, because the tough polyurethane varnish finish will prevent even soft-textured paints from being rubbed off. Even flat emulsion [latex] paints are suitable, provided they are heavily varnished. I find their dry powdery surface an excellent base for decoration. The degree of shine in the paint is not really important, since the finish will be provided by the type of polyurethane varnish you choose – matt, semigloss, or gloss. For this reason there seems little point in using the more expensive gloss [enamel] paint on floors – especially as it does not take overpainting well either. Professional decorators prefer flat white oil-based paint, tinted with universal stainers [tinting colours] or artists' oils, because of its pleasant brushing qualities and velvety texture. It is particularly suited to reproducing textile patterns that were originally woven in a matt fibre, and would look brash painted in a shiny colour topped with a gloss varnish. Flat white has exceptionally good coverage and is nice to use, but if you have problems finding it, use undercoat instead. An eggshell paint is especially suitable for designs, like those imitating tiles or china, where a hard, poreless ground is an advantage.

The room should be cleared, cleaned and sealed off as far as possible while you are working – but keep one window open to let out the paint smells.

Like walls, floors should be painted a section at a time, brushed out well and laid off to avoid pronounced brushmarks, see page 24. The chief thing to remember is to plan your floor painting so that you end up at the exit, not boxed up in a corner surrounded by sticky wet paint.

It makes a great difference to the final result if you sand lightly between coats, to smooth new paint surfaces and get rid of any grit, dust or fibres. Use medium sandpaper, vacuum away the dust, then use a tack rag, see page 25, to remove any remaining grit and nibs.

When you have obtained the opaque colour you want, leave the floor to dry out thoroughly. If you are not going to add any further decoration, all

Plain colour

Method

Opposite Motifs copied from those in a Turkish palace transform the floor of a long sitting room tucked under the eaves of a city house. Laid on freehand in flat white paint tinted with artists' oils, the design is protected by 12 coats of clear polyurethane varnish. The furnishings, although unusual enough to hold their own, are played down to allow the floor its due precedence.

123

that is left is to varnish it – matt, semigloss or gloss, depending on the degree of shine required. See page 120 on varnishing.

Stripes

An easy decorative treatment is to paint separate boards in individual, but harmonizing colours. See above for how to prepare and paint a floor. For the best effect, the boards should be fairly wide.

If you look closely at your floor, you will see that each board covers only about two-thirds of the distance from wall to wall, because few planks are long enough to do it in one. The idea is to paint a plank in one colour as far as the join, and the remaining shorter length in another. This gives the floor an attractive staggered look – prettier than if it were simply painted in regular stripes.

Chequers

A simple way to paint a floor – and a design that looks good in every material from marble to linoleum – is to use diamonds arranged in a chequered pattern, alternating two contrasting colours. Because the diamonds are placed sideways on, they create an instant perspective to lead the eye onward, giving an illusion of space and a touch of formal elegance. Black-and-white chequers usually look best in a hallway, but other colour combinations, imitating old tiles rather than marble, look good in dining rooms and kitchens. This technique works best, however, if the room is a regular rectangle – if it is not, the pattern will draw attention to the irregularities. A plain border in the darker colour makes a satisfying way to finish off this design, and also allows you a little leeway to offset any crookedness in the walls.

Preparation

If the wood is new, prime it. After a layer of undercoat, lay on enough coats of the lighter of your two colours to provide a good opaque colour.

See pages 128–9 for how to square up the floor. Measure up your floor and mark it out in chalk in exactly the same way; then mark in all the diagonals, cutting through each point where a horizontal and vertical line cross. You now have your diamond shapes, which will be a little smaller in area than the original squares.

Materials

Flat or mid-sheen oil-based paint; standard decorators' brush 25 or 50 mm [1 or 2 in] wide; pointed artists' brush or lining fitch; wooden batten or straight-edge; white spirit [mineral spirits]; rags.

Method

Paint in the outline of your darker chequers using a pointed artists' brush or a lining fitch and a straight-edge or batten. Then fill them in, using your decorators' brush. Alternatively cut a stencil or a template the size of a chequer, and use fast-drying paint. Begin painting the chequers in the corner furthest from the door, so that you will end up with space to escape. Once the floor has dried completely, paint in the border.

124

Varnishing Finish by giving the floor at least 3 coats of polyurethane varnish – matt, semigloss or gloss, depending on how band-boxy you want it to look. Use 5 coats for a hall that is going to take a lot of traffic.

Decorating chequers

Chequered designs can look rather dazzling in straight colour contrasts like black and white or red and yellow. They can be softened by lightly marbling over the paler squares – see pages 104–8 and 136–9 for marbling techniques. Alternatively, you can stencil over the chequers, reversing your original two colours, or using other complementary ones.

If you are really confident, try painting the chequers to imitate fabrics, picking up colours and patterns used elsewhere in the room, for a stunning patchwork effect.

Floor stencils

The most successful floor stencils I have seen kept quite close to effects created by more traditional types of flooring, using fairly dark and subdued colours and regular, repetitive designs. Apart from the practical consideration of not showing dirt and dust, there is an aesthetic or psychological point behind this preference. Visually, a room gains from being weighted at the bottom with a solid-looking floor – a delicate flowered porcelain effect on a pale ground may look pretty, but it can make one feel vaguely uneasy unless the other colours in the room have been chosen with care to balance the insubstantial-looking floor. Study

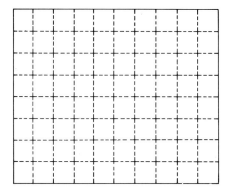

To mark out a chequered floor, first follow the instructions on pages 128–9 for squaring it off. Having chalked out your squares, draw in the diagonals, *above*, passing through every point where a horizontal and a vertical line cross. Start in a corner and work out across the room. For larger chequers, *right*, put in diagonals through alternate crossing-points only.

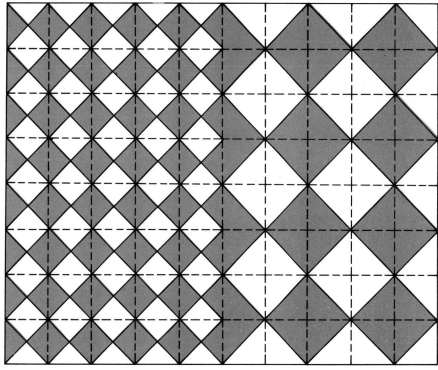

125

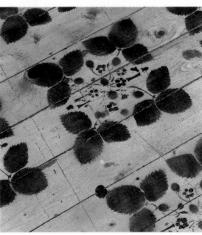

Above Stencilled in signwriters' paint [bulletin colour], this unpretentious but positive pattern gives character to a plain kitchen floor. Several coats of gloss varnish mean it can be mopped down easily.

Right Strawberries cluster in an orderly fashion over sanded planks, and show how spray paints can be used to get an attractively muzzy effect.

Far right The colours and shapes on this stencilled 'rug' echo those on the armchair. Many thin coats of pure colour were used to build up the brilliant red of the poppies.

Squaring off a floor

To square off a floor (whether for a chequered or squared, stencilled design) you will need a pencil, ruler and squared paper; chalk, ball of string and/or a long wooden batten; a set square for checking angles. Two people will speed up this slow and rather fiddly operation.

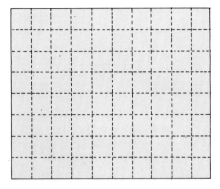

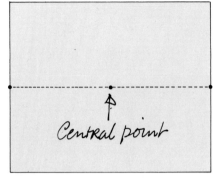

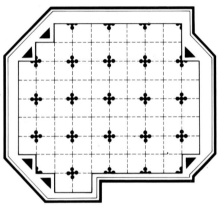

1 Measure the room or floor space and draw it out to scale on a sheet of squared paper. Having decided on the size of the squares (or pattern blocks for stencils) mark these off in pencil along the sides of the floor plan, working outwards from the central point of each wall. You may have to adjust the size of the squares to suit the floor space, because most simple patterns look best if they complete a run. A border (see illustration *left*) gives room for adjustment here.

2 Find and mark the centres of two opposite walls. Using chalk and a long batten, or a length of heavily chalked string pulled taut across the floor and snapped in the middle, mark a straight line across the floor between these points. The centre of this line is the centre of the room.

3 Working from the central point, measure off the width of the squares in both directions along the line you have just drawn. Through the two outer points draw two more lines, parallel to each other and at right angles to the first line, running the length of the room. Accuracy is important in measuring a floor as small mistakes soon become large ones when the lines drawn are very long. Check the right angles with a set square, or better still by the following simple formula. Measure 90 cm [3 ft] along one parallel, 120 cm [4 ft] along the central line, mark these points and draw a line between them. This third line should measure exactly 150 cm [5 ft], if it doesn't the angle is not a right angle.

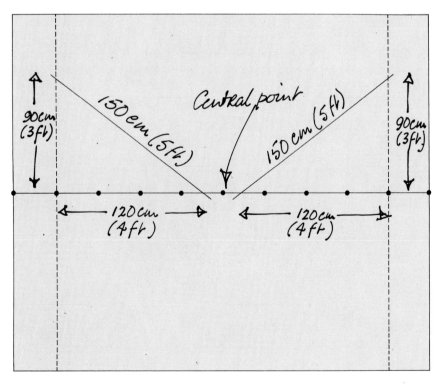

the examples shown here, as well as traditional floorings – tiles, carpets, old stencilled floors – and decide for yourself.

Technically speaking, floors are stencilled in exactly the same way as walls. See pages 55–65 on how to design, prepare and cut stencils.

Preparation

The floor surface must be fairly good for stencilling, and, if you want a painted ground, smoothly finished in an opaque colour with a flat or mid-sheen oil-based paint. See page 123 for how to paint a floor.

Materials for painting stencils

Paint Some decorators advocate spray paints (as sold for touching up car bodywork) for floor stencils, on the grounds of speed and convenience. I find spray paints quite difficult to control when used pointing downwards, as they are apt to become blocked. Spraying at an angle – with the can held a little way above the floor – gives more even coverage, but the paint is liable to creep under the stencil, smudging the edges of the design, which then have to be cleaned off with a rag. Scoring round the design with a knife, before spraying, will help avoid this.

The paints to choose for stencilling floors, as well as walls, are those that dry quickly, give maximum coverage and come in good colours. Fastest drying are acrylic colours thinned with water or acrylic medium, signwriters' colours [bulletin colours] thinned with a little varnish, and, for American readers, japan colours thinned with white spirit [mineral spirits]. These have the advantage that the stencils dry almost as you do

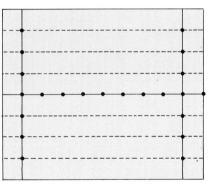

4 Having drawn these lines with chalked string or batten, mark off the squares along them, as for line one. You are now in a position to draw in all the lines in one direction by joining up the points across the floor as shown.

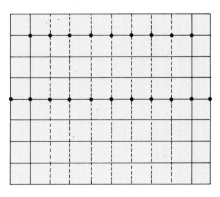

5 Choose one of the outer lines (parallel to line one) and again mark off the width of the squares from the centre outwards. Complete the grid by joining the two sets of points as before.

129

A stencilled border delineates a floor area just as it does a wall, with the added advantage that it allows you to cheat if you're marking out a regularly spaced stencil design on an irregularly shaped floor.

Above A plain, chunky border stencilled in signwriters' paint [bulletin colour] on a sanded floor proves that less, decoratively, can often be more.

Right Emphatic allover motifs look best with the simplest border – in this case merely a repeating leaf shape.

them, so there is little risk of smudging as you move across the floor.

Flat oil-based paint or undercoat gives good coverage, for widely spaced stencils. If you use flat emulsion [latex] paint, varnish it well.

Brushes The regular stencil brush, used in a pouncing or jabbing movement, gives the crispest definition, with a nice, textured look, but when painting a repetitive floor stencil this rapidly becomes very tiring. On the whole, I think a standard decorators' brush, 25 or 50 mm [1 or 2 in] wide, is the most convenient tool for fairly simple floor stencils. Use it to brush the design in rather than pounce it. This goes much faster though it gives a less immaculate outline. If you are stencilling with more than one colour at a time, use a different brush for each colour.

Other equipment Squared paper; chalked string or chalk and straight-edge; the usual supply of rags for mopping up; saucers for mixing paints; the relevant solvent for your paint; masking tape.

Method Before beginning to stencil, make a floor plan on squared paper. Mark guide lines on the floor, using a chalked string or a straight-edge to help you place your stencils. For an allover, regularly spaced pattern, square off the floor as shown on pages 128–9. To plan a border, divide the wall lengths by the size of the motifs to calculate how many repeats will fit in. Chalk a guide line the length of the floor at the required distance from the skirting, and mark off short lines along it at the central point of each motif. On each stencil again mark the centre of the motif and draw two lines at right angles through this point so that the stencil can be accurately positioned at each 'cross' on the guide line.

For instructions on how to mix colours, and place and paint stencils, see stencilling on walls, pages 55–69. Stencilling floors is a strain on the back muscles, so it is best not to try to cover too much ground in each session. Also, because of the heavier pressure one tends to exert on the brush in this position, there is more likelihood of smudges and blobs. Have a good supply of clean rags or tissues handy to wipe these away as you go along, and clean the back of the stencil frequently. Lift off the stencil carefully each time so as not to slide it over the wet paint. But a *bit* of sloppiness in the stencilling here and there will not show up too much when the floor is finished.

Leave the completed floor for no fewer than 24 hours before varnishing. The paint must be perfectly dry. Give it at least 3 coats of matt, semigloss or gloss polyurethane varnish.

Below left One of my favourite floor stencils, simple and very elegant. The outlines were scored into the boards before the wood stain colours were applied. The double track border is all it needs for discreet emphasis.

Below right A border treatment like this startles a room into life, and beautifully demonstrates that going over the top, too, can be visually stimulating. These stylized geese were executed freehand, but similarly sophisticated motifs can be stencilled – although bear in mind, before committing yourself, that they will take hours of patient work to perfect.

Hardboard is the cheapest possible floor covering, strong, easy to cut and lay, and a first choice with hard-up householders looking for a way to hide disgraceful boards or to block off draughts that howl up between them. [Hardboard, with one rough and one smooth side, is often called

Stencilled hardboard

particleboard or masonite.] It is a good solution, too, for people with little working space, since an entire floor covering can be prepared, right through to the final varnishing, in shifts on the kitchen table. The chief objection to hardboard is that its drab brown colour can be depressing to live with, but there are various ways to cheer it up.

One way to do so is with stencilling. You could banish the brown altogether by painting over the entire surface first with a coat of oil-based mid-sheen paint over a layer of acrylic primer, standard undercoat or thinned emulsion [latex] paint. You will need 2 top coats if painting a light colour, but with a dark one you can get away with one.

Another possibility is to use the natural hardboard colour for your background, and stencil directly on to it. Stencil alternate squares in two colours harmonizing with each other and with the brown – dark brown and Indian red, red and black, or green and dirty yellow. Otherwise try using one of these pairs of colours to make a two-colour stencil to go in every square.

Method Measure the entire floor area and cut standard sheets of hardboard into enough large tiles of about 120 cm [4 ft] square to cover it. Many builders' merchants or hardware stores will do the cutting for you if you give them prior notice. When cutting hardboard yourself, use a panel saw for straight cuts, a coping saw or hacksaw to cut round curves or corners, and cut from the smooth side to prevent crumbling. If you are going to paint the entire surface, prime it first, before you do so.

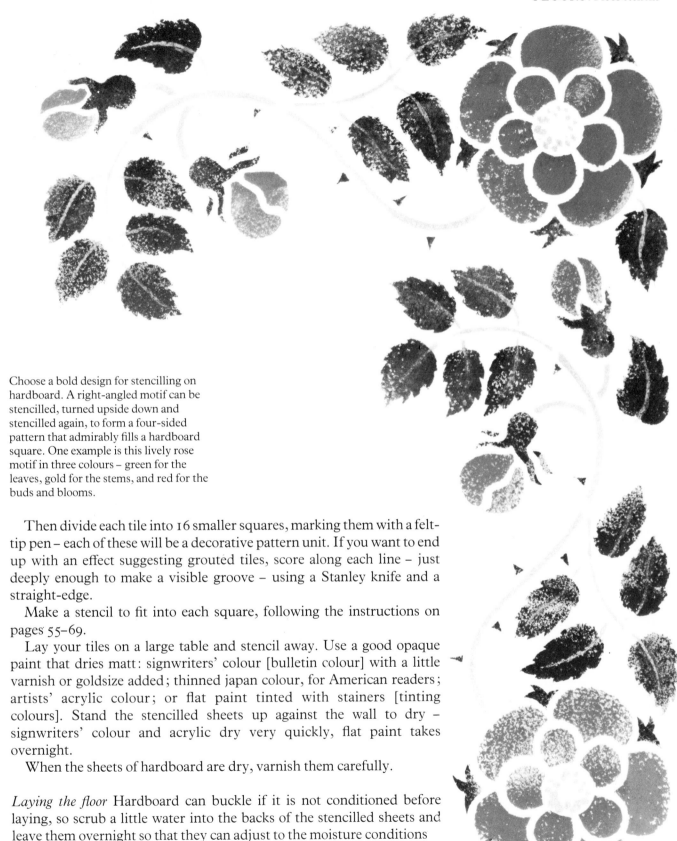

Choose a bold design for stencilling on hardboard. A right-angled motif can be stencilled, turned upside down and stencilled again, to form a four-sided pattern that admirably fills a hardboard square. One example is this lively rose motif in three colours – green for the leaves, gold for the stems, and red for the buds and blooms.

Then divide each tile into 16 smaller squares, marking them with a felt-tip pen – each of these will be a decorative pattern unit. If you want to end up with an effect suggesting grouted tiles, score along each line – just deeply enough to make a visible groove – using a Stanley knife and a straight-edge.

Make a stencil to fit into each square, following the instructions on pages 55–69.

Lay your tiles on a large table and stencil away. Use a good opaque paint that dries matt: signwriters' colour [bulletin colour] with a little varnish or goldsize added; thinned japan colour, for American readers; artists' acrylic colour; or flat paint tinted with stainers [tinting colours]. Stand the stencilled sheets up against the wall to dry – signwriters' colour and acrylic dry very quickly, flat paint takes overnight.

When the sheets of hardboard are dry, varnish them carefully.

Laying the floor Hardboard can buckle if it is not conditioned before laying, so scrub a little water into the backs of the stencilled sheets and leave them overnight so that they can adjust to the moisture conditions of the room. The next day, tack or glue (or both) the squares down on to the floor, butting the joins carefully so that they are tight.

Fossilstone marbling

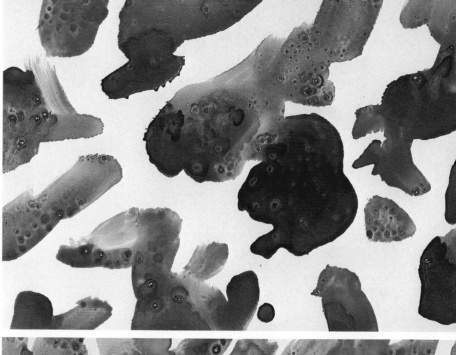

Apply a ground of white or off-white oil-based mid-sheen paint. When dry, sand it. With a soft cloth rub on a thin film of linseed oil. Mix up two paint glazes, from 1 part of the ground paint thinned with 2 parts white spirit [mineral spirits] and tinted with artists' oils or stainers [tinting colours]. Here, glaze 1 has been tinted with burnt sienna and yellow ochre, and glaze 2 with cobalt and raw umber. Dab glaze 1 with a stiff brush fairly regularly over the surface.

Using the same brush, apply glaze 2 roughly in the spaces left by glaze 1. Clean the brush.

Go lightly over the entire surface with a marine sponge or crumpled paper tissue to soak up excess glaze and give a softened effect.

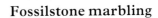

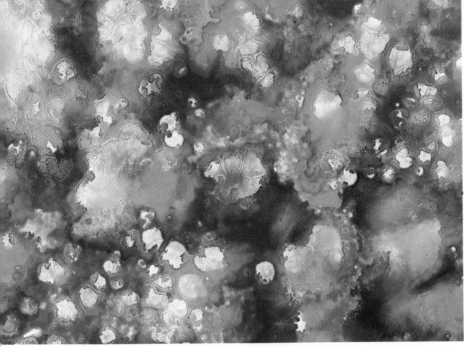

Take up some white spirit [mineral spirits] on the brush. Flick the bristles with your thumb to spatter the glazed surface liberally. Little holes will open out where the solvent lands.

To add extra variety to the pattern, flick on drops of methylated spirits [denatured alcohol].

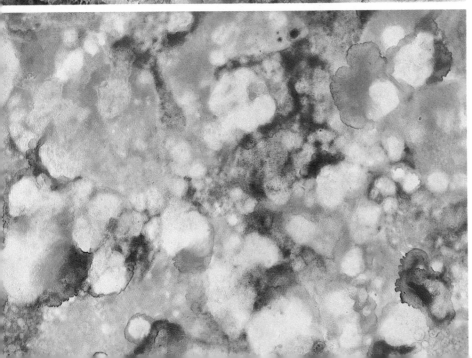

Soften again with a sponge or paper tissue. When the surface is quite dry, give it 3 to 5 coats of gloss polyurethane varnish, thinned 3 parts to 1 of white spirit. Lightly sand down each coat except the first.

Marbled floors

Painting a floor to look like marble adds a palatial air to any room. It is not as difficult as it sounds, because over a large surface the marbling can be done in a very loose and impressionistic way and still look convincing. You will find the technique easier to handle if you divide the floor into squares, to imitate paving slabs.

At the other end of the scale, marbling the floor in pale, cool colours adds a look of space and light to small, confined areas like hallways, landings and corridors. As long as it is given several protective coats of polyurethane varnish, a painted marble floor stands up well to foot traffic. For cut-price luxury, marble the bathroom floor and extend the treatment over bath surround and woodwork.

Fossilstone marbling

The marbling technique described below is particularly effective. It is suitable for any flat, horizontal surface – table top, picture frame – but do not try it on a vertical one because the colours will run off. Its fossilstone appearance is achieved by spattering wet glaze with solvent – easy and surprisingly convincing. It looks best using low-keyed pebble colours – greeny-grey, dull blue and tawny brown – and is especially impressive on hardboard tiles used as a floor covering.

Preparation

As when stencilling, cut the hardboard into large tiles of about 120 cm [4 ft] square. Prime it with acrylic primer, standard undercoat or thinned emulsion [latex] paint.

Cover your working area with newspaper or sheets of plastic. Paint over the tiles with white or off-white oil-based mid-sheen paint. When the surface is dry, sand it smooth with medium sandpaper. The finish should be not only smooth, but also opaquely white, so it will probably need as many as 3 coats of paint, each one sanded down. Smoothness matters with this marbling technique, because brushmarks or bumps left on the paint surface interfere with the opening-out movement of the glaze that produces the fossil shapes. Rub over the surface with the thinnest smear of raw or boiled linseed oil, just enough to give a faint sheen. This will stop the moving glaze from spreading uncontrollably.

Filling woodgrain If you plan to marble a table top and the wood is coarse textured and open grained, you will get much better results by filling the wood grain before painting. Use proprietary wood filler, all-purpose filler or synthetic gesso, applying as many coats as necessary to level up the grain. Rub the surface smooth with sandpaper, then undercoat it and paint it with oil-based mid-sheen paint for a hard, fine-textured surface. Table tops undergo closer inspection than floors, so it is worth taking extra trouble to get a first-rate finish.

Materials

Two paint glazes, made by mixing 1 part white flat or mid-sheen oil-based paint with 2 parts white spirit [mineral spirits], and tinting with

136

artists' oil colours or universal stainers [tinting colours]. The glazes should be as thin as milk, and dark enough to show up well on the white ground – test them on a corner of a hardboard tile.

You will also need a 75 mm [3 in] brush; a stiff stencil brush; white spirit [mineral spirits]; methylated spirits [denatured alcohol]; a marine sponge or some crumpled paper tissue.

Method

Work on one tile at a time, laying it flat, face-up, on your protected work area. Dip your brush into one of the glazes, and with it dab a roughly chequered pattern over the surface, like the black squares on a chessboard. Then dip the brush into the other glaze and use it to fill in the gaps, not worrying too much about keeping the sections apart. Go over the whole surface with the sponge or paper tissue to remove some of the heaviest glaze and produce a crumpled-looking, slightly blended effect.

Now take up some white spirit on the stiff stencil brush, and flick this with your thumb, to spatter the wet glazed surface quite thickly. In seconds, the glaze will start 'cissing' – little holes opening up and radiating outwards to suggest round fossil shapes. For more variety you can flick on some methylated spirits at this stage – it also cisses, but produces rather different shapes. Small drops of water will leave neat little rings. If you spatter on any extra large blobs that threaten to ciss rampageously, mop up the excess liquid quickly with a corner of paper tissue. See the photographs on pages 134–35 for an idea of the effect.

This is a technique to have fun with – the difficulty is knowing when to stop. When you are quite satisfied with it, leave the tile to dry perfectly flat.

Varnishing Once the marbled tiles are completely dry, varnish them with up to 5 coats of clear gloss polyurethane varnish – thinned 3 parts varnish to 1 part solvent. Rub lightly with sandpaper after every coat except the first.

When the sheets are finished, scrub water into the back and condition them overnight, as above, before laying.

For a superbly smooth finish on a table top, do not sand the last coat of varnish, but rub it over with powdered pumice, rottenstone or household scouring powder and a little baby oil, lemon oil or salad oil. Apply this goo with a piece of felt or with a soft flannel cloth, using long strokes and following the direction of the grain underneath. Wipe it off with a damp cloth, and when dry, polish the surface with a soft, clean one.

Marbled floorboards

You can also marble directly on to the floorboards, provided that the cracks are not too noticeable and the surfaces are reasonably smooth. See pages 113–17 for how to get them that way. New wood should be primed; over 1 or 2 undercoats, paint the ground colour in oil-based mid-sheen paint, which gives the best surface for marbling. Use the marbling method described on pages 104–8, but divide the floor area into large squares – see

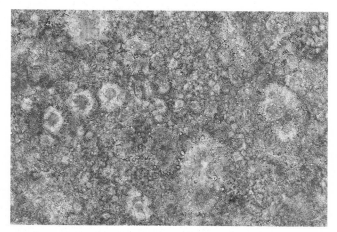

Glaze 1: burnt sienna, a little burnt umber, a little yellow ochre. Glaze 2: yellow ochre, raw umber.

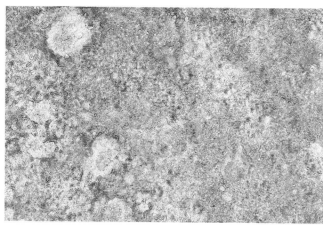

Glaze 1: raw umber. Glaze 2: lots of cobalt, a little raw umber.

Glaze 1: burnt sienna, yellow ochre. Glaze 2: cobalt, raw umber. Extra splashes of solvent and extra sponging.

Glaze 1: burnt umber. Glaze 2: raw umber.

Glaze 1: raw umber. Glaze 2: cobalt and raw umber.

Glaze 1: grey. Glaze 2: indigo. Spotted with red oxide.

pages 128–9 for squaring off a floor. Mark these out carefully on the surface with ruler and black felt-tip pen, since they become part of the design. Marble one square at a time; this breaks the job up into manageable units and it will look better too, since you can vary the direction of the veining from square to square in a naturalistic way. Finish with 3 to 5 coats of thinned clear gloss varnish (3 parts varnish to 1 part solvent) for protection.

Opposite Each fossilstone marble was produced from two glazes made of thinned oil-based paint tinted as indicated.

Above Paint turns plain deal boards into cool marble chequers, here edged with a band of fossilstone marbling.

Combed floors

Use pieces of stiff cardboard or plastic to make your own graining combs, giving them notched teeth of various widths.

Combed paint effects are like woodgraining writ large, and look stunning done in boldly contrasting colours. One American designer has had the idea of adapting the technique to decorate floors, using bright, candy colours, and combing alternate squares this way and then that. This is a quick and easy way of adding pattern to a painted floor, but you can also use it to decorate squares of hardboard, see page 131, which has the

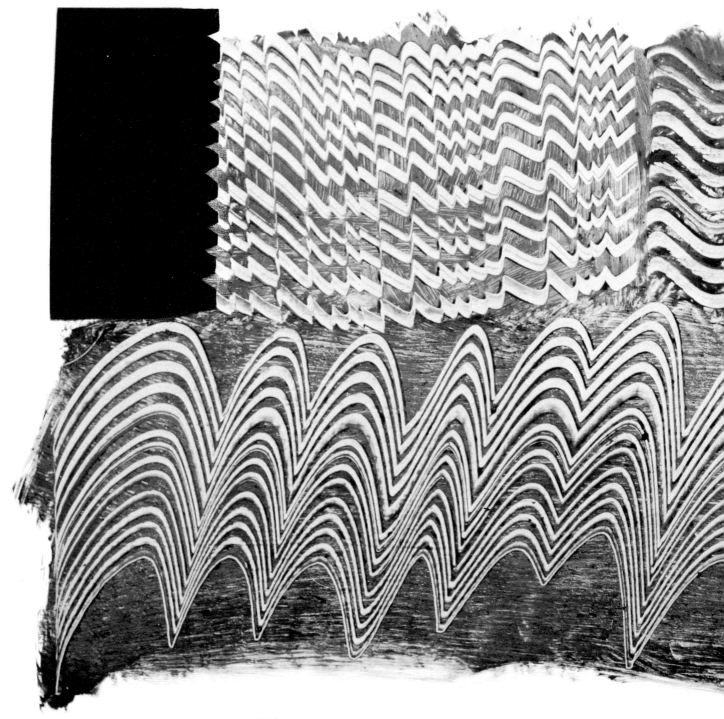

141

advantage that all the painting and varnishing can be done before you lay your floor covering – useful if you need to use the room in the meantime.

Preparation New wood should be primed. After undercoating, the floor surface or hardboard should be given enough coats of oil-based mid-sheen or flat paint to provide a good opaque cover. Choose a base that will do nice things for the colour you plan to comb. Try a straight contrast like green or red, or, for a more restrained effect, use different shades of a single vivid colour.

See pages 128–29 on stencilling for how to square off a floor, and mark off your floor accordingly. If you want the painted squares to end up with crisp edges, fix strips of narrow masking tape over your chalk lines.

Materials for combing Oil-based mid-sheen or flat paint; stainers [tinting colours]; graining combs; 75 mm [3 in] brush; white spirit [mineral spirits]; masking tape; rags.

Builders' merchants and hardware stores stock graining combs, but it is easier and cheaper to make your own. You can use cardboard, stencil board, thick plastic, plywood – any rigid material that can be cut into a comb shape with evenly spaced teeth. The size of the teeth determines the scale of the combed patterns. Make your combs quite wide so that each chequer can be combed in as few movements as possible.

Method Thin your top colour with about 1 part solvent to 3 parts paint. If it is too thin it will not cover the ground colour properly.

Plan your painting to provide yourself with an exit, starting at one edge of the room. It is best to paint half the floor in one go, and, when that has dried, to do the rest in the same way. Brush your combing colour over two or three adjacent squares at a time – if you try to cover too large an area the paint may dry before you can finish the combing. Lay on enough paint to cover the ground evenly but not too thickly. Then place the comb at one edge of a square and draw it across the wet paint to the opposite edge to give a striped effect. Comb the next square in just the same way but with the stripes at a right angle to those in the first one. Carry on square by square, alternating vertical and horizontal stripes. The second row of chequers should go alongside the first, again alternating the directions of the combed stripes. Wipe the comb clean of excess paint with a rag every few squares.

It does not matter if the stripes wobble a little, or if you do not achieve perfectly neat edges to your squares – combing looks all the better for a bit of variety. But do not drag paint over the edge from one row of squares to the next, or you will get a smudgy line where the overspill has dried and cannot be combed. Laying masking tape over your guide lines will prevent this happening.

Varnishing When the combed paint is thoroughly hard and dry, cover it with polyurethane varnish.

Combing is a quick way to get a lively texture over a floor, and dividing the area up into large squares makes the process easy. Alternatively, apply the technique to large hardboard squares, laying them when the decoration is complete.

Left Raw umber tones elegantly dress up the floor of a cool modern room.

Below Green is not always a popular decorating colour, but this kitchen floor shows how crisp and clean it can look, particularly when it contrasts with plain pine furniture and pretty ceramics. And take another look at the dresser behind – it's really a painted trompe l'oeil screen.

Floorcloths

Floorcloths are usually described as the forerunners of linoleum, but you will get a better idea of their special qualities if you think of them as painted canvases spread underfoot, where they add comfort and beauty, plus excluding draughts and providing a smooth surface that can rapidly be swept clean.

Floorcloths reached the height of their popularity in Europe and America in the late eighteenth century, before they were superseded by factory-made floor coverings. With fast-drying modern primers, paints and varnishes, however, they are far easier and quicker to make than they were two hundred years ago. If you want something quite individual, handsome and practical for a kitchen, bathroom, hallway or child's bedroom, a homemade floorcloth is an excellent solution. The first question people ask when they see a hand-painted floorcloth is 'can I walk on it?' The answer is yes, even with stiletto heels. A properly primed and varnished floorcloth stands up to normal traffic extremely well – even on stairs – and, of course, when varnish or decoration do get shabby or worn, it is quite simple to touch them up again.

The critical factor in deciding the size of a floorcloth is the amount of space you have available in which to work. A small floorcloth, say the size of a bedside mat, can be done on the kitchen table, as long as you have somewhere it can be laid out to dry between coats. A room-sized cloth is best painted *in situ*, which of course puts the room in question out of bounds until the project is completed. The intermediate sizes are probably the biggest problem because the cloth should be stretched during priming and drying. One solution is to pin the cloth out on a reasonably flat stretch of lawn during a spell of fine weather.

Designs Plenty of scope here – the deciding factor may well be your skill with the brush. The simplest designs to reproduce, using stencils and templates, are the eighteenth-century favourites, which were based on floor tiles or marble paving. Paint imitation tiles to look like the interlocking, unglazed Provençal shapes; or for a colourful pattern borrow designs from antique tiles of Delft, Italy, Spain and Islam. Consult books on ceramics for photographic inspiration. Make the most of the colour opportunities and use colours that blend with your furnishings for a custom-made look that no one could mistake for one of the commercial floor coverings.

Another idea is to turn for inspiration to the delectable field of old appliqué quilts. Their simple decorative shapes and vivid colours are ideal for reproduction, via stencils, on canvas. A light final glazing in raw umber or raw sienna to suggest faded age, followed by a matt varnish finish, plays up the quilt effect. A point to remember when planning the design and ordering canvas is that appliqué blocks are invariably square – whatever size block you decide on, it should complete a run both ways with perhaps a little extra all round for a border design.

If you decide to try freehand painted decoration, you could borrow ideas from Etruscan wall-paintings or old tapestries, or a cut paper work by Matisse. Oddly enough, the design source to be approached with most caution is that of conventional rugs and carpets, most of which are devised with the rich texture of wool pile in mind. Flat-weave designs, like Kelims or Navajo rugs, might provide inspiration, but study any example carefully before attempting to reproduce it and try to determine how effective it will look shorn of the rich texture and tones of its original material.

Canvas; a sharp Stanley knife for trimming it; a frame for stretching it on (optional); drawing pins [thumb tacks] or a staple gun for pinning down small canvases, thin 50 mm [2 in] nails for staking out larger ones; primer; paint; various brushes; adhesive, and varnish. You will also need the usual white spirit [mineral spirits]; ruler or tape measure; saucers or jamjars for mixing colours; chalk or pencil for marking designs; medium sandpaper; rags and waste paper.

Equipment

    If you decide to stencil your design, see pages 56–8 for equipment.

Canvas Buy a close-woven canvas, in the dimensions you want your floorcloth to be plus 25 to 50 mm [1 to 2 in] all round, for turning under. Sailmakers sell the greatest range of widths. Artists' suppliers are more expensive but stock a variety of different weights of canvas for painting on. Narrow widths of canvas can be machined together – some sailmakers will do this for you.

Frame This is not essential, but a properly stretched canvas makes a more professional-looking floorcloth, without creases or cockled edges. Nail together light wooden battens, 25 by 25 mm [1 by 1 in] to make a frame on which to stretch the canvas, and pin it tightly into place with drawing pins [thumb tacks] or a staple gun. A frame also makes the cloth easier to stow away out of harm's reach while paint and varnish are drying. Alternatively, small floorcloths can be pinned out on a table, floor or shed wall,

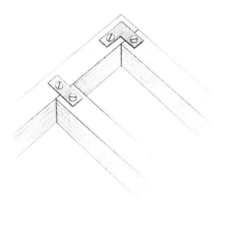
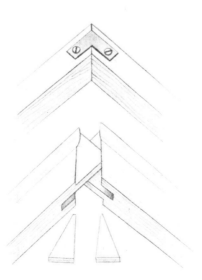

To make a sturdy frame, *far left*, join four wooden battens, 25 by 25 mm [1 by 1 in], using metal plates. To give further support to a large canvas, and to prevent the frame from twisting, you can add middle struts, too. If you possess a mitre-box, mitring the corners, *top left*, produces a neater fit. Otherwise, *bottom left*, you can use an artists' frame made from prepared lengths of wood that have been carved to form a mortise and tenon, for a secure joint.

Simple geometric designs, popular on 18th-century
floorcloths, look equally good on modern ones, *top* and *right*.
Paint them to echo existing colours in the room. The floorcloth
above was sponged to match the colours of the Whieldon ware
pottery in a corner cabinet. Painted to match the colours and
pattern of an old Pennsylvanian decorated chest, the floorcloth
opposite makes a colourful and hardwearing covering for a busy
attic landing.

146

and larger ones staked out with long, thin nails on the lawn; as soon as the cloth is *dry*, it can be unpinned, rolled up and temporarily put away.

Primer This does various jobs – it helps to level up the weave and provide a good painting surface, and protects the canvas in wear, but it must remain flexible enough to allow the finished floorcloth to be rolled up for cleaning and transporting.

The cheapest possibility is standard emulsion [latex] paint, with a little PVA added to give greater adhesion and flexibility. PVA is stocked by most artists' suppliers and some builders' merchants or hardware stores: you need 1 part of it to about 5 parts emulsion paint. A floorcloth 240 × 180 cm [8 × 6 ft] will need about 2 litres [2 US quarts] of emulsion [latex] and $\frac{1}{2}$ a litre [1 US pint] of PVA. Although the first couple of coats are slow to brush on, it dries fast and gives a smooth surface after sanding. You can paint directly on to it – if you want a coloured ground, tint the last 2 coats with stainers [tinting colours] or artists' acrylics.

Acrylic primer – sold in large cans from builders' merchants – is more expensive than emulsion paint, but it dries extremely fast and gives more build in fewer coats. This is also true of synthetic gesso, the most expensive of the lot, sold only through leading artists' suppliers. Delicious to use, it rapidly builds up a smooth, chalky, immaculate surface.

Paint Synthetic gesso and acrylic primer should be given a coat of emulsion [latex] paint plus PVA, or flat oil-based paint, suitably tinted, before decoration is applied.

For the decorative painting, or stencilling, use fast-drying, highly pigmented paints with good hiding power. Artists' acrylics can be used almost neat for density, or thinned with water or acrylic medium for transparency. Signwriters' colours [bulletin colours], mixed with a little polyurethane varnish or goldsize for extra elasticity, are cheaper but more restricted in range. Artists' oils thinned with solvent give a rich, juicy colour but are slow drying – add a few drops of drier. American readers will find thinned japan colours ideal.

Brushes For applying primer you need a large, preferably old brush, 100 mm [4 in] or 125 mm [5 in] or more – the bigger the brush the more time you save. For putting on the base coat of paint a large decorators' brush of the same size. You will also require brushes suitable to the design and medium you are using – an extra-large stencil brush, a velour pad, or a fine-textured sponge could all be used for stencilling. You will also need a large varnishing brush, or a brush reserved for applying varnish, see page 231.

Adhesive Use one of the milky-looking PVA-based adhesives that remain flexible when dry and do not stain to stick down the floorcloth edges, after decoration is done.

Cut your canvas to the required size, allowing 25 to 50 mm [1 to 2 in] extra all round to be turned over eventually and stuck down flat.

Any seaming should be done now. Make a flat join by edge stitching two selvedges, using an oversewing stitch, strong needle and sailmakers' twine or waxed thread. Alternatively, machine stitch a seam along two selvedges, open it out and glue it flat.

Priming Pin the canvas out taut on frame, table, floor or lawn. Priming protects the canvas and builds up a smoother surface for decoration. To

Preparation

To sew two pieces of canvas together you require waxed thread or sailmakers' twine and a strong needle with a large eye. Use an overlapping stitch. Open the seam out and glue it down on either side with PVA-based adhesive. For priming and painting, stretch the canvas tightly and fix it in place on a frame or flat surface with a staple gun, thin nails or drawing pins [thumb tacks]. Make these about 50 mm [2 in] apart.

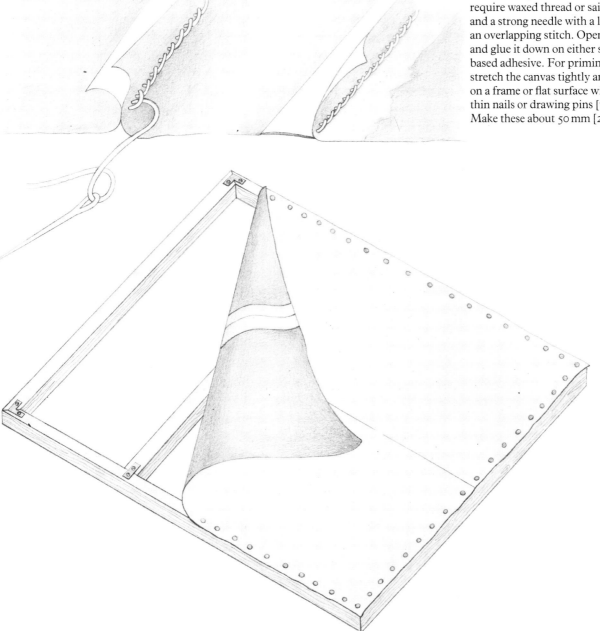

Above Notches on a square stencil enable you to position it exactly on a grid to make up a perfectly regular repeat pattern.

Right One example of a repeat design is this floorcloth using the hearty red and green and the crisp, formalized motifs of an old appliqué quilt.

Far right Make a separate stencil for each colour in a motif: registration marks on the acetate mean that you can align each one accurately over the previous ones.

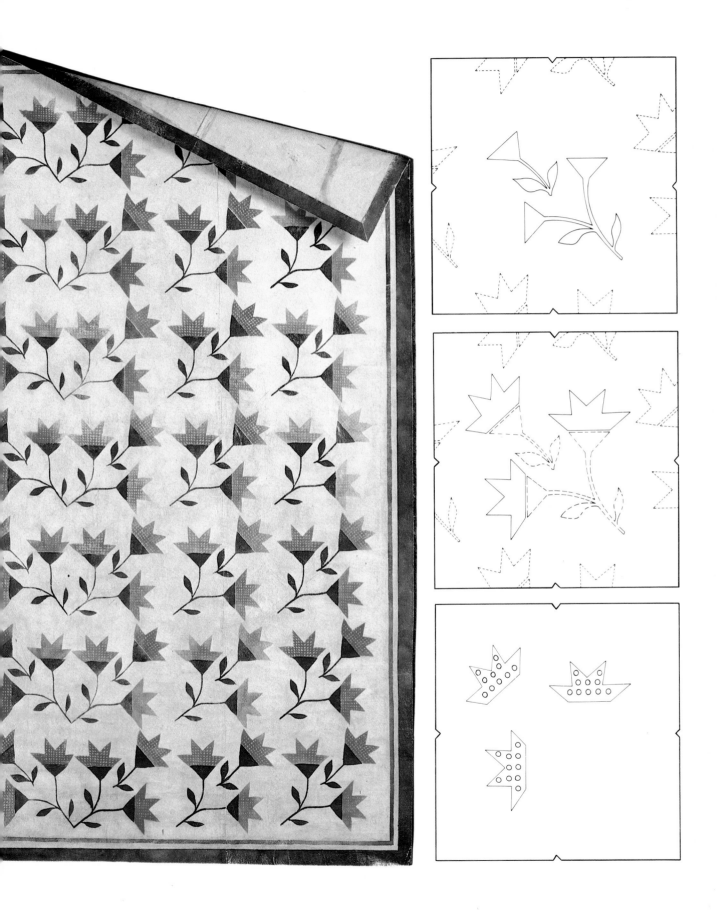

level up the weave takes 3 or 4 coats of artists' gesso or acrylic primer, or 5 coats of emulsion [latex] and PVA primer. The more coats of primer, the smoother and tougher the floorcloth. Give the underside a couple of priming coats, too, for protection.

Brush the primer on evenly with a large brush, taking it right up to the edges of the canvas. The edges may wrinkle at first, but when you eventually stick them down you will find that they flatten out quite satisfactorily.

The first couple of coats will take some time to apply, since the canvas will absorb the primer unevenly, but after that it will go on speedily, each coat taking only a few minutes to apply. After the third priming coat has dried, rub it over with medium sandpaper to smooth it and to remove grit and stray fibres, and sand lightly after any succeeding priming coats. This will make the cloth more supple as well as smoother.

If you want a coloured ground for your design, the last coats of emulsion and PVA primer should be tinted to the required shade with artists' acrylics or stainers [tinting colours] – a dark colour will need 3 coats to build up the required density, a lighter colour, two. Sand them lightly when dry.

Always leave the floorcloth stretched while it dries. Once dry, it can be unpinned, rolled up and put out of the way. Try not to make any sharp creases in it when handling it because these crack the delicate paint skin, causing the fine crazing one sees on old paintings. Although the effect is quite pleasing, it means that the paint surface is slightly weakened.

Painting and stencilling Use coloured chalk or tiny pencil dots to plot the design on the floorcloth before setting to work with paint and brushes. Regular repeat motifs, such as appliqué blocks or tile patterns, can be positioned by chalking in the centre line of the cloth both ways and working outwards from the middle; see pages 128–9 on stencilling floors. Designs relying on templates should be drawn in all over before you start. These can then either be painted in by hand, or, if this seems too longwinded and the pattern is suitable, you can make a stencil of the main part of the design in acetate, register it over each of your drawn shapes and paint it in.

It is probably a matter of temperament how long you spend over getting your design mathematically aligned on the floorcloth. Some people will want to mark in the position of each stencil block or pattern before painting, others will position them by eye as they go along – quicker, but it does lead to errors. However, if you allow a generous margin for a border all the way round, any major slip-ups can be corrected later by reducing the size or style of the border.

In a multi-coloured stencil, paint in all the elements in one colour at a time. The first colour is usually dry by the time you are ready to apply the second. Mix up less colour than you think you will need – stencilling uses it very sparingly and a couple of tablespoons in a saucer will be enough for a floorcloth as large as 180 by 240 cm [6 by 8 ft]. For a soft, shadowed effect use very little colour on the stencil brush (test it on waste paper each

152

time) and pounce it on to the canvas with a jabbing movement through the holes in the stencil. More appealing than flat, hard-edged colour, this effect looks just right for colouring in appliqué designs, as it suggests aged and faded fabrics. For juicy, slick opaque colour, on the other hand, use colour mixed in a little varnish and brushed in place carefully so that it does not fuzz out under the stencil edges. Gloss varnish to finish will supply the shine that brings these colours up handsomely.

You can alter or mellow the colours of a floorcloth after decoration, but before varnishing, by applying a tinted wash or glaze, see page 224. One tinted with raw umber, for instance, will soften and unify harsh or bright colours. Sponge it over a square metre or yard at a time, count to thirty, then wipe it off with a rag, so that just a little is left ingrained in the weave. To lighten patches that are too dark, dampen the rag a little with water or solvent, and wipe them again.

    Washes and glazes

You will have no problems if you apply oil-based glaze over acrylic or oil-based colours or an acrylic-tinted wash over oil-based colours. However, if you are putting an acrylic wash over an acrylic-decorated ground, take care that the latter is completely dry, or you may rub it off when you rub off the excess wash. To make quite sure, test the wash on a corner first. Alternatively give the floorcloth a quick coat of clear varnish beforehand. Washes and glazes can safely be played about with over a tough protective barrier like this, which seals in the colours underneath.

To modify the ground colour a little (or in a hurry) *before* you decorate the cloth, use a glaze or wash in the same way: raw sienna with a speck of black transforms a white base into a creamy calico colour, perfect for a quilt background. A little cobalt blue and a dash of black give a white ground a faintly blue cast, suitable for ceramic-type designs.

Another even faster way to alter the colours on your floorcloth is to mix a little colour into the first coat of varnish – blend thoroughly so that you do not get streaks, and do not overdo the tinting, or the cloth could end up simply looking grubby. Once again, test it on a corner first.

Varnishing

Polyurethane varnish dries very fast on a well-primed painted canvas, especially under warm, dry conditions. All the same it is a good idea to leave a coat to dry 6 to 8 hours, or overnight, before re-varnishing, because varnishes continue to harden some while after they are touch-dry. If possible, varnish the cloth while it is spread so that light from a window falls obliquely on to it – you will be less likely to omit patches. Thin the first 2 coats of varnish with white spirit [mineral spirits], 3 parts varnish to 1 part solvent; the subsequent coats should be thinned 4 or 5 parts varnish to 1 part solvent. Brush it on thinly and fast with as large a brush as you can manage. The more coats of varnish the tougher the surface of your floorcloth – 4 or 5 are about right. Too much varnish will darken the colours noticeably, even so-called clear varnish has a distinctively yellowy cast. Brush a coat or two over the back of the floorcloth, too.

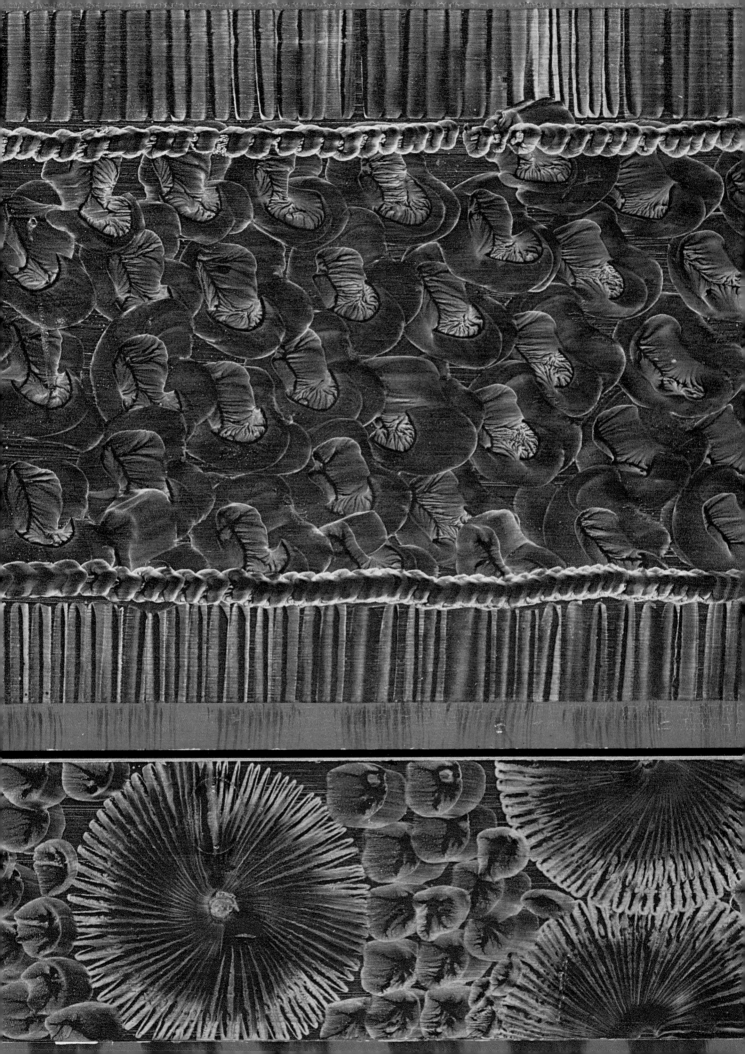

Furniture

155

Furniture has been painted since earliest times, usually to add surface colour and texture, sometimes to protect or conceal inferior wood, or to disguise crude workmanship. Each creative historical period has added some particular refinement of technique or decorative flourish.

There has never been a more beautiful plain finish than the old lacquer that the Chinese made from the sap of the lac tree. The 'japanning' techniques used by later European craftsmen to simulate lacquer are flimsy by comparison, although they do have a witty sophistication.

No painted furniture is more poetic in its fantastic decoration and tender colouring than that produced by the Venetians from the time of the Renaissance onwards, yet their very refinement of the gesso and tempera finish served the more prosaic purpose of disguising inferior woods and joinery. For elegance of a highly strung sort, French and English furniture of the late eighteenth century is unrivalled, the colours and decoration applied with taste, discretion and consummate technique. Regency craftsmen added the spice of wit, sparkling colours and a great deal of gilt to shapes that are a lively spoof of the Gothic and the Chinese. Later in the nineteenth century, painted furniture entered a brief new phase under the inspiration of William Morris in England, who produced perhaps the most theatrical and romantic pieces ever devised.

Such painted furniture belonged to the world of rich patrons, but alongside it evolved a democratic form – usually now called folk, rustic or provincial furniture. The workmanship is solid rather than refined, the shapes often clumsy, while the painted decoration itself tends to be bold and uninhibitedly colourful. It is often spirited, and like the decoration on Delft tiles or Staffordshire figures, skilful for all its apparent slapdashedness. Its brash colouring softened by time and use, much of this folk-style furniture is highly endearing, and perfectly at ease in the informal homes of today.

Unless one is very lucky, the chances of picking up an attractive old piece cheaply are getting smaller all the time. The only really inexpensive items around seem to be the boarding-house and office furniture of twenty or thirty years ago, often solidly made, usually of oak, but with a treacly varnished finish that looks unhappy anywhere. Painting them in the ordinary way makes them inconspicuous, but decorative finishes can transform them into really attractive, colourful pieces that are a pleasure to look at and use.

Painting furniture is tempting to try, because the preparation and work can be done in a small space without making too much mess or disrupting the household. In most cases the materials are cheap and easily available – filler, paint, stainers or artists' colours, varnish.

There is a decorative finish to enhance any type of piece and emphasize its attractive features while camouflaging its worst points. Ugly, coarse-grained wood texture is easily hidden by priming with the modern equivalent of the old Venetian gesso, to build up a hard, poreless surface for paint. Large, looming wardrobes, sideboards or chests of drawers

Previous page No half measures about the way the painter of this early 19th-century American chest handled his effects: simple painting is combined with wild sponging, combed borders, and rosette patterns produced by pressing fans of crisply pleated cartridge paper into the wet paint. Vinegar paint is the ideal medium for these effects, but follow the example of this gifted craftsman and handle it boldly.

undergo a visual shrinking process when given a simple distressed finish in quiet colours that match or tone with the wall colour. Such outsize pieces are always improved by a matt or at most a semigloss finish because non-shiny surfaces seem to look smaller than glossy, reflecting ones.

Look for items in good working order: drawers that slide, hinges in place, doors that fit, chairs that do not wobble. Choose a simple shape, an air of solidity, sensible proportions – in other words a piece with recognizable kinship to the classic models. Superfluous twiddly bits or gimcrack detail like nasty handles can simply be removed, while some more stylish ornament can be made a feature of, with a suitable finish. Furniture with built-in decoration – relief carving on panels, turned knobs or curlicues – can be painted, too. A fantastic Gothic-style piece responds to a folk approach using strong, contrasting colours, but keeping the finish quite matt to resemble the powdery texture of old paint. Offbeat colours are best: dull reds, maroon, pea green, murky yellows, faded indigo, bistre, all of which can be achieved by mixing raw umber into a basic tint. In total contrast, furniture with shallow relief carving, the sort that looks more pressed than carved and usually goes with thirties shapes, looks surprisingly urbane and attractive if given a finish of that period – ultra-sleek creamy 'lacquered' paint achieved by patient rubbing down and varnishing. Good colours are cream, black and vermilion red.

Odd dining chairs can be given a visual link by sponging or spattering, see pages 175 and 176, techniques so simple that a child could tackle them. Paint cane-seated chairs of almost any style in soft, matt blues and greens, with the caning itself painted in a trellis pattern. Use the same colours and patterns to give a French provincial charm to the most ordinary, battered kitchen units – useful again if you want to link up pieces with disparate finishes.

Furniture does not, of course, have to be in a hideous condition to qualify for decorative painting. No one would be rash enough to paint anything made of rare or expensive hardwood, or wood with attractive figuring. As a general rule, the best articles to paint are those of wood that looks better covered up, and these are usually of recent make. Sometimes an old piece may need painting to conceal unsightly repairs in wood that does not match, or to replace an old finish that has worn off – though be careful here, since old paintwork in tolerable condition adds to the value of a good item. If you do repaint, make sure the technique and finish are appropriate to the piece.

Small wooden items, such as picture frames, boxes, trays or hanging shelves are great fun to decorate and one can afford to lavish more pains over a small thing that takes only a few minutes for each step. Marbled picture frames look immensely chic, as do blonde tortoiseshell painted boxes. Trays and table tops look elegant covered with neat, formal stencil patterns, while angular modern tables are transformed by a porphyry finish – easy to do as long as you have somewhere outdoors where you can safely spatter paint about.

157

Although fantasy graining has been used all over Europe, the splendid boldness of these early American pieces makes them veritable tigers among painted furniture.

Above A grained early 19th-century chest from New England.

Above A Pennsylvanian pine chest of about 1830, grained in stylized forms of traditional German motifs – a six-pointed star on the top, eyes on the front, tulips on the ends.

Left A pine chest, painted in New England around 1835, decorated in a combination of sponging and graining.

Left A pine blanket chest – the two top drawers are false – grained with uninhibited vigour in red and green on a yellow ground.

Below A pine chest with drawers, from Massachusetts, decorated with a combination of dramatic effects. For a closer view of them, see pages 154–55.

Above Like the rosette decoration on the chest *left*, the circular graining on this New England chest was probably achieved by pressing crisp, folded paper into the wet glaze.

159

Preparing furniture for painting

Decorative finishes of the sort discussed in this section are wasted effort unless the surface beneath is prepared to a high standard. Any surface imperfections like rough grain and unfilled scars or screw-holes will show through the finish you put on top, and detract from the overall effect. Although giving a first-class finish to an old item of furniture usually involves painstaking preparation, extra time and trouble taken at this stage are well worthwhile since the result is an elegant piece that looks as though it comes from a professional studio.

Stripping down

The most important step is to take off the old finish and get back to clean bare wood. Occasionally old paint is in good enough condition to paint over. Paint that has gone thin and chalky with time makes an excellent undercoat and small chips and cracks can be filled in with all-purpose filler [spackle]. But more often the old paint has been badly applied, sometimes straight over varnish, and is flaky, blistered and wrinkled. If you sand it down, wear a paper mask (as bought from a chemist [druggist]) or a scarf tied over nose and mouth, because old paints contain lead, the dust of which should not be inhaled. Unless you are going to gesso a piece, varnish should always be removed since it never bonds satisfactorily with paint on top. It is easily dissolved either with proprietary paint stripper or, in the case of a shellac finish like French polish, with methylated spirits [denatured alcohol]. It is often difficult to tell what the finish is, so try a little methylated spirits on the piece first, and if that fails to soften the finish quickly, progress to paint stripper. In any case, use proprietary stripper for smaller pieces, especially those with fine detail such as carving, fretwork and turned ornament, or on pieces that may prove to be made of superior wood. Unscrew hinged doors and remove drawer pulls and other metal attachments. Cover the surrounding floor with sheets of plastic, wear gloves, and apply the stripper with an old paintbrush, following the maker's instructions. When the top layers of paint have softened, which usually takes 10 minutes or so, scrape the sticky paste off large surfaces with a flat scraper, taking care not to scratch and scar the wood. Then clean up tricky surfaces with coarse, then finer, old steel wool. It can take several applications of paint remover to work through many old paint layers. Small pointed knives or nail files are handy for digging paint out of cracks or carving.

Caustic Large pieces, covered with numerous layers of paint, are best cleaned with a strong caustic solution, see page 116 for the recipe. This should be done out of doors, using rubber gloves and applying the mixture with the type of spatula sold for putting on oven cleaner. Loosen the paint layers with an old scrubbing brush. A hose is handy for rinsing off the sludgy dissolved paint. Removing layers of paint may take several successive applications, and the mess is considerable, but over a large area it is infinitely cheaper to use caustic than proprietary stripper. To make things easier for yourself, lay as many sections as possible flat before rubbing it on. This will concentrate its action, since it tends to run off vertical surfaces. Caustic leaves wood fuzzy and discoloured, but patient, gentle sanding down with finer and finer grades of sandpaper will restore a smooth finish. Some firms advertise a paint-stripping service using tubs of caustic – useful if you live in an apartment block.

Primer

As the name suggests, primer is the first coat of paint in a system. Experts insist that it should always be used if you are painting new wood, as it protects the wood by counteracting its natural porosity, so that subsequent coats of paint do not sink in. Of the various types available, the toughest is the traditional pink or white oil-based primer, sold for use on wood alone; it should be thinned 3 parts primer to 1 part white spirit [mineral spirits], applied liberally and brushed well into the wood. White universal primer can be used on wood or plaster, while aluminium primer goes over any highly resinous woods or varnished surfaces. Acrylic primer, for use on wood, acts as a combined primer and undercoat. Metal has its own primers.

The knots in pine and deal must be sealed with patent knotting [knot sealer] before priming. Do not skip this; knots exude resin for years, and unsealed ones will cause surface paint to crack and discolour. Use it according to the maker's directions, applying 2 coats – more if the wood is really raw – over each knot. Dabbing it on with a rag goes faster than brushing.

Filler

Coarse woodgrain, cracks and scars should be filled to present an even surface for painting. Use a proprietary woodwork filler or standard all-purpose filler [spackle]. Mix it to a creamy consistency and apply it with a brush. Apply the first layer with the grain; allow it to dry and then, if necessary, apply a second layer against the grain. When it is dry rub it down firmly, with the grain, with medium sandpaper. Coarse-grained woods like oak may need 2 applications to level them up.

Larger holes, dents or chips should be filled with a stiffer mix of filler, applied with a palette knife, left proud (above wood level) and sanded flat when dry. Really bad holes should be filled with a harder substance such as plastic wood – follow the manufacturer's instructions.

Sand down the primed and filled surface until smooth before going on to the undercoat stage. It is a good idea to apply a coat of shellac to any extra special piece, or one that will get a lot of handling, now – it really does improve the look and feel of the paint finish, giving a fine surface for paint. Thin it with 1 part methylated spirits [denatured alcohol] to 2 of shellac. See pages 169–70 on applying shellac.

Undercoat

More highly pigmented than most paints, undercoat does a good cover-up job on furniture, as well as providing the ideal flat, 'hungry' surface for subsequent paints. Undercoat should be brushed out well to give even coverage and laid off lightly with the bristle tips to flatten out brushmarks. Apply 1 or 2 coats (thin it with a little white spirit [mineral spirits] if you are applying 2), depending on the state of the surface beneath. American readers can use an enamel undercoater, which

161

The more northerly the climate, it seems, the more colourful its native painted furniture. The three pieces from Sweden and Denmark on these pages have an exuberance far from the simple lines and blonde wood we now associate with Scandinavian furniture.

Left A magnificent 18th-century Swedish corner cupboard combining vigorous marbling in shades of blue with rich red mouldings and plain cream panels decorated in raw umber and black.

doubles as a primer as well. Under pale colours, white undercoat is fine, but under dark ones it will need tinting to something near the final colour.

Rub it down firmly when dry with medium then fine sandpaper. On large surfaces begin rubbing in a circular motion, and end by rubbing in the direction of the grain beneath; on smaller pieces, rub with the grain throughout. For a supersmooth finish, use a special quick-drying fine filler, which comes ready mixed, to level up any little blemishes remaining at this stage. Keep the lid on this, since it hardens quickly if exposed to the air.

The routine of primer, filler and undercoat can be replaced by the application of synthetic gesso, which fulfils all requirements in one and takes less time.

Above The little gentleman surrounded by admiring birds – a detail from a 19th-century Danish cupboard – epitomizes the innocent style of early folk decoration. Rather than copying a detail like this, try substituting a similar portrait of one of the family. Mix raw umber into your basic paints to imitate these beautiful colours.

Right Another gorgeous painted piece from Denmark, using the same colours as the Swedish cupboard, *opposite*, but in a vernacular style.

Left This somewhat geometrical style of decoration was popular in an area of Massachusetts in the early 18th century. The designs are easy to imitate, if you·use a compass, but half of the charm lies in the scarred texture of the cream ground. Try painting on a strongly grained wood such as oak, then rub it down to reveal the grain patchily, give it an umber antique glaze, and finish it with matt varnish.

163

Gesso Traditionally used by makers of high-quality painted furniture, gesso is a fine plaster bound with glue size that builds up – after many coats (sometimes as many as 40) and much smoothing – a surface as hard and poreless as porcelain. It not only provides an immaculate surface for fine finishes but also helpfully obliterates coarse texture and crude joinery in the piece itself.

Professional decorators, and restorers particularly, still use traditional gesso, but making and using it properly is a skill in itself, involving trial and error, correct drying temperatures and constant attention. Altogether too much bother for an amateur who simply wants the advantages of a gesso-type base on a few picture frames, or a piece of furniture.

Thankfully, there is a less troublesome modern alternative. Modern synthetic gesso, sold by artists' suppliers for priming canvases, is more expensive and a little less versatile than the traditional type, but it answers ordinary needs perfectly, brushing on as easily as a good paint.

A ground of synthetic gesso works a positive transformation on any piece of unpleasant texture and coarse construction but reasonable shape. It is absolutely ideal, for instance, for any pieces of veneered blockboard or chipboard, as well as for any of the items that can still be picked up really cheaply because they are too recent to be 'period' and too mass-produced to be interesting. Cover them with a fine, hard shell of gesso before painting them and they mysteriously acquire dignity and presence, their shoddy materials and construction becoming invisible.

Applying synthetic gesso Synthetic gesso is delightfully easy to use. The piece of furniture does not even need to be stripped of paint or varnish first, although gesso adheres better and builds more rapidly if the surfaces are well sanded first to provide tooth. Depending on the state of the original finish, sand it first with coarse, then medium sandpaper. Fill in cracks and chipped veneer with plastic wood or all-purpose filler [spackle], and sand it level when dry. Wipe over the whole piece with a rag dipped in white spirit [mineral spirits] to remove grease.

Using an old brush – these plastery substances are hard on brushes – paint a thin coat of synthetic gesso over the entire piece. Do not bother with the insides and unseen parts of furniture, but paint over all the previously finished surfaces, which usually include the edges of doors and tops of drawers.

The first coat takes about an hour to dry, subsequent ones about three-quarters of an hour. Rub over the gesso with folded medium sandpaper in the direction of the woodgrain, using firm pressure and long, level strokes. Dust off with a rag, and recoat with gesso, repeating the whole routine several times, until you have built up a smooth, white, level surface over the whole piece.

Rub the gesso down harder on door and drawer edges or they may not fit properly. If you are rubbing down correctly the gesso will be so fine and compacted that the original finish will just show through on sharp edges. Beginners tend to go too gently from a natural reluctance to remove too much of what they have just laboriously put on – the ideal result is a thin, level and very smooth surface.

The number of coats needed varies with the type and condition of the wood and its previous finish. Open-grained wood with a poor varnished finish will require 4 or 5 coats, previously painted wood only 2 or 3. Pieces that get a lot of handling, like chairs, should have fewer coats, and these should be rubbed down harder in between. You will need at least 5 coats of gesso if you are going to put transparent watercolour on top, to build up a white, shadow-free surface.

All-purpose filler [spackle] It is worthwhile using synthetic gesso for special pieces. For less important items use all-purpose filler [spackle] thinned with water to a creamy, brushable consistency. Apply and rub it down in exactly the same way as synthetic gesso, although you will find that it takes longer to build up, to dry hard and to rub smooth.

Sanding down

Sanding between layers of filler, undercoat, gesso, paint and varnish smooths the surface, while providing tooth for the next coat. Scrupulous sanding makes a difference to the final look and feel of a painted piece out of all proportion to the time involved. Professional work is *always* sanded, at every stage.

What we tend to call 'sandpaper' is, strictly speaking, abrasive paper, which may be coated with one of a number of substances such as glass, garnet or silicon carbide. These papers come in grades between coarse and fine, which are split into progressively finer subdivisions. The routine is to begin with a coarse paper and work down to a fine one. The finer you want your finish to be, the finer the grade of paper you must end up with.

When sanding a flat surface wrap your paper round a sanding block. This distributes your hand pressure evenly. Use firm pressure, and long, smooth strokes. Rub backwards and forwards in the general direction of the grain beneath, going gently over sharp edges, relief carving and turned detail. To sand a narrow, rounded surface, such as a chair arm or leg, wrap a small piece of sandpaper round it, like a scratchy collar.

Wet-or-dry (silicon carbide) paper, as its name suggests, can be used in either condition. Use it dry over bare wood. For rubbing down paint and varnish, it should be used with soapy water to soften the abrasive action and prevent scratching. Mix pure soap flakes with water and pat the sudsy solution over the surface. Rub the paper smoothly with long strokes from edge to edge of the surface, following the direction of the grain and going easy on projecting areas. Test the surface with your fingertips for smoothness from time to time, and wipe off the soapy mixture to check your progress. When you have gone over the whole piece, wipe it dry with a clean, damp rag, and then go over it with a tack rag, see page 25.

As an alternative to wet-or-dry paper you can use steel wool, also with soapy water, but throw away the pads after use, since they rust up quickly. Like abrasive paper, steel wool comes in coarse to fine grades.

Painting Furniture

The chief difference between applying a high-class paint finish and the average do-it-yourself cover-up is that with the former you linger longer over each stage. The aim is to achieve a sleek, level paint surface, thin enough not to obscure any carved or turned detail, flat and smooth enough for any decorative finish to glide gratefully into place. The more thoroughly you do the base painting, the better the final finish will look and the more gracefully it will age.

Mix your colours by hand, tinting your own paint as in the instructions on pages 218–21. This not only allows for much finer colour adjustments, but is also more convenient, since one can of paint plus the various tints takes up less room than an equivalent range of cans of bought colours.

Gloss [enamel] paints are not used in good quality furniture painting. Shiny paint does not provide enough tooth for subsequent decoration, and it looks wrong, especially on old pieces. Any shine required is added later by means of clear or tinted varnish coats, rubbed and polished for a supple sheen.

Flat white oil-based paint is the one commonly used for most furniture painting by professional decorators and restorers. Being relatively soft-textured, it needs several coats of varnish as protection against use and handling. Flat paint protected with matt varnish is the ideal finish for large, vividly decorated country-style pieces that look brash given a gloss finish. Mid-sheen oil-based paint, see page 214, is suitable too, and harder wearing, but the finish should be rubbed down to dull the sheen.

Emulsion [latex] paint and acrylic colours are widely available, easy to use, quick-drying, and give a pleasantly chalky texture very close to that of the aged lead paint found on many old country pieces. Use flat emulsion to paint any piece that would look best with a simple, rustic finish, and acrylic colours for any decorative painting on top. This gives a quick and passable imitation of the old gouache over gesso decoration. Varnish renders an emulsion finish as durable as any other. Use 2 coats of clear matt varnish to give protection while retaining the flat, lean look.

Paint

Opposite When artists turn their talents to decorating they invariably bring off delicious effects with an enviable economy of means. This bedroom corner in the house of the famed early-20th-century Swedish illustrator, Carl Larsson, uses a few well-balanced colours on ceiling, wall and cot, and a simple border, with a result whose sophistication lies in its apparent artlessness. A closer look reveals that the same room features in the Carl Larsson original hanging over the cot.

Brushes

Use a standard paintbrush on large pieces. On small, delicately detailed ones, a brush with soft, fine bristles, such as a round squirrel artists' brush, helps to flow the paint on so that it needs less rubbing down afterwards.

Method

Applying oil-based paint After tinting, mix the paint thoroughly with white spirit [mineral spirits] to a thin cream consistency – about 1 part white spirit to about 4 of paint.

167

Make sure that you leave each paint coat plenty of time – say overnight – to dry hard, before applying the next. Most of the troubles that arise in painting come from applying paint before the surface beneath is hard and dry. You will need between 2 and 5 coats of coloured paint to provide a good finish, or a ground for subsequent decoration. More but thinner coats give a professional appearance, and rubbing down is crucial. Use medium-grade sandpaper for the first coat, fine wet-or-dry paper with soap and water for the following ones.

Applying emulsion paint Although emulsion can be applied directly to bare wood, it tends to sink in and raise the grain. It is better to apply primer first, rubbed smooth when dry. You will need 2 or 3 coats of emulsion paint over primer, 3 or 4 over bare wood, each sanded down with medium sandpaper.

To capitalize on the inherent dry texture of this finish, apply further decoration in acrylics straight on to the emulsion ground. Be warned, however, that this does not allow for correcting mistakes – as with any watercolour painting, once a colour is brushed on to the emulsion surface, it is pretty permanent. You can apply a barrier coat of clear matt varnish, but this means some loss of texture. However, you can always paint out a real disaster area with a couple more coats of emulsion and start again from scratch.

Glazes and washes For how to make and apply these, see pages 224–29. Although tinted glazes are traditionally used in furniture decoration, their slow drying time means that they are often rejected in favour of quicker-drying tinted varnish.

Transparent paint

Tinted flat paint gives opaque colour. For a special richness, an inimitable depth and glow unmodified by white pigment, you can also make a sort of transparent paint, by mixing pure colour into clear polyurethane varnish.

Tinting

Blend artists' oils – more delicate in hue than universal stainers [tinting colours], although you can use these, too – with a little white spirit [mineral spirits] in a saucer, using a palette knife. Add clear, semigloss polyurethane varnish, a spoonful at a time, and mix thoroughly. The end result will have a slightly thicker consistency than varnish. If it does not brush on easily, thin it further with white spirit. If you are using slow-drying colours like alizarin crimson or vandyke brown, add some drier.

Test the colour on a piece of paper. Transparent paint will not produce a colour change in the way an opaque paint does, but 2 coats superimposed add up to quite intense colour, so do not make it too dark.

Application

Clean the surface with a rag moistened in white spirit [mineral spirits] or in vinegar, to remove grease. Brush on the transparent paint like varnish, see pages 170–72, thinly and rapidly. When it is dry, rub it down with fine steel wool and soap and water, and then rinse it clean. The steel wool cuts down the gloss completely – if you want a shine, give the piece top coats of clear gloss varnish.

Shellac

A spirit varnish, soluble only in methylated spirits [denatured alcohol], shellac comes in various colours ranging from orange (also called button polish) to clear white. It is most frequently used in French polishing, but because of its imperviousness to most solvents and its quick drying time – an hour for 1 coat, a little longer for 2 – it is often used in furniture restoration and painting as a barrier between different stages in the work. It is also used in high-class work to seal surfaces after priming and filling and before undercoating. At a later stage, it can be added after painting in the body colour but before glazing, so that the glaze can be rubbed down, or even wiped off altogether, without fear of disturbing the coat beneath. In effects involving media and colours of possibly conflicting ingredients, a coat of shellac is a useful insurance against what the textbooks sinisterly describe as a 'breakdown' of the paint system.

Do not buy too much shellac at a time since it does not keep well. For this reason, try to buy it from a shop that has a quick turnover of stock.

Brushes

You can paint furniture without ever using shellac, but since it is not expensive, it is worth keeping to hand. Reserve a special brush – it need not be large, but it should be soft-bristled. After use, wash it out in methylated spirits [denatured alcohol], and then in warm water with a little ammonia added, *not* soap or detergent. If the bristles harden, they can be softened before use by dipping again into methylated spirits.

Application

Manufacturers often recommend shaking shellac before it is applied, but this creates bubbles that show up on the finish. It is better to tip it into a saucer, add 1 part methylated spirits to 2 of shellac, and stir gently. This thins and blends it nicely. Shellac should be used in a dry, warm atmosphere – if it is applied in damp conditions a white bloom appears on the surface, although this usually fades as the shellac dries. If the weather is damp, close the windows and heat the room to noticeable warmth.

Shellac can be awkward to brush on, drying so fast that one brushstroke is half-dry before the next overlaps with it, which creates build-ups of colour and a patchy look. Charge the bristles quite generously with shellac, press out the surplus against the inner sides of the can. Lay it on in the middle of the surface and with quick strokes draw it out toward the outer edges, trying not to overlap. Smooth it out by brushing from edge to edge, lightly and fast. A little patchiness in the final result is not too serious – correct the worst mistakes by rubbing down gently with fine steel wool and a little soapy water.

Varnish as a barrier coat

In place of shellac, you can use a coat of clear polyurethane varnish to seal off a surface or finish. Although this is much tougher – shellac is not water- or alcohol-proof – it has the disadvantage of being slower drying.

Varnish

For furniture finishing the three widely available types of clear polyurethane varnish – matt, semigloss and gloss – cover most needs and are easy to use and durable. Specify a clear varnish, since some polyurethane varnishes have a distinctly greenish-yellow tinge and several coats will darken the colours of a painted piece.

Matt varnish dries with no shine, is almost invisible and does not need rubbing down. It is right for pieces that need a simple, rustic finish, and is useful, too, where the wood and paint texture are rough and uneven, since, unlike an allover shine, it does not make these defects conspicuous. Semigloss varnish is the most useful allround finish; it dries with a soft sheen that looks good over most decorative treatments.

Gloss varnish, which dries shiny, is the toughest and most protective of the three types. Use it for small pieces that get a lot of handling like trays, boxes and tinware, as well as surfaces like table tops that need frequent wiping down. If the finish seems too brilliant, it can be softened by rubbing down. Alternatively, 2 or 3 protective coats of gloss varnish may be finished with one of semigloss to tone down the shine. Gloss varnish is also used for a high-shine lacquer finish, meticulously rubbed, and finally polished. In this case it should be used diluted 3 parts varnish to 2 parts white spirit [mineral spirits], to ensure thin, even coats.

Preparation

Varnish should be applied on a dry day in a clean, warm room – 21°C (70°F). If you must varnish in damp weather, close the windows and keep the room heated. Damp is the worst enemy of varnish; it slows its drying and prevents it from flowing nicely. On the other hand, do not try to accelerate drying by standing a freshly varnished piece next to a heater or fire or in bright sunshine, since concentrated heat can raise blisters.

If the varnish has thickened with cold, stand the can in hot water for a couple of minutes; if it is lumpy, strain it through an old stocking into a clean container. Some professional decorators decant varnish through a plastic funnel into a long-necked bottle, to decrease the exposed surface area. This is because prolonged exposure to air can cause varnish to solidify and eventually become useless.

Grease prevents varnish from adhering evenly, so wipe over the surface of the piece first with a rag moistened with white spirit or vinegar and water. Handle it as little as possible since fingermarks leave a greasy film. If you rub the piece down, wipe it afterwards, and go over it with a tack rag, if you have one, see page 25.

Brushes

A special varnish brush, see page 231, is a worthwhile buy if you plan to do a lot of varnishing. The bristles hold more varnish than a standard brush, and help it to flow on smoothly. Otherwise, use a standard paintbrush, 50 or 75 mm [2 or 3 in] wide, and keep it only for varnishing.

170

Protective varnishing is vital if your decorative flights of fancy are not to chip and flake with the passing years. While a bit of threadbare paint can look charming, too much and you are back to square one. Exuberant decoration like the garlands on this chair and wooden dado looks best with matt or semigloss polyurethane varnish – a gloss finish would tend to make it look cheap.

For smaller pieces a 25 mm [1 in] oxhair artists' brush is excellent. Varnish brushes can be stored overnight in a can of white spirit, the handle pushed through a slot cut in a cardboard lid. The solvent must be brushed out on paper before use.

Application Varnish is not applied like paint. The brush should be dipped into the varnish up to about half the length of the bristles and then transferred straight to the surface of the piece. If it seems overloaded to the point of dripping, press the bristles against the inner sides of the can – do not stroke them across the rim, as this creates bubbles. Start varnishing in the middle of a surface, flowing the wet varnish toward the outer edges. Then very lightly brush over the wet varnish again from edge to edge to even it out and break any bubbles. Brush out any runs and

Method

drips, and flick out hairs or grit with the edge of the brush. Repeat this procedure until the whole area is covered, then repeat over the rest of the piece, taking one surface at a time. In the case of a fiddly item, such as a chair, turn it upside down and begin with the legs, using a narrow brush. Then turn it the right way up and varnish the back, front, arms and seat, in that order.

Leave the freshly varnished piece in a warm, dry, dust-free place to set for at least 24 hours – longer in damp weather. If it is small enough, protect it from dust by setting it under a large box with holes punched in the sides to let air circulate.

To get a really professional finish – worthwhile in the case of a fine old piece – brush the first coat of varnish *with* the grain, the second against it, and the third with it again. After the first 2 coats some restorers use a pad made of old nylon stockings rather than a brush. This goes quicker than brushing and allows one to float on the thinnest possible coat. Tip a little varnish into a saucer and dip the pad in; if the varnish does not glide on smoothly, add a little white spirit and mix gently.

As usual, more thin coats are better than fewer thick ones. A matt varnish needs only 2 or 3 coats, a semigloss one 4 or 5, while a gloss finish – especially if it needs to withstand washing down, alcohol stains and hot plates – can do with as many as 7; 5 to 7 coats are usually recommended for painted tin. Repeated coats of varnish not only increase protection, but also level off the surface, especially if you rub down carefully between coats.

Rubbing down varnish To create a finish that is fine, smooth and delicious to touch, and to give a wellbred air to any piece, the last few coats of varnish can be rubbed down. The first 2 coats should not be rubbed, since this could cut through the thin layers and damage the paint beneath, so it is only a matter of spending a few extra minutes on each subsequent coat. Do not rub down the last coat.

Matt varnish does not need rubbing down, but semigloss and gloss definitely do, for good results. Use fine wet-or-dry paper or fine steel wool. Rubbed varnish looks less transparent when dry, but its dulled surface has enough tooth for the next varnish coat to flow on smoothly and adhere well.

Polishing For an immaculate finish, the last coat of varnish is given a handpolishing. Professional restorers use a paste made of rottenstone – a fine, grey powder that can be bought at specialist trade and artists' suppliers – mixed with lemon oil, baby oil or salad oil. Rub this on in a circular motion with a felt or nylon pad, then wipe it off with a clean cloth and buff up the surface with a piece of soft flannel.

If you cannot get rottenstone, use powdered pumice, French chalk or household flour instead. If the varnish is thick and the piece not too precious, you can use household scouring powder, but this contains harsher abrasives, so apply it with a light hand.

I bet some readers are wondering whether the end really justifies the means, and whether all this extra effort can make a visible difference. The answer is an unqualified yes. The difference between a high-class paint job and the standard do-it-yourself finish of undercoat plus one or two layers of fast-drying, non-drip paint is so obvious, it fairly leaps out at you. Let us say it is a bit like the difference between homemade bread and a factory loaf, and leave it at that. For any piece with a suggestion of quality, or of potential to be developed, a really painstaking professional paint finish is the most substantial step toward the wished-for transformation. Slow it may be, but not boring. There is a keen, sensuous pleasure, which experience confirms, in doing a thing thoroughly and well.

Is it worth it?

Quick colour

There is, however, no denying that the perfectionist paintwork I have been advocating is a long-drawn-out affair. Although it does not take so long to apply each coat, the necessary drying time in between means that the whole job must extend over many days. But there are going to be occasions when short cuts are not just a help but a necessity – you might want to decorate a box, tray or frame quickly to give away as a present.

This is where modern super-quick-drying paints come in useful. Acrylic colours dry so fast and immovably that you can complete the basic colouring of a piece in a few hours. They are expensive used over a large piece, but for something small they are excellent.

This is the routine for painting a piece in a tearing hurry. After basic filling and tidying of cracks and scars and rubbing down – a process that cannot be rushed – give the piece 5 coats of synthetic gesso. This takes maybe half a day to apply, as compared with two or three days for equivalent primer and undercoat. Over this, once the last coat is dry, put 2 or 3 coats of acrylic colour, mixed to the required shade and thinned with a very little water. The second and third of these should be rubbed down gently with fine steel wool when dry. Decoration can be painted straight onto this acrylic base, using acrylic colours again or, for gilding, metal powder in gum arabic, see pages 68–9, but I usually give it a coat of thinned fast-drying orange or white shellac first, to bind, protect and make a hard, smooth ground for decoration, see pages 169–70. It also allows mistakes to be wiped off safely without disturbing the base colour. When the decoration dries, give the piece whatever antiquing it may need, by sponging a thin wash of acrylic colour over the whole surface. Then give the piece 2 coats of thinned polyurethane varnish, matt, semigloss or gloss as required. Rub the first down lightly with fine steel wool and polish the second with rottenstone or scouring powder, see opposite. Then polish the piece with a soft cloth.

In this way you can complete a piece to a high standard in about 48 hours, instead of the usual week to ten days. Most of the time is spent waiting for the varnish to dry. If you cannot spare the time for a second coat of varnish, try polishing over the first one with floor or furniture wax. This gives a nice, soft sheen and adds some protection.

173

Paint Finishes & Decorative Flourishes

Sponging

Sponging colour onto a painted surface is a quick way of producing a pleasantly variegated finish. Sponging with oil paint glaze in two tones of the same colour makes an effective disguise for junk furniture of undistinguished shape or odd proportions. It gently softens the contours (think of camouflage) and de-materializes the whole piece, while you can use lining in a contrast colour to call attention to the features that are worth playing up.

Preparation

The piece should have the usual smooth, well-sanded coats of tinted flat oil-based paint. Make up what is called a 'flatting oil', by mixing 6 parts of white spirit [mineral spirits] with 1 part of boiled linseed oil. Wipe this with a soft rag over the whole piece, so that just a film is left behind. This oil will help your glaze to go on smoothly and transparently, rather than in clots that give a bumpy surface.

Materials

Flat white oil-based paint; universal stainers [tinting colours] or artists' oils; white spirit [mineral spirits]; soft lint-free rags; marine sponge; a stiff-bristled square-ended brush for pouncing – a stencil brush, a fitch or a glue brush are good.

Method for two-tone sponging

Mix up a thinned paint glaze, see page 225, in the lighter of your chosen tones, and apply it while the film of flatting oil is still wet. With a bunched-up rag, pat it lightly but loosely over the piece so that about three-quarters of the surface area is covered, but keeping the effect pale and cloudy.

To the remaining glaze, add enough of the original tinting colours to deepen the tone noticeably but not too strongly. This time apply it with a sponge – it will give a tighter, sharper print that contrasts attractively with the ragged pattern. For a blurry effect, sponge the second glaze straight over the first without a drying interval. If the first glaze is dry, the sponged prints stand out more sharply. You can also spot in a very little dark colour here and there, like flecks in homespun cloth.

Then, using the stencil brush in a jabbing, pouncing motion, go over the whole sponged surface, while it is still wet and malleable, to soften any hard edges and to drive the glaze into all the awkward joins, turned ridges and crevices where the rag and sponge have not reached. Lines of base colour showing at these points spoil the effect. When the sponged glaze is quite dry a gentle rubbing over with very fine steel wool and a soapy solution will smooth the surfaces if necessary – but keep checking that you are not rubbing off the glaze.

Opposite The simplest effects can often be the most charming. There was nothing special about these modern rush-seated chairs until someone set to work sponging and painting them. Now, although they complement one another perfectly, each is unique.

Lining Decorative painted lines, see pages 184–88, can be added directly over the sponged surfaces; if you are afraid of making mistakes, do it over an intervening coat of clear matt varnish or white shellac. Use lining sparingly. It is tempting to add it to every turned ridge on chair legs, rails and so on, but this tends to look heavy and amateurish.

Watercolour sponging on gesso

Exceedingly pretty and rapid finishes can be had by applying watercolour directly to gesso. Synthetic gesso soaks up water like blotting paper, so the colour remains in a fine drift on the surface. French and Italian cabinetmakers were fond of this beguiling feminine finish. It looks particularly appealing in sophisticated pale colours – greyed blue, brownish pink, celadon green. Emphasis can be given by adding painted lines in a contrasting colour, or a little freehand decoration.

Method Mix gouache or acrylic colour to watery thinness in a saucer, and test the colour on a sheet of clean white paper. Brush or sponge it swiftly over the gessoed surfaces of the piece. A little streakiness where strokes overlap is to be expected, and adds to the charm of the effect – in any case, it will be less obtrusive when the piece is dry. For a two-tone effect, leave the first colour to dry and sponge or rag a second colour lightly over the top – don't rub too hard or the first colour may lift off.

Lining See pages 184–88, this can be painted, in gouache or acrylic colour, directly onto the painted gesso, but this needs a confident hand. It is safer to interpose a barrier coat of varnish or shellac – water-based colours are apt to 'crawl' over varnish, but this can be overcome by mixing the lining colours into clear varnish, instead of water.

Varnishing

Finish sponged pieces with 2 coats of clear matt or semigloss poly-urethane varnish.

Spattering

Spattering – the name decorators use for showering a surface with flecks of coloured paint – is one of the easiest and most artful ways of distressing a painted surface. Since the colour is broken up into such tiny particles, it never looks heavy or clumsy, as can happen with brushed-on glazes.

Use it to give a rich flick of extra colour to a plain painted surface. A heavy spatter of bright green over turquoise, for instance, creates a vivid blue-green with far more depth and vivacity than if you had mixed the two colours together in the pot, or even brushed the green over the turquoise in the form of transparent glaze. A fine spatter of black over a red, mock-lacquer surface adds the merest suggestion of texture without obscuring the glossy colour beneath. Use spattering in a neutralizing colour like umber or black, to tone down or simply add a texture to whatever is beneath.

Colours It is helpful to keep in mind the principle that complementary

176

colours of the same intensity, viewed at a distance, neutralize each other. Thus, two spatter coats of roughly equal density, one of red and one of green (or orange and blue, or purple and yellow), will appear softened to an indeterminate neutral.

Preparation

The snag with spattering is that it makes a fair mess over a pretty wide area – especially if you are trying it for the first time. Ideally, take the piece into the garden, if it is a fine day. Indoors, cover the floor with newspaper, rigging some more up to form a protective screen behind.

The ground coat should be of flat paint, tinted with artists' oils, stainers [tinting colours] or, for American readers, japan colours.

Materials

Paint You can spatter with any kind of paint or glaze, as long as it is thinned to a watery, flickable consistency. If you are experimenting, the water-based colours – gouache or acrylic – are a good idea, since they can readily be wiped off with a damp sponge. Gouache, particularly, can be used for several spatter coats one on top of the other, and the whole lot can still be washed off if you are not satisfied. It will, however, need extra heavy protective varnishing.

Brush The best type to use is a long-handled stencil brush. A stiff, round hogshair brush or a fitch are good, too. Or use an old artists' brush, with about half the bristle length sliced off to leave it stiff and straight-ended.

Spattering is done by passing your finger or a metal blade (a knife, ruler or comb) over the painty bristles. You can get very even spattering by rubbing your paint-laden brush through a medium-mesh, round wire sieve. For spattering as fine as mist use a 'diffuser' [atomizer], which can be bought from artists' suppliers, see page 180.

Other equipment The appropriate solvent for the paint; paper for practising on; rags; paper tissues; saucers for mixing colours.

Method

Having made a watery thin paint, pick up a little on the bristle tips of your stiff brush. Then pass your finger steadily over them, releasing a few at a time. Try this out on sheets of white paper until you get the hang of it – with a little practice you will find that you can aim your coloured spray quite evenly and accurately from a short distance away. Avoid overloading the brush, as this gives a much heavier spray, with some blobs that might start to run like raindrops. If they do run, blot them up quickly with a corner of paper tissue.

Very fine spattering dries almost immediately, heavier coats should be left to dry before applying further colours. Finish off with varnish.

Porphyry

Natural porphyry is an igneous rock of granite-like texture often containing glints of fool's gold. Deep red with a maroon cast is the characteristic colour, but it is also found in green, violet, grey, and brown flecked with pink. Spatters of colour over a sponged ground give a convincing look of porphyry. In the past this was a fashionable treatment for table tops and mantelpieces, and it is a finish that suits today's severely rectilinear furniture.

Method for red porphyry spattering

Make up a terracotta base colour by tinting flat white oil-based paint with a lot of burnt sienna and a little burnt umber and yellow ochre. Sponge this over a ground of flat white oil-based paint and leave it until touch-dry, about 2 hours.

Make up your spatter coats; for porphyry you will require 2 – a cream-coloured one, made of flat white oil-based paint tinted with yellow ochre, and a black one made simply of black artists' oil colour. Both should be thinned with solvent to a watery consistency.

Spatter your sponged surface with the off-white mixture first. Keep the spattering fine in texture and evenly diffused over the terracotta colour. When it has dried – in a few minutes – repeat with the black, but keep this spattering much lighter.

Gold spatter For a richer effect, especially striking with dark porphyry colours, try a spatter of gold. Mix metal powder into gum arabic to make a thin paint and spatter it sparingly over the surface.

Blue porphyry For a fantasy porphyry finish, mix up a base colour of flat white oil-based paint tinted with cobalt blue and a dash of black and red. Sponge this on a white base as for red porphyry, and spatter it with off-white and black in exactly the same way.

Varnish

Red porphyry can be given 2 coats of orange shellac to enhance the colour and give some protection, but a coat of clear gloss varnish on top will make it stronger. Rub it down gently, but do not polish.

Spatter prints

The technique of spattering over templates to leave negative prints was a favourite in the heyday of hobbies, the mid-nineteenth century, when use was often made of the elegant lacy outlines of that beloved Victorian pot-plant, the common fern. Fern fronds, dried flat, still make ideal templates, arranged into patterns with plainer leaves as borders. You can also try cut paper, doilies or any other decorative shapes. Spattering for this technique is most easily done with a diffuser.

Colours Early examples imitated marquetry using dark spatters over colours like red-brown or golden-brown. This looks pretty with fern patterns, which then appear in gentle relief against a dark ground. Another good combination is olive green over a light or golden brown ground. For a more imposing effect, suggestive of inlaid marble, try the sponge and spatter mixtures suggested for porphyry over templates fixed to a black or grey ground.

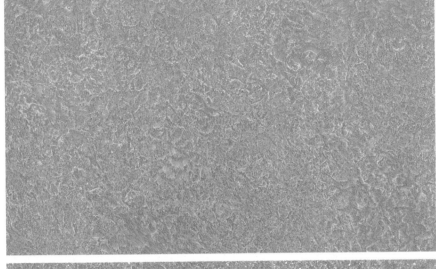

Apply a ground of flat white oil-based paint and leave it 6 to 12 hours to dry before lightly sanding. Mix terracotta colour by tinting flat white paint with a good squeeze of burnt sienna and a little burnt umber and yellow ochre. Sponge this over the ground and leave about 2 hours to dry.

Mix a cream-coloured spatter paint by tinting flat white paint with yellow ochre; thin it with white spirit [mineral spirits] to watery consistency. Take up a little on the bristle tips of a stiff brush and draw your finger firmly across them to produce a spatter. Direct it over your piece. Leave a few minutes to dry. Clean the brush.

Thin black oil colour with white spirit as above. Spatter it in the same way but less thickly. Allow it to dry thoroughly. Then give the porphyry 2 coats of orange shellac to bring up the colour.

For protection apply a coat of clear gloss polyurethane varnish on top, and rub it down with fine wet-or-dry paper or fine steel wool to cut the shine.

Spattering with a diffuser [atomizer]

For best results with spatter prints, use a diffuser [atomizer]. Place the end of the vertical tube in the paint container, direct the right-angled joint toward the template to be spattered, and blow through the mouthpiece.

You can make up the spatter paint with oil-based colours as for porphyry, but for a softer, mistier spray, use gouache colours in water. Other possibilities are acrylics or coloured drawing inks. Whatever type of colour you use, it should be poured into a jamjar or similar container and stirred well. Then place one end of the diffuser in the paint, and blow hard through the other, mouthpiece, end. Blowing creates a vacuum that forces the contents of the jar to rush up the tube. If you point the angle formed by the two sections toward the surface to be spattered, and puff, the paint will flow over it in a fine mist of colour. Practise on sheets of paper laid flat and propped up vertically, to get an idea of how to control the spray.

A diffused spray of paint is too fine to run so you need not confine this spattering to horizontal surfaces. Tackle each surface separately, beginning at one end and working across to the other, and moving the piece as necessary. Let the spatter dry, remove the templates, and touch up any holidays in the spatter by stippling in dots of the same paint with the tip of a small stiff brush. Use a fine sable artists' brush and the same paint to add further detail such as leaf veins or vine tendrils.

Lacquering or japanning

True Oriental lacquer ware, made from the milky sap of the lac tree, must qualify as the most painstaking finish ever devised by man. Built up through as many as 40 separate layers, each rubbed and polished smooth with a paste of oil and bone ash applied with the fingers, it is the hardest, most lustrous surface imaginable, so rich to the eye that it looks at its most handsome unadorned.

Not surprisingly, when examples of this superb craftsmanship reached the West, European craftsmen were soon earnestly trying to imitate the prized imported wares. More confusion arose when an identically named but intrinsically different resin, 'lac' made from the secretions of insects, *Coccus lacca*, reached the West. After processing, this became 'seedlac', which we now call shellac, an ultra-fast-drying resinous varnish differing from other varnishes in being soluble only in alcohol. By combining paint with shellac, Western craftsmen came up with a variety of technically incorrect, but aesthetically pleasing, pseudo-lacquers, which they called japan. Wooden pieces were smoothly primed, painted and decorated, often lavishly gilded, and finished with many coats of shellac, to simulate the depth and richness of the Oriental wares. Japanned wares bore only a superficial resemblance to their eastern models, but as time passed and innovators added further refinements, the pieces developed a style and charm of their own.

The lesson to be learned from studying examples of old lacquer and japanning is that it is quite possible to emulate their warmth of colour and patina by painting a piece in suitable colours, decorating it with Oriental-inspired motifs, and finishing it with as many coats of varnish or white shellac as you have the patience to apply. The result may be only a pastiche of a pastiche, but it is still extravagantly pretty. The more effort you put into it – gilt or bronze powder decoration, streaky tortoiseshell ground, stencilled or hand-painted scenes, tinted varnishes – the more sumptuous the final result. At the opposite extreme, you could explore a modern, starkly simple lacquer effect, relying on brilliant glazed colours and many coats of rubbed-down clear gloss varnish.

Furniture of a plain, strong shape is the best choice for these rather gorgeous lacquer treatments. Modern-style lacquer looks especially good on dining chairs and coffee tables. The wood beneath does not have to be anything special: the tattiest veneered blockboard by the time it has been gessoed, decorated and varnished to the nines is perfectly adequate, as long as it is structurally sound and sturdy.

Preparation

Synthetic gesso greatly improves the surface of open-grained or inferior wood and adds to the final appearance of your handiwork. Unless the wood you are working on is fine-grained and smooth, in which case it need only be undercoated, give the piece 4 or 5 coats of synthetic gesso, or all-purpose filler [spackle] watered-down to paint consistency, see pages 164–65. When it is dry, rub each coat down with medium steel wool or medium sandpaper. Aim for bone-hard smoothness. When the last coat of gesso is dry, brush shellac, diluted with 1 part methylated spirits [denatured alcohol] to 2 parts shellac, over the whole piece, to bind the gesso and give a sleek base for paint.

Materials for black 'lacquer'

Flat black oil-based paint, bought at any ironmongers or hardware store; burnt umber artists' oil colour; gloss polyurethane varnish; brush; wet-or-dry paper.

Method for black 'lacquer'

The first 2 or 3 coats should be of flat black paint, the last one rubbed down with wet-or-dry paper and soapy water. For the subsequent 2 coats, mix 5 parts flat black paint with 1 part burnt umber and half a part gloss varnish. Rub these 2 coats down in the same way.

At this stage the lacquer may be gilded or otherwise decorated.

Varnishing If you want a warm black, add a little burnt umber artists' oil colour, or dark oak varnish stain, to the last of your 2 or 3 coats of protective polyurethane gloss varnish. Each coat of varnish should be rubbed down and the final one polished with rottenstone – for a higher lustre, wax it and polish with a soft cloth.

Materials for red 'lacquer'

Flat white oil-based paint; vermilion artists' oil colour or universal stainer [tinting colour] or, for American readers, orange-red japan colour, to colour the ground coat; white spirit [mineral spirits]; gloss polyurethane varnish; crimson and burnt sienna artists' oil colours for top coats; wet-or-dry paper.

Method for red 'lacquer'

Mix the red oil colour, stainer or japan colour with just enough white spirit and flat white paint to give a little body and flow without making the colour too chalky. Paint the piece with 2 or 3 coats of this, rubbing down with wet-or-dry paper after the first 2. For the next 2 coats, make a rich transparent paint by substituting gloss varnish for the flat white paint, and adding a squeeze of crimson and burnt sienna oil colours. This changes the effect of the opaque vermilion beneath quite astonishingly.

Varnishing If the red is too bright, it can be softened before final varnishing by applying a thin burnt umber wash or glaze, or by spattering it with sepia or black ink. Alternatively, your 2 or 3 coats of protective gloss varnish – thinned 3 parts varnish to 2 of white spirit – could be tinted, as above, with a little burnt umber artists' oil colour or dark oak varnish stain, and rubbed down and finished in the same way.

Other 'lacquer' colours

As well as the classic black and vermilion, japanned furniture exhibited a wide range of colours – white, sharp yellow, olive, chestnut, blue and purple. The point to bear in mind when reproducing these is that the glow and brilliance of the final effect is greatly enhanced by brushing on a tinted varnish or, even more subtle, a glaze, in a slightly different tone of the ground colour. This can be brushed solidly over the ground, or

182

Right A porphyry finish suits modern rectilinear shapes. To achieve this unusual effect, blue paint was sponged over a white ground, spattered with off-white thinned paint, then black. The whole thing was finished with coats of matt polyurethane varnish.

Below A modern folding table frame, lacquered and gilded to match the antique japanned tray that now forms its top.

Right The top of this 18th-century lacquered table has been given a witty contemporary trompe l'oeil treatment, then topped with coats of shellac for further shine.

183

dragged on with a brush in fine stripes, so that the two colours interact more vibrantly. Thus a ground of flat yellow – made by mixing Indian yellow into flat white – is sharpened by a glaze of chrome yellow or yellow lake; a blue ground of cobalt in flat white is made brilliant by glazing with Prussian blue or ultramarine.

Lining

Lining or striping in a contrasting colour is often used to trim painted furniture, to underline and strengthen its contours and to draw attention to decorative details. Like braid on a military uniform, painted lines serve to tighten and emphasize structure and proportion. Traditionally the lining decoration used varied with the type of furniture. On curvy French and Italian provincial pieces, wide bands of watery thin colour often edged table tops and chair frames. On the whippet-slim pieces by such eighteenth-century designers as Robert Adam, the lining had a calligraphic tautness. But it was on coachwork, the supreme test of a painter's skill, that lining displayed the utmost in slender precision – all of it executed freehand with a control born of years of practice.

Anyone can manage wide decorative edge lining, which looks tremendous even when painted quite crudely, but to paint immaculately fine lining freehand, you require confidence, practice and a steady wrist. However, there are cheating ways to get a similar effect which are worthwhile experimenting with. Applying an intervening coat of clear varnish or thinned white shellac allows botched lines to be wiped off and redrawn. A straight-edge used with a lining fitch or a fine sable brush enables one to produce satisfactory straight lines on flat surfaces; I have even known professional decorators to use a felt-tip pen for the purpose.

Preparation

Lining is usually applied toward the end of decorating a piece, after the glazing has been done, but before antiquing, see pages 205–9. This makes for crisper definition. As always, the smoother the paint surface, the more fluently the painted lines will flow. If you are unsure of your brushwork, apply a barrier coat first, see pages 169–70, before lining.

Materials for lining

Paint For transparent, watery edge lining, use artists' gouache or acrylic colour diluted in a little water. To help watercolour to stay put, add a drop of detergent; alternatively, mix the paint into a little clear matt varnish for an extra-flowing line. This effect is best suited to pieces that have been given a matt finish.

For fine lining, professional decorators generally use artists' oil colour or universal stainer [tinting colour], dissolved in a little white spirit [mineral spirits] and then mixed with clear varnish for body. Quick-drying goldsize is a useful substitute for varnish, since it dries fast, which means that there is less risk of smudging. Indian ink gives fine, distinct black lines but should be applied over a varnish barrier coat since it can be difficult to remove – if you have to wipe it off, use methylated spirits [denatured alcohol] on a rag.

184

Brushes For broad edging lines, use a No 6 sable artists' brush, for fine lines, a No 3 sable brush. Professional decorators often use a sword liner, see page 234, because the curved, tapering bristles give greater control for freehand lines.

Other equipment You will also need the appropriate solvent for your paint; rags or cotton wool [absorbent cotton] swabs; a saucer for mixing colour. Optional: a notched card, to keep a measured line even; a lining fitch; felt-tip pens; a straight-edge.

Method

Make sure that the piece is placed at a convenient height. A low table, with solid legs, makes an ideal platform for most items. Test the paint mixture on a board, to get the feel of your lining brush, and to check that the paint flows nicely and that the colour is sufficiently intense. Do not overload the brush, or your neat line may blob if you press harder. The thickness of the line depends on your hand pressure as well as on the width of the brush itself. For freehand lining, the professionals stand a little way back, hold the brush quite far up the handle, not close to the ferrule, and *draw* in the line with a steady, relaxed sweeping movement. Your eye should travel fractionally ahead of your brush – 'eye leads, hand follows' is the experts' formula. Otherwise you may hesitate, which will lead to wobbles and breaks in continuity.

Correct any mistakes after you have reached an obvious break but before the paint hardens. If the paint has set, leave it to dry thoroughly, then gently rub it away with fine steel wool. Rubbing down, which emulates the worn effect found on an old piece, is a useful trick for softening less than perfect lining. Retouch lines after the paint has dried, but with a light hand, or you will get noticeable variations in colour. After lining, a piece can be finished with matt or semigloss clear polyurethane varnish.

Having sketched your first, fine careless line, keep its width even, as you fill it in, with the help of a notched card.

Edge lining Chunky folk pieces often look good with really emphatic edge lining, anything from 12 to 25 mm [$\frac{1}{2}$ to 1 in] wide. It is the easiest kind to do, because the line is broad and you can use your little finger to guide the brush. Use a notched card to make little paint marks all the way along before painting, to keep the width of the band even. Slight variations do not matter, but you may find that some kind of mechanical aid will increase your confidence.

Water-thinned paints produce delicate faded-looking lines, appropriate to antique pieces, but take care when retouching them, because thin colour builds up fast if you go over the same spot too often.

Along straight edges a helpful cheat is to set a boundary of masking tape at the requisite distance in from the edge. Before painting, run a knife blade firmly along the tape edge to help it to grip, and peel it off immediately after painting each section, for a clean edge. To keep the old and faded look, the paint should be matt, but not so thick it builds a raised line, and the piece can be finished with matt varnish.

Left This 18th-century wooden table, turned in imitation of bamboo, has recently been bambooed in dark ochre over a light ochre ground.

Below A modern folding table, picked out in colour to imitate female bamboo.

Left A turn-of-the-century junk-shop find, bamboo-striped in tinted and thinned varnish. The wicker surfaces are painted freehand in the same three shades of blue.

Right To achieve the marbling on this contemporary table, a white ground was given a coat of blue glaze which was sponged, before veins were added in white, red and black. The colours were 'knocked back' by a coat of tinted varnish.

Below A coffee table, dragged in buff and lined in a dark brown.

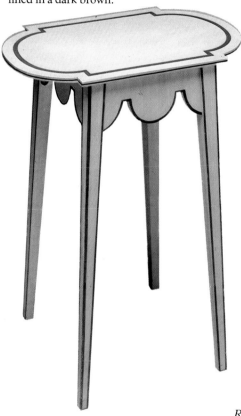

Right An antique washstand with a fold-out top, dragged in off-white and lined in green.

Below Lined in a combination of sophisticated colours, this mid-19th-century painted box from New England looks surprisingly up-to-date.

187

Fine lining This is usually painted a little way inside the edge of a piece, following the curves of a chair back or the taper of a flat chair leg. A chair back is best tackled with the chair laid on its back at normal table height, where it can be approached from three sides. Paint the inner surfaces first so that you won't risk smudging one line as you lean across to tackle another.

It is no good pretending that it is easy to paint a fine, even line freehand. However, confidence quickly grows with practice. Give the surface a coat of thinned shellac or clear varnish first, and strike out boldly in the knowledge that mistakes can be wiped off with a cotton wool swab moistened in solvent once you have completed the section; touch them up when they are dry. Use a felt-tip pen and/or a straight-edge if you cannot live with imperfections.

Fine lining has no end of decorative uses; to trim plates, trays, boxes and tins, picture mounts or matts, most antique furniture. It is a natural way to decorate flat surfaces, making a visual break between plain and decorated painted areas, tightening and strengthening shapes. Study examples the next time you find yourself in a museum – their variety will surprise you.

Bambooing

During the eighteenth-century craze for Chinoiserie, one of the materials in vogue was bamboo, which reached Europe from the Far East in the form of fantastical furniture and bibelots. Cheap and commonplace in the Orient, bamboo was both scarce and expensive in the West. It was not long before craftsmen were producing imitation bamboo from turned and carved wood. Made, as a rule, of inferior wood, this imitation bamboo was invariably painted, after the style of the natural wood to begin with, but later in increasingly fantastic colours.

Different craftsmen favoured different effects, but most imitation bamboo kept to certain conventions. The prominent knots at the intersections were emphasized with painted lines in one, two or even three colours, and the same colours were used to add the little eyes and tapering spines characteristic of natural female bamboo. The hand-painted detail would sometimes be done in discreetly complementary colours – grey-green on yellow buff, for instance – sometimes in flamboyant contrasts like pink on white, or black and gold on vermilion.

Bambooing remains an easy way to add colour and fantasy to a simple painted piece, breaking up uniformly coloured surfaces in a decorative and witty fashion.

Suitable furniture

First candidates are any pieces in turned imitation bamboo. Choose emphatic colour schemes for the elegant shapes that can take it – black, red, cockatoo pinks and greens – with bambooing in lighter, contrasting colours. For pieces with only a little turned bamboo decoration – on chair backs and legs, round table tops and drawers – stick to sophisticated neutrals with details painted in discreet colours: sepia on buff, green on yellow, dark green or brown on green and any middle-toned colour on cream or greyish-white.

Any simple, rounded wooden moulding can be smartened up with a stylized bamboo treatment. Frames on mirrors, or screens, simple bedsteads, small tables with plain, round legs – once your eye is receptive, it is easy to pick out pieces that will gain from this treatment, and judge the lengths to which you can go without arriving at a visual joke. If you give caned or rush-seated chairs a bamboo finish, paint the seats to match the chair frame and then, in the bambooing colours, paint a trellis pattern over the top of woven cane, or stripes on rush.

Bambooing can also be used to freshen up those spotted turn-of-the-century pieces, made of real bamboo varnished and scorched to produce a brown mottling, that have broken out like a rash in so many junk shops. It would be a pity to paint fine examples, but there are many inferior pieces that would look all the better for cleaning, rubbing down and painting in a restrained eighteenth-century painted finish.

There are two commonly used techniques for bambooing. The first, picking out in colour, can be done only where the distinctive bamboo knots, or knobbly joints, are present – either on turned wood or genuine bamboo. The decoration consists of picking out the knots with fine lines and, if you wish, adding painted eyes and spines.

The second technique is bamboo striping. This has the advantage that it can also be used on plain round mouldings. The striping consists of graduated rings – in tones of the same colour – painted one on top of the other. English country-house bedrooms often contain pieces painted in greyish-white, bamboo-striped to pick up a dominant colour in the room – pink, blue, green – which always look fresh and pretty. Shades of sepia on a straw-coloured ground, echoing natural bamboo colours, look especially effective on plain round mouldings. Over dark colours, paint bamboo striping in light, sludgy colours like white tinted with raw umber, raw sienna or yellow ochre, to give sufficient contrast without being garish.

Any piece to be bambooed needs a sleek, carefully painted and rubbed-down ground coat, applied over a suitably smooth surface, see pages 160–65 for how to achieve this. Turn-of-the-century scorched bamboo must be rubbed down first with steel wool and methylated spirits [denatured alcohol] to remove old French polish.

Use at least 3 coats of undercoat or flat oil-based paint, tinted to your chosen colour, thinly applied and gently rubbed down in between with fine wet-or-dry paper and soapy water.

Paint For picking out in colour, fast-drying paints with good opacity are a sensible choice. Acrylic colours or, for American readers, japan colours are both good. Acrylics give dense colour if thinned with very little water, or a thin transparent wash when heavily diluted. Japan colour should be

Bambooing styles

Preparation

Materials

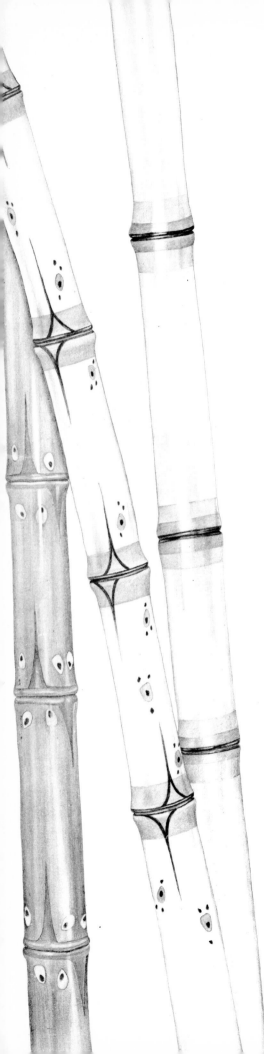

dissolved in solvent and mixed into clear matt varnish, the proportions used depending on how strong a colour is needed. Flat oil-based paint tinted with universal stainers [tinting colours] or artists' oils can also be used, but this will take many hours to dry.

For bamboo striping, decorators tend to use transparent paint made by tinting clear matt varnish with artists' oils or universal stainers, dissolved first in a little white spirit [mineral spirits]. The proportions of solvent to varnish are about half and half for the palest stripe colour, ranging to 1 teaspoon of solvent to 1 tablespoon varnish for the darkest tone. The palest stripe should be transparently thin; over a dark colour it must contain some white pigment to show up sufficiently. This transparent paint is fast-drying, because of its high solvent content, which means that all three rings can be painted in a few minutes.

Brushes Fine, pointed sable artists' brushes, Nos 3 and 6, for painting details; a square-cut oxhair artists' brush for stroking on transparent colour. For bamboo striping you will also need a 17 mm [$\frac{3}{4}$ in] standard decorators' paintbrush or a fat soft-bristled artists' brush and a similar brush about 12 mm [$\frac{1}{2}$ in] wide.

Other equipment Masking tape; rags; saucers for mixing.

Method for picking out in colour
Mix up a little paint in a saucer – a couple of tablespoonfuls is enough to do a chair. The mixture should be opaque enough to cover the ground colour, but thin enough to flow smoothly from the brush.

With the fatter brush (No 6), paint a neat band of colour round each knot, pressing on the bristles so that the colour extends a fraction over either side of the ridges. For further decorative effect, the fine spines and speckled eyes that distinguish the female bamboo may be painted in with the No 3 sable brush. The spines should be painted with two curving lines joining to form a delicate spike, not more than a third of the bamboo section in length.

In nature the eyes appear either side of the spine. They are slightly oval dots, surrounded by tiny freckles of colour. Paint a few on the more prominent sections, placing them asymmetrically – not two spines and four dots per section. Tempting as it is to go on embellishing one's work with more and more pretty details, my advice is to be sparing with them.

When the paint has dried hard, you can add a little tinted varnish to bring out the modelling of the bamboo. Dip the square-ended brush into the mixture, brush off the excess on rough paper, and stroke it in fine stripes over the plain sections between the painted knots. Keep the brush pressure light, and the colour unemphatic.

Method for bamboo striping
The widest stripe is painted in the lightest tone of your transparent paint, usually about 25 mm [1 in] wide, using the widest brush. Centre it

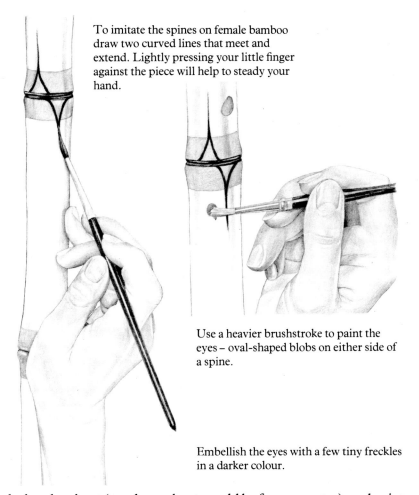

To imitate the spines on female bamboo draw two curved lines that meet and extend. Lightly pressing your little finger against the piece will help to steady your hand.

Use a heavier brushstroke to paint the eyes – oval-shaped blobs on either side of a spine.

Embellish the eyes with a few tiny freckles in a darker colour.

over the bamboo knot (or where a knot would be for symmetry), and paint a smooth ring of the thinnest possible colour right around it. Paint all the wide rings on the piece in one go, and wait a moment for them to dry.

Now add enough colour to the paint to tint it a few tones darker, and paint a second narrower ring in the centre of the wide ones, about 12 mm [$\frac{1}{2}$ in] wide. Then mix enough colour into the remaining paint to give it a decidedly dark colour. Using a fine, pointed brush, No 3, paint in a slender central ring, about 6 mm [$\frac{1}{4}$ in] wide.

You can also use this darkest tone to paint in eyes, and, on chair backs and table legs, coloured lines to emphasize the shape of the piece – for lining, see pages 184–88.

When it is dry, you can brush or drag on a darker tinted varnish, for dragging, see pages 27–32.

Varnishing

When the surface is completely dry (if you have used tinted varnish, this could take 3 or 4 days), give the whole piece 2 protective coats of clear matt varnish. To strengthen it further, and add a soft sheen, give it a light coat of soft, colourless wax.

Bambooed pieces finished in dark, Oriental colours may look better covered with gloss varnish for a lacquer effect.

Gilding

Something of a mystique surrounds the art of gilding – understandably, in view of the expense and fragility of true gold leaf, and the elaborate technique involved in traditional water gilding. The current price of gold leaf certainly puts it outside the reach of amateur furniture decorators – there is no fun in experimenting with a material so expensive that every mistake hurts.

There are other ways of adding a rich metallic gleam to a painted surface, using lesser metals in the form of transfer leaf or of powder. These are far cheaper and easier to apply, and can be boosted with various professional tricks to give a pleasing suggestion of the real thing.

The fake gold materials look best treated lightheartedly as one shiny element in an overall decorative scheme rather than as a serious imitation of true gold. A touch of gold or silver, outlining drawer fronts and table tops or highlighting relief carving, turned chair legs and backs, adds considerable class. More throwaway still, delicious effects can be obtained by using aluminium leaf as a luminous ground for tortoiseshell finishes. This treatment makes smaller objects like picture frames and boxes look precious and important. The simple gilding techniques described here can be confidently undertaken by any reasonably neat-fingered person.

Metallic powder decoration

Bronze, silver and aluminium powders are cheap enough to have fun with, so start with these if you want to add a Midas touch. They come in a wide range of colours – from silvery white to rich bronze gold – and look most attractive when several colours are used together. Use them for stencilling, freehand decoration or lining.

They can be applied straight over a tacky surface, usually painted in a dark colour such as black or red to set off the metal, or over motifs filled in with a sympathetic colour, say yellow ochre or Venetian red, which enriches the metallic finish.

All metal powders tarnish quickly, so must be varnished for protection. They look effective shaded with tinted varnish or antiquing glazes, to suggest patina and modelling. Knocking back the metallic gleam in this way makes the untreated areas, paradoxically, shine more brightly.

Neatness and patience are the chief requirements for handling metal powders. They are so light and clinging that some care is needed to stop them from going where they are not wanted. Do not use them to cover large, flat areas, in imitation of gold leaf, because this shows up their powdery thinness. Instead, use metal transfer leaf.

Preparation

Surfaces for powder decoration should be covered with opaque flat or mid-sheen oil-based paint. Rich, dark colours set it off best – brownish red, black, dull green, chestnut or fake tortoiseshell. The ground colour must be left to dry completely hard, without a hint of tackiness.

Nervous practitioners might like to give the surface a coat of clear semigloss varnish or thinned shellac; this not only allows more scope for correcting mistakes but will encourage even drying in the varnish subsequently used as a size. This barrier coat should be rubbed down lightly with very fine steel wool, wiped clean with a rag moistened with white spirit [mineral spirits] and gone over with a tack rag, see page 25.

This alternative to the method described on pages 68–9 produces greater subtlety of shading and highlight. Stencils and metal powders were traditionally used for lacy borders, but also make effective allover patterns and large single motifs. The stencils should be neatly cut, since any raggedness shows more with powder than it does with paint, and should be small enough to be easily controlled. Press them flat before use – ironing with a warm iron over paper flattens them quickly.

Stencilling with metal powder

Stencils, see pages 55–69; metal powders; clear semigloss or gloss polyurethane varnish; small pieces of silk, velvet or chamois leather; varnish brush, see page 231; small brush for shading; square-tipped artists' hoghair brush, for floating on colours; artists' oils, or japan colours (for American readers) for tinting varnish; saucers or plastic jamjar lids; paper to hold excess powder; rags; masking tape.

Materials for metal powder stencilling

First varnish the entire surface with semigloss or gloss varnish. Leave this to dry until there is a just perceptible 'tack' left – if you press the stencil on a corner it should come off with a faint pull but leave no mark. The tacky varnish will act as a size or adhesive for the metal powders.

Method for powder stencilling

Tip a little powder into a saucer or jamjar lid – if you are using more than one powder, use a separate container for each one. Place your stencil on the varnished surface, masking off the surrounding area, if possible, with paper fixed with strips of masking tape. The stencils should cleave tightly to the surface or powder may seep underneath.

Wrap a piece of velvet or chamois leather round your index finger, adjusting it so no creases appear. Dip the covered finger into the powder, then rub it on a piece of spare paper to remove the excess – very little powder is needed at any time. Place your finger on what is to be the highlight of your stencil design and, starting from there, rotate it gently, to polish in the highlight. From there work outwards, lessening the finger pressure so that the solid highlights blend to a softer bloom at the edges. When you need to pick up more powder, use the surplus on your spare paper first.

Use a different piece of fabric for each powder colour. Pale colours can be shaded with a darker one – use the lighter shade as highlight, and blend the two colours gently into each other for a modelled effect.

When your motif is completed, lift up the stencil and move it along to the next spot; repeat in the same way until the design is complete. Leave the varnish to dry hard – this usually takes about 24 hours. Then wash it gently with soapy water and a rag to remove any loose powder. Any powder that has landed on the wrong areas can be rubbed off patiently with a rag or swab dipped in a little household scouring powder.

Floating on colour When the powder stencilling is dry and clean, brush on a barrier coat of clear gloss varnish, to give yourself leeway for experiment.

Floated colours are made by mixing a little artists' oil colour with clear polyurethane varnish. Apply this tinted varnish smoothly over the metallic motif with a soft, square-tipped artists' brush. Keep the colour intense in, say, the deeper folds of petals or the crease of a leaf, and thin it out over the rest. The effect should be very smooth and a little melodramatic. It does not matter if the floated colour goes over the edges,

since being transparent it will scarcely show over a dark ground colour.

Use this technique with raw or burnt umbers or siennas, if you want to add richness to metallic decoration without too strong a contrast.

Freehand metallic decoration

Use this for large central motifs, where you need more impact and shading. The technique here is a bit different: instead of covering the whole surface with a tacky varnish, you fill in only the areas to be powdered, using a mixture of varnish and paint. This both gives enough tack to hold the powder down, and delineates the motif against the background. If you are using metal powders just to highlight a coloured motif, the paint should of course be of the appropriate colour, but if the design is to be solidly powdered, you can use any colour that shows up clearly – black over a light ground, white or yellow ochre over a dark one.

On to your chosen ground coat, sketch out simple designs with white chalk or wax crayons. Complex ones can be pounced out in talc sprinkled

Preparation

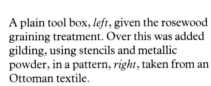

A plain tool box, *left*, given the rosewood graining treatment. Over this was added gilding, using stencils and metallic powder, in a pattern, *right*, taken from an Ottoman textile.

195

through holes pricked along the lines of a paper pattern.

Materials *Paint* The paint used for your design should be fast-drying and opaque enough to cover the ground coat properly. Use universal stainers [tinting colours], signwriters' colours [bulletin colours] or, for American readers, japan colours, mixed into clear gloss varnish. You can use artists' oil colours but even when mixed in varnish these take longer to dry. A little flat white paint added to any of these will improve opacity.

Other equipment The same materials as for powder stencilling; a plate or other surface for mixing; a sharpened charcoal stump; a rubber eraser.

Method Mix your colour or colours on a plate. Dip your brush in your first colour and load it well, then squeeze out the surplus on the side of the plate. Test the colour on paper.

Paint in your design elements carefully and smoothly, leaving them to dry until just tacky. Then apply the metal powders with a velvet or chamois leather pad, as for powder stencilling, pressing harder for highlights, gently for faded-out effects. Try to stop the powders from going over the edges of the painted area, although overspills can be cleaned off later with an eraser.

Short, fine strokes can be put in with a sharpened charcoal stump dipped in metal powder. Fold a piece of velvet to make a point for adding tiny dots and highlights.

When it is dry, add floated colour, as above, to give the metallic decoration an effect of inward-lit radiance.

Lining The easiest way to apply metallic lining is to use this coloured paint approach. Paint in the coloured lines freehand or using a straight-edge. When the paint is tacky, use the narrowly folded velvet point to run metal powder carefully along it – keep the pressure even and use very little powder. You may find it better to run two faint layers of powder rather than a single heavy one that keeps thinning out in patches.

Varnishing When all decoration is dry and the surface has been washed of any loose powder, cover the whole piece with clear gloss polyurethane varnish, rubbed down and polished, see pages 170–72.

Transfer metal leaf

This consists of squares of leaf mounted on sheets of waxed tissue, which come in booklets. It is much easier to handle and lay than loose leaf, which is so light and fragile that it readily disintegrates. The most suitable types for use on furniture are Dutch metal – an alloy that closely resembles gold in colour and gleam – and aluminium. The latter is considerably cheaper, and can be coated with button polish (orange shellac) to imitate gold, or shaded with a little umber or diluted Indian ink to suggest aged and tarnished silver.

Transfer leaf can be applied over small or large areas, as fine line trimming, and on raised or carved surfaces as well as flat ones. Once laid, it can be etched through with a sharp stylus or pointed instrument to reveal the paint colour beneath. It is not particularly difficult to lay – provided the tack is right, and the size accurately applied, it goes on as easily as any other type of transfer. To avoid waste, transfer leaf can be cut into smaller pieces with scissors or a sharp knife, cutting from the waxed paper side.

Preparation

As for metal powder decoration.

Materials

Dutch metal or aluminium transfer leaf; quick-drying goldsize, and soft artists' brush in suitable size for applying it; soft cotton wool [absorbent cotton]; orange shellac or diluted Indian ink.

Method

Sketch or pounce out your design as for freehand metal powder decoration. Fill in the parts that are to be gilded, using goldsize mixed with a little colour so that you can see where you have put it. Leave it to dry until it is just tacky – it should be a little drier than varnish on which you apply powders.

The leaf is more lustrous when laid at the right time – if the size is too wet, it will tend to look dull. The time this takes depends on the conditions in which you apply it – the only way to be sure is to test it. Extract a sheet of waxed paper with leaf attached from the booklet, and turn it leaf side down on the sized area. Rub over the back quite firmly with a pad of cotton wool or your fingertips. Then lift the paper off gently – if the tack is right, and your pressure even, the leaf will be stuck to the sized portions. Lay the next sheet to slightly overlap the first, and repeat the procedure, continuing until you come to the end of the design. Carefully brush off any loose metal with a soft paintbrush. Repair any skips or holidays in the leafed surface by pressing on scraps of metal while the size is still sticky. When the size has dried, which will take a few hours, rub the surface over with soft cotton wool to smooth it and remove any loose bits, taking particular care with the overlaps.

To turn applied aluminium leaf a convincing bright gold, give it 1 or 2 coats of orange shellac, which dries in less than an hour. Brush diluted Indian ink over it for a soft, silvery finish. Shading and antiquing can be added by applying raw or burnt umber oil colour mixed into a little thinned varnish.

Applying metal leaf over carving Over raised or carved areas, such as picture frames, paint the surface first with a little flat white oil-based paint tinted with Venetian red or yellow ochre. When this has dried, cover it with a coat of clear gloss varnish, and when that is dry, apply the goldsize and wait for it to become tacky. Then apply the leaf to the prominent areas of the carving, not attempting to cover every crevice, but just to suggest gilding worn and weathered over the years. This selective use of

197

leaf used to be known as 'parcel gilding' and has always been a sensible economy – no sense in wasting gold where it will not show. When the size has dried, any surface patchiness can be softened by rubbing down very gently with fine steel wool to reveal a little red or yellow underlay here and there.

Varnishing Varnish the whole surface with clear semigloss polyurethane varnish, rubbed and polished, see pages 170–72.

Tortoiseshelling

The tortoiseshell finish described on pages 108–9 is a stylized effect especially suited to large surfaces, with its strong directional flow and slightly exaggerated markings. For furniture the whole effect needs scaling down and simplifying if it is to be a background for further decoration. There are several traditional methods of achieving the rich tones and varied markings that belong to the natural shell.

Streaky black and red tortoiseshell

A bold and stunning finish this, often found on early American japanned pieces. It looks superb under gilt decoration, raised or flat, and is best used on furniture, not on walls, where it would be overpowering. The technique is based on the standard one for tortoiseshell, with some modifications. Where possible, paint a horizontal surface, laying cupboards and so forth on their backs or sides on the floor. It is possible to work on a vertical surface, but with less control and comfort. Paint one surface at a time and try to see each surface as a whole, painting it that way, so that the black and red streaks carry on parallel over drawer fronts and doors.

Use dark bronze powder for gilding on top of it, antiqued with earth-coloured glazes, see pages 205–9. This is a finish worth working for, because it is so boldly beautiful, but I would reserve it for pieces with an aristocratic cut to their jib.

Preparation The ground should be smoothly painted with a strong, opaque orange-red. American readers can buy japan colour in just the right shade; otherwise, it can be achieved by tinting flat or mid-sheen oil-based paint with universal stainers [tinting colours] or artists' oil colours in raw sienna and scarlet.

Materials Dark oak gloss varnish stain: this is an essential ingredient – nothing else has the right consistency to stop the streaks running all over the place; black artists' oil colour; pointed artists' brush; 50 mm [2 in] decorators' paintbrush; a wider, clean, dry decorators' brush; white spirit [mineral spirits]; paper tissue.

Method Dilute the varnish stain, about 1 part white spirit to 2 parts varnish. Paint this over the surface. It will bubble excitedly. Fidget the brush diagonally

198

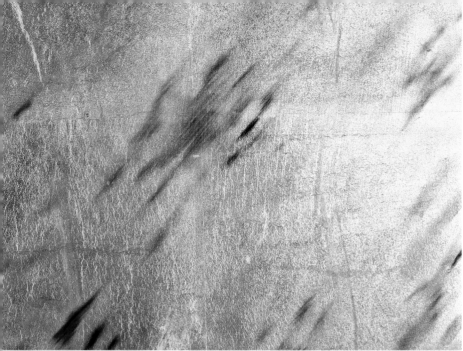

Left Blonde tortoiseshell over metal leaf.

Centre left Rich brunette tortoiseshell achieved by doubling up the standard technique over a metal ground: a second layer of dark oak varnish stain is applied when the first has dried, and is tortoiseshelled in the same way.

Bottom left Black and red streaked tortoiseshell which, *below*, decorates the top of a folding table.

over the wet surface, or dab with crumpled paper tissue, to distress it and remove surplus varnish. Mix a little varnish stain into the black oil colour, to make it flow, and streak it into the wet surface, with a pointed artists' brush, using a sideways rolling motion and jerking it a little as you go, to produce highly irregular black streaks. These should all follow a parallel course in the same direction as your fidgeted diagonals, and should be spaced roughly 5 cm [2 in] apart. Leave the varnish to harden for just a minute or two. Then with the bristle tips of a clean, dry brush, stroke the black streaks gently in the same diagonal direction as they were painted, teasing them out to give wispy ends. Some of the wet black will flow out over the red – this is correct. Now stroke the streaks in the opposite diagonal direction. This opens them out and merges some together, generally loosening up the parallel movement of the pattern. You can work over odd areas further in the same way, to even up the design, but do not go on until all the original red has been darkened over. The colour ratio in this technique should be about three-fifths of the surface black and two-fifths thinned black fading into shaded red. Leave it to dry hard before applying further decoration.

Varnishing   Since the oak stain is a hard gloss finish, further varnishing is not mandatory, but if you want a surface that is alluring to touch, and which will last a hundred years, varnish and rub down and polish in the usual way, see pages 170–72. Do not rub down the tortoiseshell surface itself, or you may leave scars.

Tortoiseshell over metal leaf

On small objects – boxes, frames, trays – where a rich effect is not going to be overwhelming, tortoise mottling over shiny metal leaf looks beautiful. Aluminium leaf makes a cheap and satisfactory substitute for the traditional silver leaf.

Preparation   The object to be leafed should have as smooth a surface as possible.

Materials   Aluminium transfer leaf – as many sheets as needed to cover the object with a little over; goldsize, on which to apply the leaf; dark oak gloss varnish stain; burnt umber and black oil colours; 50 mm [2 in] decorators' paint brush; a wider, clean, dry decorators' brush; pointed artists' brush; cotton wool [absorbent cotton].

Method   See pages 196–97 for how to apply metal leaf. When it is dry, smooth and burnished, give it a coat of quick-drying white shellac. When quite dry, it is ready for tortoiseshelling, which is done just as described on pages 108–9. Do not fret if the overlapped squares of leaf are discerned through the final finish – this is hard to avoid and has its own appeal. But do smooth off any irregularities in the leaf since these are apt to surface through the finish – all right over a large area, but messy on a little box.

For a darkly glowing effect, try doubling up the technique – just enough of the silver shows through to give cool depth, like moonlight filtered through cloud.

Blonde tortoiseshell over metal leaf A blonde version of this technique gives a softer, quite different look. The only difference here is that you use a light oak gloss varnish stain, instead of a dark one. Use your burnt umber and black oil colours a little more thinly and sparingly, and brush out the markings less.

Though not essential, further coats of clear varnish, rubbed and polished, will strengthen the finish.

Varnishing

Vinegar painting or putty graining

This intriguingly named technique is one of many devised by busy country craftsmen of the nineteenth century to meet the increasing demand for 'fancy graining' on furniture and woodwork. Compared with the convincing wood effects produced by master grainers, vinegar painting was a wild parody, but it was quick and easy to do, and the materials were few, cheap and handy. The irony is that to modern eyes the early American pieces in this vigorous style, with their bold patterning, often look more attractive than the expertly grained pieces they were trying to imitate.

It remains a beguilingly simple method of decorating large, flat surfaces rapidly, and looks prettiest in purely decorative colour mixtures: dark over light red, dark over light blue, dark over light green, or any of these colours over off-white. It is a technique that one can really have fun with, since the vinegar medium takes clear, bold impressions of almost anything that comes to hand – a cork, a roll of Plasticine [modelling clay] or the putty traditionally used, crumpled paper or fingerprints. The more playful and bizarre the effects, the better they look, especially on large pieces like chests and dressers, where tight, repetitive patterns could look monotonous. For small things like trays, boxes or table-lampstands, elegant little patterns can easily be built up with close-printed impressions made with a cork or a blob of Plasticine.

Let your imagination rip. There is plenty of time to experiment in the fifteen or so minutes before the colour dries, and if you do not like what you have done, you can easily wash it all off again in a minute. Vinegar-painted pieces, like all those finished in watercolour, need thorough varnishing as a final protection.

The piece to be vinegar-painted should be finished in flat oil-based paint, tinted to the required colour, and when dry rubbed smooth with fine wet-or-dry paper and soapy water. Mid-sheen oil-based paint can be used instead, but it should be rubbed down thoroughly to cut the sheen.

Preparation

Vinegar and sugar (the traditional grainer's alternative to vinegar and sugar was stale ale – by all means use that if you have it to hand); a squeeze

Materials

201

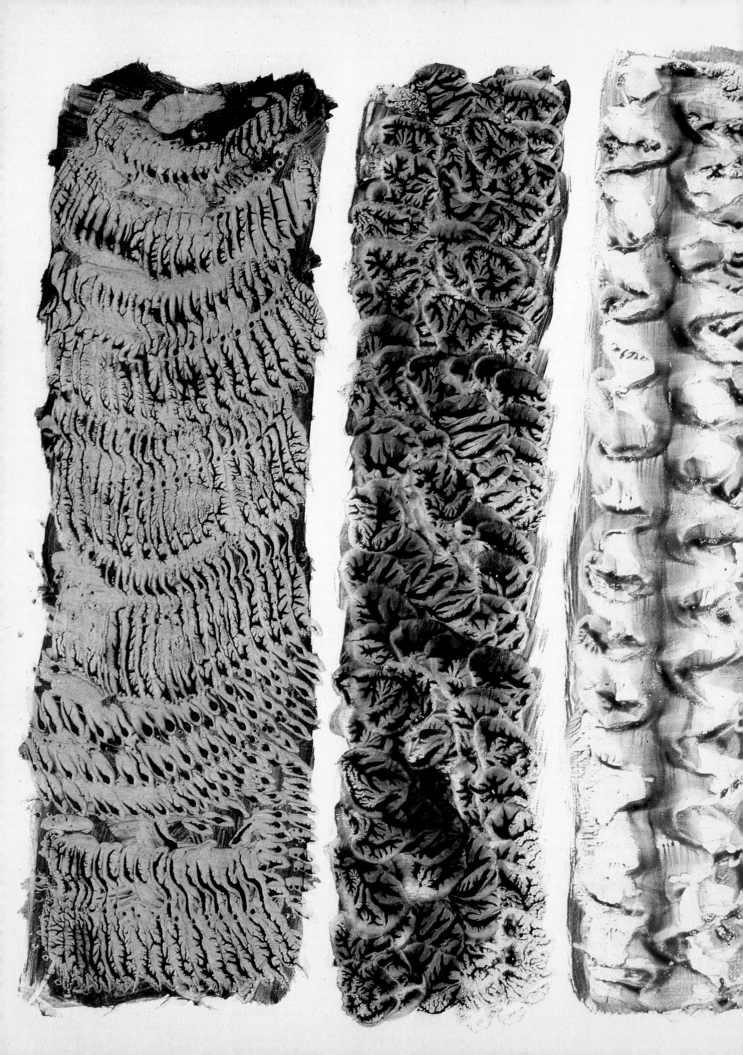

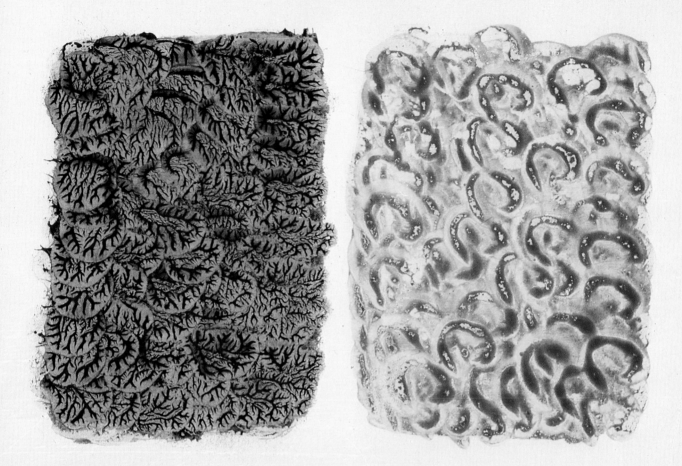

of detergent; dry powder colour: if you cannot get artists' quality powder pigment, children's poster colours will do; 2 jamjars; standard decorators' brush; sundry objects with which to make patterns: for example, a cork, Plasticine or putty, cardboard cut into comb shapes, a rag or crumpled paper.

You can achieve an astonishing variety of effects by pressing a piece of Plasticine [modelling clay] into wet vinegar paint.

Method

Mix half a cupful of vinegar with a teaspoon of sugar and a squeeze of detergent in one jamjar. Take some powder colour and pour this into a second jamjar. Add a little of the vinegar solution and blend it to a paste, then pour in the rest and mix the whole lot together thoroughly. Test the colour on a piece of paper. Hold it vertical for a minute or two – if the mixture runs, it is too thick – dilute with more vinegar and test again.

Before you get to work on your piece in earnest, spend a few minutes experimenting with different effects: brush a little mixture on to it and try stamping, combing and cross-combing (for a woven effect), dabbing with crumpled rag or paper or printing with a coiled roll of Plasticine to leave delicate whorls.

When you have hit on an effective combination, wipe the surface clean again with a rag moistened with plain vinegar. Then brush the vinegar mixture over a large area and begin making your patterns. Its slow drying-speed leaves enough time for patterning an area as large as a dresser door or the side of a chest, but if the colour begins to dry out and gets harder to work, simply brush more vinegar mixture over it, and start that bit afresh. The real problem is knowing when to stop, and being sufficiently disciplined to impose a coherent design over the whole piece.

Brushed out finely, the vinegar solution makes a pleasant semi-transparent wash in itself, which can be used to create a restful space among the wilder patterns.

Varnishing When the vinegar paint is quite dry, in about an hour, varnish it overall with clear semigloss or gloss polyurethane varnish – 2 or 3 coats on a piece that will not get much handling, 4 or 5 on a piece that will. Rub down the last coat lightly with wet-or-dry paper lubricated with soapy water, followed, if you like, by a rub with rottenstone and oil, see pages 170–72. Polish it with a soft cloth for a mellow shine.

Rosewood graining

The quickest, simplest version of rosewood graining consists of dragging a thinned brownish black glaze over a rich brownish red ground. Well varnished, this looks fine over large areas where it would be dauntingly slow to attempt really elaborate graining, or as a base for gold stencils. The other, more complicated version would be suited to something a bit special. It involves more preparation and final coats of transparent colour, so takes longer to do. The reward is a glowing intensity of colour, with something of the depth of natural wood. This longer method is described below.

Preparation The finer the painted surface the more lustrous and convincing the finish. To imitate the dense, finegrained texture of rosewood, most cheap wood or veneered boards will need preliminary filling. Use proprietary wood filler or all-purpose filler [spackle], watered down to paint consistency, or else synthetic gesso, see pages 164–65. Two or 3 coats may be needed, depending on the wood texture and type of filler. Finish with 1 coat of standard undercoat, also sanded when dry.

Materials *Flat red paint* Flat white oil-based paint tinted with 4 parts alizarin crimson, 2 parts burnt sienna and 1 part vermilion artists' oil colours mixed in white spirit [mineral spirits], with a teaspoon of liquid drier (optional).

Transparent red paint The same artists' oil colours as above mixed into clear gloss varnish thinned with white spirit – 3 parts varnish to 1 part solvent.

Dark glaze 4 parts raw umber, 1 part burnt umber and 1 part black artists' oil colours, mixed in equal parts of gloss polyurethane varnish and white spirit. Add a little boiled linseed oil, about $\frac{1}{8}$ as much as the white spirit (measuring in tablespoons helps with these sums), also $\frac{1}{2}$ teaspoon of liquid drier.

Other equipment Orange shellac; methylated spirits [denatured alcohol]; a brush for shellac; a 50mm [2in] decorators' brush for the red paint; a dragging brush or dusting brush, see page 232, or other paintbrush for streaking the glaze; wet-or-dry paper; very fine steel wool; a soft cloth dipped in solvent or vinegar, for removing grease.

Method

Red ground Apply 2 coats of flat red paint. Make this as instructed, so that you have a rich red-brown colour a little thinner than conventional paint. A teaspoon of drier can be added to counteract the slow drying oils in the paint colours. Mix more paint than you need for 1 coat and store the remainder in a jar sealed with clingfilm [Saran wrap]. Follow the flat paint with 2 or 3 coats of the transparent red paint. As usual rub down all but the first 2 coats of paint using wet-or-dry paper with soapy water for the finest, smoothest surface. Now give 2 coats of orange shellac diluted half and half with methylated spirits. This seals off the red body colour, allowing more play with the dark glaze.

Glaze Before streaking, wipe down the red surfaces with a pad dipped in vinegar or white spirit to remove grease and fingermarks. Dip the brush bristle tips into the glaze and test on a piece of paper for colour and consistency. More burnt umber will make a warmer colour, but remember the red base is going to show through the dark streaks. Streak the glaze on by drawing the bristles firmly over the red ground to give even dark fairly parallel stripes. Cover the whole surface in this way. You will find the glaze easy to manipulate, drying slowly enough to allow bits to be gone over again until the graining effect looks right. Don't aim for a ruled regularity, which is hard to achieve anyway – a little build-up of glaze on corners, or where strokes overlap helps give a naturalistic effect. Leave the glaze to harden for at least 24 hours. When it is hard dry, smooth it over using a pad of very fine steel wool and soapy water, following the direction of the graining. This leaves a dulled, but deliciously sleek surface.

Varnish

Apply two coats of clear gloss varnish. Rub the second coat over with steel wool and soapy water and polish with a soft cloth when dry.

Quick method

Fast rosewood graining for less precious pieces requires 3 coats of flat red paint, followed by the dark streaked glaze and 2 coats of varnish. Omit the transparent red and shellac stages altogether.

Antiquing

Antiquing with paint, as distinct from the rough stuff with bunches of keys, chains and dropped bricks that restorers use to match reproduction pieces to time-scarred antiques, is of interest to anyone who paints furniture, because it is a process that not only ages a piece in a trice but makes it look more convincing. Imitating the complex patina acquired imperceptibly over years of use is an effective way to restore character to a refinished old piece and to enrich the appearance of a newer one. It should be done with some understanding of the way in which wear and tear operate naturally on painted surfaces – abrading the finish on parts that get the most handling and along exposed sharp edges, while darkening and softening the parts that collect dust or grime. This is not to say that antiquing should make a piece look merely dirty; if it appears grubby and smeary, the technique has been misjudged. Properly handled, it is more like subtle shading in half-tones, emphasizing structure and modelling, and delicately softening paint texture and colour.

A combination of techniques, sparingly applied, gives a more convincing effect of age and patina than any single one pushed to the limits. Shading with neutral, earth-coloured glazes distressed in some way is one method; a light spattering of brown or black dots another; or give varnish a final rub with rottenstone and leave some of the dusty powder behind in corners and carvings. Brash new gilding looks better dulled, and hard painted lines or stencils can look more appealing discreetly rubbed away here and there. An isolating coat of shellac or varnish over the paint finish will allow you to experiment with various antiquing effects, and rub away the ones you do not like, without affecting the finish.

Antiquing glazes and washes

For antiquing effects, glazes and washes are usually tinted with the duller earth colours, but grey or much-thinned black is sometimes used. A little of the ground colour of the piece can be added to the antiquing glaze to soften the contrast. Glazes are usually thinned to transparency, applied overall and then gently manipulated as they begin to set, to create a softly shaded effect.

Materials

Oil-based paint glazes These give imperceptibly graduated colour. A glaze containing flat white oil-based paint, see page 225–26 will be slightly opaque: for a completely transparent one, blend artists' oil colour with a little boiled linseed oil, a lot of white spirit [mineral spirits] and a

A painted wooden blanket chest *right* from Connecticut, decorated in a combination of freehand painting and sponging, about 1825. The junk-shop piece *left* was recently decorated in the same style, using flat oil-based paint and artists' oils. The effects of age have been reproduced by applying an antiquing glaze of thinned oil-based paint tinted with raw umber.

dash of drier. But these glazes may take as long as a week to dry, which could be the straw that breaks an impatient camel's back.

Washes For instant antiquing on flat or well rubbed-down finishes, use watered-down acrylic colour or gouache, see page 228 for recipes. These do have two disadvantages: they require careful blending to soften the edges, and they do not spread or stick evenly over semigloss or gloss finishes (although adding a little detergent will help). However, being so quick, they deserve a try.

Colours Tint the glaze or wash with earth colours – raw or burnt sienna, raw or burnt umber, plus a speck of black. Raw umber is the standard antiquing colour, because it ages and softens almost every other hue without muddying it. It is a safe standby when in doubt. Raw sienna adds a warmer tinge to glazes applied over cold colours. A speck of black with each intensifies their effect. A little rottenstone mixed with the glaze medium or with polyurethane varnish makes a very convincing, dust-coloured antiquing liquid.

The tint of the glaze or wash should be a couple of tones darker than the base colour.

Other equipment Soft brush; rags or a marine sponge; fine steel wool. Optional: shellac; brush for shellac.

Method *Applying a glaze* With a soft brush, cover all the surfaces of the piece thinly and evenly. The longer the glaze is left to dry before blending and rubbing down, the heavier the antiquing effect. Heavy antiquing looks better on rustic-looking pieces – for this effect, leave a glaze overnight. Light, urbane furniture needs a much gentler nuance of colour, achieved by leaving the glaze until just tacky, and then rubbing it down.

Rub the surfaces gently with a pad of fine steel wool so as to lift the glaze from the parts that would get most wear, while leaving it like a dark bloom over the rest. Rub down harder on places like chair arms and backs that get worn naturally. Rub away, too, over the centre of flat tops, sides and drawer fronts. Any prominent mouldings or raised carving should be rubbed down hard on the highest points, leaving the glaze darker in the recesses. The glaze should blend very gradually from highlight to dark, without streaks or smears or sudden transitions. Even where you have rubbed most of it away, just enough will remain embedded in the minuscule flaws of the paint finish. As you work, stand back from time to time to judge the overall effect. Go gently when rubbing over any applied painted decoration unless you want it to emerge slightly worn and tattered. If you do not, apply an isolating coat of clear varnish or thinned shellac first.

Distressed antiquing glaze The glaze can be finely dragged, sponged or stippled over the paint finish to give more texture than the method described above – see pages 27–32, 37–41 and 175, and 32–37. Rub down a distressed glaze in the same way, when drying or dry, to soften it.

Applying a wash A wash should be sponged on with a rag or sponge, left to dry for a moment or two, and then rubbed with lint-free rags bunched to make a soft pad, and finally blended with fine steel wool. It works best over a flat and slightly absorbent paint finish.

Spatter antiquing

One soon acquires the knack of producing an even shower of colour that does not go all over the room, and spattering is an elegant way to antique a slender, shapely piece in light or medium colours, giving artful shading and emphasis that never looks crude.

Another trick, often used in combination with a heavily rubbed, or dragged, glaze, is to use just a scattering of spots in a strongly contrasting colour – brown or black – to suggest the sort of freckled look one finds on old painted surfaces.

Method

Spatters of neutral colour used to suggest age, or to tone down colour or pattern, should not be applied too uniformly – the effect looks more natural if the spatter colour is denser in some spots than others.

Make up your antiquing glaze or wash as above, but a little thinner. Spatter it with a stiff brush, using the method suggested on page 177, practising first over a piece of paper, before directing the spatter over the painted surface. When it is dry, you can apply a second coat, concentrating on the parts that you want deeply shaded. When the whole surface is quite dry and the colour sufficiently softened, the spatter coats can be blended a little by very gently rubbing down with fine steel wool.

Freckles For a coarse, random spatter, use a little black or sepia drawing ink. If it is permanent ink, either use it over a barrier coat of varnish or shellac, or dilute it a little with water so that blobs and mistakes can be wiped off with rags. Diluted Indian ink, blotted as it falls, leaves faint grey rings that look most convincing on rather delicate pastel finishes. Take a little ink up on your brush, and knock it on a stick with a quick, jerky movement to direct the spatter where you want it. This coarse spatter can be used anywhere on a previously antiqued piece, to add contrast and texture, but go sparingly, as it is an effect that can easily be overdone.

Varnishing

Antiquing is usually done before the final protective coats of varnish. Over antiqued paint the most suitable varnish is matt or semigloss polyurethane – if you use gloss you should rub it down well, to dull it. Use a clear varnish, unless you want to emphasize the antiquing tone further, in which case you can add a little of the same tint to the varnish.

On a special piece, use a rottenstone rub and polish for a very fine finish, see page 172; allow a little of the dusty powder to remain in cracks and recesses.

FURNITURE

Frames, small and large, are good subjects for decorative finishes. Painting and distressing go quickly over such a little area, and the variety of shapes and mouldings is a stimulus to the imagination. A painted finish makes a frame look special and expensive, and can be chosen to flatter and enhance a favourite painting or print.

1 Vinegar painting – the wet vinegar medium distressed with blobs of Plasticine.

2 Graining to imitate birds' eye maple.

3 A deliciously spotted tortoiseshell treatment over a greenery-yallery base.

4 Crosswise graining in sludge green, edge-lined in darker green.

5 A tortoiseshell finish over a ground of bronze powder mixed with gum arabic.

6 Light buff dragging and khaki edge lining.

7 Marbling in tones of sepia.

Fundamentals

Paints, stains and varnishes

A little background knowledge about the way paints, stains, varnishes and so on are made, and why some do some jobs better than others, is helpful to anyone contemplating the bewildering array of cans displayed in most paint shops and do-it-yourself centres. I have not attempted to give an all-inclusive list of every variety of paint available, since many of these fall outside the scope of a book concerned with paint used decoratively rather than functionally, that is, as a protection from weather, rust or damp. Practicality does come into the picture, of course, since no one wants to be left with peeling, flaking walls, but decorative painting is concerned first with the look of a finish, and only secondly with its ability to withstand hot plates, alcohol or dirty little fingers.

I have therefore classified the paints, varnishes and so on in this book simply by their finish – flat, mid-sheen, glossy or transparent. Primers have not been included in these paint charts, since they are not used as final finishes: follow the maker's instructions when using them.

FLAT FINISHES

Type	Composition	Appearance
Undercoat [UK]	Pigments, drying oil, synthetic resins	Perfectly flat, slightly chalky texture. Gives thin, dry coats of colour
Flat paint [UK]; alkyd flat paint [US]	Pigments, drying oil, alkyd resin	Perfectly flat, a thicker and more uniform film than undercoat. Good coverage
Flat emulsion and matt vinyl paint [UK]; latex flat paint and latex flat enamel [US]	Pigments, synthetic resins – usually polyvinyl acetate (PVA) or polyacrylic resin – dispersed in water to form an emulsion binder	Less matt than flat paint, tends to have faint sheen. Gives a thick, slightly plastic coat that looks better in pale colours – dark or bright ones lack resonance
Distemper; limewash; whitewash	Dry pigments, whiting, glue size, water. Limewash contains slaked lime instead of whiting	Absolutely matt. Soft, powdery texture. Good cover and clear colour
Buttermilk paint	Dry pigments, buttermilk	Perfectly flat, but not as powdery as distemper. Exceptionally clear colour since no white pigment is present
Floor paint, liquid lino [UK]	Pigments, drying oil, alkyd resin	Neither quite flat nor shiny. Very thick, rubbery coat. Dull colour

The secret of using paint finishes successfully today, when there are so many formulations available, seems to me to lie in intelligent experiment plus common sense. There may be several ways of achieving a similar effect – you must decide which one best suits your taste, the sort of wear it can expect to get, and the amount of time and money you can invest in it.

Look here for information about paints with matt, or flat, finishes. The most versatile and stylish one is the oil- or alkyd-based 'flat paint', which can be used on walls, woodwork, floors and furniture. Widely available in the United States, it is difficult to find in the United Kingdom, but British readers can use standard undercoat as a satisfactory substitute, although it will require protective varnishing. Incidentally, American enamel undercoater should not be used as an alternative to flat paint, since it is quite a different animal, drying to a hard, slightly shiny film, instead of a matt, chalky softness.

Flat finishes

Solvent	Uses and advantages	Disadvantages
White spirit [mineral spirits]	Not intended to be a finish but has come to be used as a readily available substitute for flat paint. Cheap, easy to apply, dries in 8 to 12 hours. Highly pigmented. Pleasant, matt, dry texture, takes colour well. Can be bought anywhere	Needs matt varnish protection on surfaces that get scuffed. Poorer quality undercoat is more absorbent than flat paint, and so takes decoration less cleanly and smoothly
White spirit [mineral spirits]	Can be used for all interior purposes, with varnish protection on floors. The best flat finish available – opaque and elegant. Takes colour well, dries in 6 to 12 hours. A favourite with decorators, either as a paint finish or as a glaze (thinned with solvent and with added drier). Alkyd flat paint is widely available in the United States	In Britain, obtainable only through specialist paint suppliers. Rather thick film, which shows scuff marks. Use over undercoat only
Water	Quickest, cheapest, easiest and fastest drying finish for walls and ceilings. Can be bought anywhere. May be tinted with stainers [tinting colours]. Can be used as a base for some decorative finishes, or thinned with water to make a wash. Recoatable in about 4 hours, washable. Can be used on new plaster or rough, porous surfaces such as brickwork. Has almost no smell. Some types have been formulated for one-coat coverage for speed, and in gel form for no drips	Too absorbent to take most decorative finishes really well. Not as soft or matt as distemper. May soil unless protected with matt varnish. Not recommended for steamy rooms such as kitchens and bathrooms; cannot be used on bare metal, since it will corrode it. Different brands should not be mixed. A wash of thinned emulsion paint dries very quickly
Water	Very cheap – you can even make it yourself, see page 45. Easy to apply, delicious texture and particularly pretty colours. Can be tinted with gouache, dry pigments or stainers. No smell, easy to clean up, can be scrubbed off. Ideal for colourwashing or for any simple rustic effects	Difficult to buy, since the do-it-yourself market rejects it as being short-lived, non-washable and susceptible to damp. It is also liable to rub off and must be removed before applying oil-based or emulsion paints on top
Water	The easiest paint to make – just mix dry pigment into buttermilk, bought or homemade, with a little fungicide to prevent mould growth. Good, clear colour. Easy to apply; smells nice (not cheesy). Used in many early American stencilled rooms and still good for the purpose	Better in paler shades – bright or dark colours look streaky. Non-washable and susceptible to damp. Must be removed before overpainting with oil-based or emulsion paint
White spirit [mineral spirits]	Exceptionally tough, hardwearing paint especially formulated for floors, wood or cement. Needs 2 coats at most, since it has great staying power. Can be applied with a mop for speed – the floor must be completely clean and dry. Washable, does not require varnishing. Ideal where a strong, cheap coat of colour is called for – bathroom, landing. Fairly widely available	Poor colours, although they can be intermixed for greater subtlety. Not to be used with stainers or other pigmented media

Mid-sheen finishes

These are the finishes that come midway between flat and gloss. If you can get trade eggshell, do, because it is a splendid all-purpose paint – strong and non-absorbent with an elegant soft sheen when dry. It makes the ideal base for many of the decorative finishes described in this book, particularly for glazes. Unfortunately, it has become hard to find, except through specialist paint suppliers, but one of the oil- or alkyd-based mid-sheen paints formulated for the do-it-yourself market will serve almost as well.

MID-SHEEN FINISHES

Type	Composition	Appearance
Trade eggshell [UK]	Pigments, synthetic alkyd resin, drying oil	Like thin cream, with a smooth, hard opaque surface and a dull sheen. The most elegant finish for woodwork
Oil- or alkyd-based mid-sheen, semi-sheen, silk or satin finish paints [UK]	As previous entry, but modified for faster application and opacity in one coat. Some may be thixotropic (gel-based), for non-drip, non-stir properties	Much as previous entry, but thicker, slightly less attractive appearance
Oil- or alkyd-based velvet, eggshell, low-lustre and satin finish paints [US]	As previous entry	As previous entry. The list is in ascending degrees of sheen, i.e. satin is the shiniest
Silk or satin emulsion, silk or satin vinyl [UK]	As for matt emulsion but with more PVA added to give extra sheen and washability	A soft but definite sheen
Latex velvet, eggshell, low-lustre and satin finish paints [US]	As previous entry	As previous entry. The list is in ascending degrees of sheen

GLOSS FINISHES

Type	Composition	Appearance
Semigloss, gloss, high gloss and hard gloss paint and enamel	Usually based on oil-modified alkyd resin, lightly pigmented with finely ground, highly opaque pigment	Brilliant gloss, hard, tough surface film. Semigloss is less shiny
Vinyl enamel [UK]; latex enamel [US]	Based on polycrylic resin plus pigments, which means it is water-thinned. May be thixotropic (gel-based) for convenience	Shiny, but not brilliant, gloss
Aerosol spray-on paint and enamel	Pigmented nitro-cellulose medium or acrylic lacquers	Very hard, shiny, thin surface film – as on car bodywork
Floor enamel [US]	Available in both alkyd-based and latex types	Alkyd type has a high gloss finish, latex type a mid-sheen

214

Gloss finishes

Glossy paint finishes are seldom used in high-class decorating circles, except perhaps for children's playrooms, kitchens, bathrooms and other places where hard-wearing properties are the first requirement, since they are the toughest of the finishes and can be washed down frequently.

In decorative painting, a shiny finish – such as that on 'lacquered' walls or furniture – is usually achieved by applying coats of gloss varnish over flat or mid-sheen paint, rather than a simple one-step shiny paint. The result is a more subtle texture, with greater colour depth and richness.

Solvent	Uses and advantages	Disadvantages
White spirit [mineral spirits]	As a finish for interior walls, woodwork and furniture, as a base for decorative treatment of any kind on a smooth, sound surface. Takes tinting well. Gives a fine, non-porous, porcelain texture that looks and feels nice, wears well and is lovely to paint on	More expensive than other mid-sheen paints and obtainable only through specialist suppliers. Takes 12 to 16 hours to dry, and needs careful brushing on and laying off
White spirit [mineral spirits]	As previous entry, though with a less satisfactory texture. Needs less brushing out. Easily available	Gives less coverage. Professional decorators prefer trade eggshell
White spirit [mineral spirits]	As previous entry	
Water	Very fast-drying, recoatable in 2 to 4 hours. More suited to walls than woodwork. Can be used as a base for decorative finishes. Tougher than matt emulsion	Not as hard-wearing as oil- or alkyd-based paints
Water	As previous entry	As previous entry

Solvent	Uses and advantages	Disadvantages
White spirit [mineral spirits]	Gloss is for any surface requiring a strong, shiny, dirt-resistant finish. Hard gloss is for places that get extra wear – exterior woodwork, kitchen fitments. These paints are all long-lasting, moisture-resistant, easy to wipe down, reasonably proof against scratching and chipping	Must be used over proprietary undercoat for proper colour solidity. Takes between 12 and 16 hours to dry. Shiny finish exaggerates surface flaws, so thorough preparation is essential. Hard gloss finishes contain less oil; this makes for harder surface film, which chips more since it is less elastic
Water	Dries in 2 to 4 hours. Easy to apply	Not as durable as oil-based gloss finish, nor as hard and shiny
Benzol, acetone	Sold at do-it-yourself centres for touching up car bodywork. Can be used for spraying large, simple stencil patterns, where it can give a softly graduated colour effect	Expensive, tricky to use evenly, apt to spatter everywhere. Unpleasant smell; requires special solvent for cleaning up. Can be applied over emulsion [latex] or acrylics, but not over oil-based paints
Alkyd – white spirit [mineral spirits]; latex – water	Fairly quick-drying. Hard-wearing. Latex floor enamel can be applied to damp (though not wet) surfaces	Quite expensive

Transparent finishes

The old-fashioned types of varnish, such as rubbing varnish and carriage varnish, have been superseded by polyurethane varnish, which is easier to apply and less likely to yellow. Shellac in its various forms is occasionally used as a finish, although it is not very tough. It is better used as a barrier coat in furniture painting to isolate a particular layer and to help to build up a smooth surface to take further decoration.

TRANSPARENT FINISHES

Type	Composition	Appearance
Polyurethane varnish	Clear or pigmented alkyd/polyurethane	Clear, only a faint yellow compared with older type varnishes. Matt, semigloss or gloss according to need
Shellac; button polish or orange shellac; white polish; knotting [knot sealer]	Natural shellac in alcohol	Transparent. Shellac itself is yellowish-brown; button polish or orange shellac is orange, as is knotting; white shellac or white polish, made from bleached shellac, is almost clear
Proprietary floor seal	Alkyd resin or polyurethane base	Clear, slightly yellowy, hard and shiny surface film
Goldsize, japan goldsize	Rapid-drying, short oil varnish with high drier content	Clear, slightly yellowy

STAINS

Type	Composition	Appearance
Water stains	Water-soluble dyes or pigment usually bought in powder form to be dissolved in boiling water and diluted to strength required	Clear, vivid colour, as with all colour using water as a medium. Can be bought in wood colours or made up from dry pigments (household dyes will do) and water
Spirit or alcohol stains	Spirit-soluble dyes in shellac solutions thinned with methylated spirits	Come in woody and other colours. Less brilliant than water stains
Oil stains	Pigments in oil or synthetic resin	More transparent than water stains
Varnish stains	Mixture of oil stain and hard-drying oil varnish	Thicker, more opaque colour, which is less flattering to woodgrain
Wax stains	Can be made by mixing artists' oil colours into beeswax or paraffin wax melted in a double boiler; allow it to cool to a soft paste. Shoe polish is a handy readymade alternative	Transparent and shiny, with a rich, waxy gloss after polishing

216

Stains

There are a number of stains available for use on wood. You can also try applying fabric, carpet or leather dyes, made up according to the instructions on the packet but with only half the recommended amount of water. Another idea is to make your own wax stains – they give a marvellously rich glow to any wood, but require a lot of elbow-grease to keep them looking good.

Solvent	Uses and advantages	Disadvantages
White spirit [mineral spirits]	The most versatile, easily used and widely obtainable varnish for most decorative purposes – walls, woodwork, floors and furniture. Hard, clear, almost non-yellowing, strong. Touch-dry in 6 to 8 hours, should be left overnight before recoating. Easier to use and cheaper than traditional varnishes	Not as elastic as traditional varnishes, less suited to rubbing down
Methylated spirits [denatured alcohol]	Almost instant-drying sealing varnish for use in French polishing and as a barrier coat in furniture painting. Button polish or orange shellac can be used over metal leaf to simulate gold. Knotting is used to seal knots in new wood	Must not be bought in large quantities, as it does not keep well. Does not make a strong final finish, since it is not alcohol- or water-proof
White spirit [mineral spirits]	Easily applied, with rags as well as brushes, water-thin protective coat for decorated floors. Hard and durable if 4 or 5 coats are superimposed	Needs dry conditions. Not as tough, and slower-drying than polyurethane varnish
White spirit [mineral spirits]	Used as adhesive for metal leaf, and as medium for some quick-drying paints. Very fast-drying – 'quick goldsize' especially so – almost clear, easily applied	Brittle, becomes tacky at temperatures above 43°C [110 °F]

Solvent	Uses and advantages	Disadvantages
Water	Cheap, easily applied, allow great range of colour effects, especially on light-coloured, close-grained woods	Lift woodgrain, so need rubbing down. Surface must be free from grease. Penetrate unevenly on porous softwoods, need sealing with shellac or goldsize before waxing
Methylated spirits [denatured alcohol]	Best stains for use under French polish, penetrate deeply. Ideal for oily or hard, fine-grained woods. 2 or 3 pale coats give better results than 1 bright or dark one	These dry so fast that they are difficult to apply evenly. They may lift the grain a little
White spirit [mineral spirits]	Easier to apply than spirit stains, give a more even, less penetrating colour. Ideal for softwoods, will take any superimposed clear finish when quite dry	Slow-drying, must be left overnight
White spirit [mineral spirits]	Cheap, easily available and quick to apply	May be brittle. Very hard to remove
White spirit [mineral spirits]	Easy to apply – simply rub in and burnish. Give a mellow, antiqued look – restorers use shoe polish on pieces of non-matching woods	Hard work to polish, harder still to remove. Will not take any other finish on top

Making colours

Although these days a paint stockist can mix most of the colours that you are likely to require, learning how to mix your own precise colours and tones is nevertheless an excellent way to develop a colour sense – probably the definitive step toward becoming a decorative painter. With a small stock of concentrated pigments and a tin of basic white, or coloured paint, you can mix up most of the colours you are likely to need on the spot, as you require them.

Pigment, or raw colour, is available in many forms – as loose powder, compressed blocks or cakes, or bound with oil, varnish, and other media

Type	Composition	Appearance
Powder paint, artists' quality	Finely ground pigments	Matt colours, vivid, clear (unless mixed with white) and intense
Poster colours	Powdered pigments, not so finely ground as artists' quality	Matt, rather thick colours, not so vivid or rich as above
Universal stainers [universal tinting colours or colorizers]	Concentrated colours bound with oil	Very strong, matt colours, clear unless mixed with white
Artists' oil colours	Highly refined pigments bound with linseed oil	Rich, varied and finely differentiated colours, matt if thinned with white spirit, otherwise the oil gives some sheen
Gouache colours	Concentrated colours in a water base	Particularly sharp, clear and fresh matt colours of great staining power. The white-pigmented base gives more opacity than ordinary watercolours
Artists' acrylics	Pigments in a water-soluble polyacrylic base	Watercolour-clear when thinned; juicy *impasto* used neat. Matt colours, a little less vivid than gouache
Signwriters' colours [bulletin colours]	Pigments in quick-drying varnish medium	Matt, intense, opaque colours
Japan colours [US only]	Pigments in quick-drying varnish medium	Similar in texture and appearance to signwriters' colours, but in superior hues
Casein colours [US only]	Pigments in casein medium	Matt, powdery, opaque, very intense but hard colours unless mixed with white casein paste

in tubes, jars and tins. One rule to bear in mind is that like should be mixed with like – thus solvent-thinned pigment with solvent-thinned paint, water-thinned pigment with water-thinned paint. But this is only a rough guide, since there are exceptions – universal stainers [tinting colours], for instance, which are bound with oil, can be used to colour almost any type of paint except gloss emulsion. However, do not add more than $\frac{1}{4}$ litre [$\frac{1}{2}$ US pint] of stainer or oil colour to 4 litres [1 US gallon] of paint, or the mixture may start to gel.

Most of the colours listed below can be obtained from artists' suppliers; many paint suppliers stock universal stainers.

Solvent	Uses and advantages	Disadvantages
Water	Can be used to tint oil- or water-based paints, or varnishes. Dark colours stain wood. Pale colours make lovely washes	In most cases they need a protective finish to prevent the colour washing off. Can be difficult to dissolve completely
Water	Cheap, easily soluble colours	Limited range of colours in rather crude shades, thick pasty texture
White spirit [mineral spirits]	Cheap, highly concentrated colours that mix easily and quickly with almost every type of paint or glaze. Limited colour range, but intermixing gives much greater colour possibilities	Rather hard colours that tend to need a touch of their complementaries to soften them. No raw umber in some ranges
White spirit [mineral spirits]	Decorators use these for a lot of smaller scale decorative painting, because the colours are excellent, comprehensive and the texture is fine. Can be used thinned with solvent or oil, or mixed into clear varnish	Not cheap. Relatively slow-drying as compared with acrylics
Water	Really beautiful colours, especially in strong pastel range. Ideal for colouring water-based paints and washes. Mix easily. Concentrated, so a little goes a long way. Used often in past to decorate furniture, on a gesso ground	Expensive
Water	Amazingly quick-drying, so stencils or painted decoration can be finished in one session. Can be used diluted with water for a transparent effect, or in a special acrylic medium for transparency with body, or straight from the tube for thick, opaque cover	Expensive. Less rich textured than oil paints. Less mellow colours too. Dry so fast they need constant wetting in use (a retarding medium is also available). There tends to be wastage because of this very rapid drying
White spirit [mineral spirits]	Very opaque, thick colours, so give good coverage with one coat – ideal for floor stencils. Large colour range	Not so rich or mellow as artists' oil colours. Need varnishing to bring out the colour
White spirit [mineral spirits]	Rapid-drying, good flat texture and excellent colour range. Ideal for furniture decoration and any stencilling; use thinned with solvent, and with clear varnish – to bind colours and improve adhesion	Give reasonable opacity when thinned, but not full coverage. Though touch-dry in less than half an hour, must be left considerably longer before applying second coat or this dissolves the first
Water	Use thinned with water only (about 1 part colour to 2 parts water) for a wash, or added to white casein paste or other water-thinned paints for creamier and pastel shades. Dry very quickly, excellent opacity and therefore economical to use. Hard finish	Must be left for some time and sealer applied before painting on second coat. Tend to solidify if not used up quickly. Unpleasant smell

Colour mixes

If the ability to combine colours inventively is a largely instinctive process, knowing what to mix with what to get a specific colour is something you pick up as you go along, making mental notes (or, better still, written ones) of happy combinations you come across. Here are some rough indications of how to get what decorators call 'good' (that is, gutsy, lively, distinguished) colours. It would take a book to go into the subject in depth, but half a loaf is better than no bread and you may find these notes helpful. Some artists' colours contain tiny amounts of harmful chemicals – the chrome range, for instance, have some lead. If you don't want to use them, say in a child's room (and in some countries they are hard to find anyway), ask your artists' supplier for substitute colours made from organic pigments.

Don't be frightened of experimenting with colours. But don't mix large quantities while you are experimenting; a few spots of likely shades on a plate or sheet of paper can be worked together with a fingertip to give a good idea of what they look like when mixed. Once you know you are on the right lines, it's safe to proceed with larger quantities.

Don't run away with the idea that there is only one way to get a particular colour. If your requirements are not too precise, if you are after a warm earthy red rather than the exact shade to match a piece of fabric or an old tile, there are probably half a dozen or more ways of arriving at a colour in that general area. Most interesting colours in decorating are, literally, mixed-up ones, but there are exceptions, generally in the pure and paler shades: for example, a mix of cobalt blue, white and a tinge of yellow does not give quite the same cerulean tint as the paint of that name, nor do cobalt, chrome yellow and white give quite the lettuce green of chrome green. But it is nevertheless sound practice and training to begin with a fairly limited standard range – such as the universal stainer [tinting colour] range plus raw umber and crimson – and see how far you can get by combining these in various proportions. Some decorators swear that they can get all the colours they want this way. Others insist that some shades can be prepared only from bought pigment. But you can always add these special colours to your collection as you need them.

Dirty, or off-whites Raw umber plus white gives a cool greenish grey, a very safe colour. A spot of yellow ochre warms it, a dot of black intensifies it – easy on the black, though, as a little goes a long way. Yellow ochre plus white gives a warm cream, which is lightened to ivory by adding more white. A dot of umber shades it to parchment. White plus black gives the coolest grey, known as French grey.

Pinks You can make good pinks by mixing burnt sienna with white. This gives delectably warm, but not sissy pinks, like faded cottage walls. Adding more white lightens them, a little yellow ochre (earth colours are mutually compatible) gives an apricot cast, a touch of cobalt and black takes them toward terracotta. Venetian red and white also make a good strong pink. Use the crimson reds to get sky blue pinks, because they contain a little blue.

Reds It is rare to find a really good commercial red, they tend to be too brash and hurtfully bright. But it is easy to mix your own. Composite reds always work better on walls, floors, woodwork and furniture than pure ones, in my experience. Burnt sienna, alizarin crimson and a little cadmium scarlet, vermilion or bright red stainer give a magnificently vital, rich but not hard red with a brownish cast. More crimson makes it deeper, cooler, more sienna makes it earthier and browner, more vermilion brings it nearer to old lacquer. Raw sienna mixed with scarlet gives a soft, warm orangey red. Venetian red, red oxide and Indian red are all good strong sympathetic slightly brownish reds. Add a dash of cadmium or one of the other red reds above to make them brighter and less earthy. A spot of cobalt blue softens red red; umber will age it.

Yellows Yellow ochre and Indian yellow are both warm friendly earthy yellows, with a creamy tone when mixed with white – nice wall colours. Chrome yellow is a hearty, sunflower colour with more orange to it. It is also the best, most opaque, one for mixing other colours, but if you prefer a lead-free substitute, use cadmium yellow or organic arylamide yellow. For the sophisticated yellow often used for lacquer wall effects, try a glaze of mixed yellows: lemon chrome (or cadmium lemon), chrome and a touch of burnt umber, over primrose: white tinted with chrome yellow.

Greens Chrome yellow mixed with black gives a strong, drab olive green much used in the eighteenth century, on furniture chiefly. Adding white to this produces a Dijon mustard colour. Cobalt and chrome yellow again give a green of olive tone. Indigo, chrome yellow, raw umber and white give strong greens paling to duck egg green as one adds more white. Some greens cannot be successfully mixed, and must be bought as colours. The sharp, light yellow-greens, such as lettuce or young beech leaves, are a case in point – chrome green is the juiciest (an organic substitute is arylamide yellow with phthalo blue). Sap green is another good one.

Blues Cobalt is the blue most used by decorators, a nice clean but soft blue, less strident than ultramarine and Prussian. A little umber dulls it, chrome yellow warms it, a spot of red knocks it back. I like indigo, a very distinguished blue, darker than cobalt, with purply sloe-berry overtones. Mixed with the above colours it gives similar, but moodier effects. To make the ethereal cerulean/thrush egg blues, best start with a bought cerulean, adding a spot of chrome and raw umber, or yellow ochre, to give the greeny cast, and then lots of white. For a terrific, vibrant stained-glass sort of blue, with green tones, use ultramarine or Hortensia, but don't try to get it in one, use a tinted glaze in one tone over a ground coat of another. To make a very pure violet, mix ultramarine and crimson, rather than Prussian blue and scarlet, which both contain yellow.

221

Reds

Burnt Sienna + Alizarin Crimson +

Cadmium Scarlet =

Raw Sienna + Cadmium Scarlet +

Venetian Red + Cadmium Scarlet =

Pinks

Burnt Sienna **+ White =**

Mixed Pink No 1

Mixed Pink No 1 +

Yellow Ochre = Mixed Pink No 2

Mixed Pink No 1 +

Black +

Cobalt = **Mixed Pink No 3**

Crimson + White =

Yellows

Yellow Ochre + White =

Lemon Chrome + Chrome + Burnt Umber

222

Greens

Chrome Yellow + Black =

Mixed Green No 1 + White = Mixed Green No 2

Chrome Green★   Sap Green★

Raw Umber + Chrome Yellow + Indigo +

White =

Blues

Cobalt +

Raw Umber =   Chrome Yellow =   Scarlet =

Cerulean +

Chrome + Raw Umber +

(varying amounts of) White =

★These bright colours cannot easily be mixed, but may be bought from artists' suppliers

223

Glazes and washes

Glaze is a word that crops up repeatedly in this book, as it is a key ingredient of so many decorative finishes, for walls, woodwork and furniture. Broadly speaking, a glaze is a semi-transparent film of oil-based colour, while a wash is a semi-transparent film of colour diluted with water. There are subtle visual differences between the two; oil-based colour tends to be richer, sleeker and more transparent, while colour in water is fresher, purer, still diaphanous, but 'brushier' looking. Both can be used over painted surfaces to soften, enrich, and otherwise modify the colours beneath.

Glazes, being slower drying, are more easily manipulated than washes. Classical painting used glazes routinely, to float delicate tints on hair and skin, deepen shadows, suggest the fragility of flower petals, the lustre of pearls. In the decorative field, the concept of colour seen through transparent colour has countless applications. Woodgrainers and marblers use glazes, and washes, to suggest patina, depth and the complex layering of colour and markings in natural materials. Furniture restorers often use murky tinted glazes to give an instantly 'aged' look, suggestive of centuries of use and wear, to newly painted furniture. Decorators are always using glazes, and, to a lesser extent, washes, to get subtle colour effects or for distressed finishes that give a soft, rich, spaced out look to any interior. A wash has a particularly vivid spontaneous effect. Whether as a glaze or a wash, transparent colour over white gives glowing pastels; over toning colour it gives a richer version of the same; over contrasting colour it creates effects of astonishing sophistication considering the simplicity of the means. Glazes are a help, too, in keeping one's colour options open – wall colours that have come out wrong can almost always be corrected by applying a suitably coloured glaze on top, distressed or plain. Since thin glazes can be applied over walls in less than half the time it would take to repaint them, this is a trick worth knowing.

Glazes

Depending what goes into a glaze, it can be shiny or matt and more or less transparent, according to the amount of white pigment it contains in proportion to the other ingredients. It should not be confused with that other transparent medium, varnish. Varnish is designed to give a hard, clear, protective coating and though it is sometimes tinted (as with lacquered walls or in furniture decoration) to give a glazed effect, it is not suited to distressing.

Glazes can be bought ready made, requiring only tinting, or they can be made up from basic ingredients that you may well have on hand.

Transparent oil glaze

Transparent oil glaze, sometimes sold under the name 'scumble glaze' in Britain [glazing liquid or glaze coat in the United States], is a ready-mixed glaze base requiring only the addition of colours. These can be the powerful universal stainers [tinting colours], which are strong, versatile, cheap and come in a basic range, or artists' oil colours, which offer a wider range of colours, but are more expensive and slower drying. Proprietary glaze is convenient and easy to work with, being formulated to 'stay put' and yet remain workable, or wet, long enough to allow decorative effects to be applied over quite a large area at a time.

Depending on what brand you buy, transparent oil glaze varies in appearance from thick golden honey to white hair cream. Brushed out on a wall, it goes transparent. It can be used full strength, but gives softer and subtler effects and goes much further when thinned with solvent – white spirit [mineral spirits]. It dries to a slight sheen, which varies according to how much it is thinned, and can be used for all wall finishes except colourwashing. Some decorators object to it on the grounds that it yellows with time, and that its 'stay put' ingredients give it a slightly hard-edged quality – although this can be modified by thinning it down well. On balance, it is probably the easiest formulation for beginners to use and be sure of getting professional results. It makes techniques like dragging, stippling and rag-rolling quite straightforward.

Recipe for homemade oil glaze Blend together in a suitable container: 1 part boiled linseed oil, 1 part pure turpentine, 1 part drier and (optional) add a little whiting – about a tablespoon to a litre [1 US quart]. All these ingredients are readily available from most paint suppliers.

Because transparent oil glaze is obtainable only through specialist paint stores or shops that cater for the decorating trade, it seemed a good idea to include a recipe for making up your own. This traditional formula gives an exceptionally soft and transparent colour on walls and dries to a definite sheen. A little whiting can be added to give 'body' for dragged painting, where it helps prevent the stripes from blurring. The snag to this glaze is that owing to its high linseed oil content it takes a good while to dry hard, a couple of weeks in some weather conditions.

Ground Transparent oil glaze should be used over an oil-based ground paint, preferably with an eggshell (mid-sheen) finish, otherwise flat, see pages 213–14. Oil glaze can be used over emulsion [latex], but because this type of paint is porous it will be more difficult to apply and the finished effect won't be so slick.

Thinning Commercial oil glazes can give good results thinned as much as 1 part glaze to 2 parts solvent – white spirit [mineral spirits]. But they vary in thickness, so it is best to start with equal quantities of glaze and solvent, and step up the amount of solvent gradually, testing as you go. The thinner the glaze, the faster it will 'set up', or harden, so this is something to take into account too. Be prepared to experiment a little – on painted boards, or the wall surface itself. The glaze can be wiped off again, with a rag moistened with solvent, if you are not satisfied. Homemade glaze should not need further thinning, but use pure turpentine again if it does.

As the name suggests, this glaze is really just very heavily thinned oil-   **Thinned paint glaze** based paint – usually white paint, tinted – and it is what most decorators use for distressed finishes, partly I suspect for convenience, and partly because they prefer its quite matt, uninsistent texture and the soft effect it gives when manipulated with brushes, rags, sponges, and so forth. Because it contains some white, opaque pigment, it is never fully transparent, like the proprietary oil glazes, but this adds to the softening effect. Beginners might find it a little more difficult to work with, because it dries a great deal faster than oil glaze, and is more affected by the weather and room temperature. A little practice soon gives one confidence, however, though applying and distressing it really is a two-person job, so make sure you conscript a helper. That done, your decorative finish goes like lightning.

For a completely matt texture the ideal paint to use is 'flat white'. Flat white is a trade paint in Britain, and not always easy to find. In this case a standard white undercoat can be substituted. In the United States alkyd flat paints are readily available, and would be the obvious choice, see page 213.

Trade eggshell paint (or any oil or alkyd mid-sheen finish, see page 214) is an alternative, always remembering that it will dry to a noticeable though faint sheen. It is not quite so elegant as flat paint as a background for pictures and furniture, but on the other hand it has definite practical advantages in rooms where a washable, tough finish is the prime requirement – bathrooms, nurseries, corridors and hallways, for instance.

Ground For the best results decorators use a flat glaze over walls finished with eggshell (mid-sheen) paint. Experience has shown this to be the ideal marriage – the eggshell surface is smooth and non-absorbent, helping the glaze to stay 'open' or workable that bit longer and allowing more subtly textured effects to be achieved. Use this ground for an eggshell glaze too. It is perfectly possible to use a thinned paint glaze over flat paint, or even emulsion [latex], and still get delicious results, but they won't have quite that immaculate professional touch.

Thinning Use paint glaze thinned about 1 part paint to 2 parts solvent – white spirit [mineral spirits]. Again, start with equal parts and then add more solvent, testing the results as you go. If the consistency seems too runny to distress properly, try adding a little drier. I add about 1 teaspoon to $\frac{1}{2}$ litre [1 US pint] of thinned glaze.

This mixture can be dragged, ragged, stippled, sponged, and so on. For colourwashing, thin the glaze a great deal more – about 1 part paint to 8 or 9 parts solvent.

Tinting a glaze Transparent oil glaze and thinned paint glaze are tinted with universal stainers [tinting colours] or artists' oil colours. To tint oil glaze, squeeze a blob of colour into a cooking tin or pan and add a little white spirit [mineral spirits] to dissolve it, stirring hard to blend. Next spoon in a

226

cupful or so of the unthinned glaze and stir well, then add the rest of the glaze, still stirring continuously. Thin as recommended.

If you are using thinned paint, again stir the dissolved colours into full-strength paint and then add white spirit to thin as instructed above. Use white paint for mixing pale glazes, and a colour somewhere near your final effect for dark ones. See pages 218–19 on making colours.

Keep the glaze coat to a thin film or it will tend to run. Take up a small amount of glaze on the bristles of a decorators' paintbrush, brush it on quickly and then smooth out lightly with the bristle tips. On a very smooth, eggshelled surface, glaze is more easily applied with a bunched-up rag – *smeared* on thinly. If a thinned paint glaze seems too fluid, add a little drier to help check the drips – about 1 teaspoon per $\frac{1}{2}$ litre [1 US pint] of thinned paint. You must expect more mess with a thinned paint glaze than with transparent oil glaze, however.

Where a glaze threatens to dry off too quickly, as it might on a hot day, one solution is to add a little boiled linseed oil – again a teaspoon to $\frac{1}{2}$ litre [1 US pint] should do the trick. But remember to allow longer for overall drying, which may take a couple of days. The end result will also be slightly shinier.

Though professional decorators, in Britain, tend to use trade paint formulations, such as trade eggshell and trade flat white, I find one can substitute do-it-yourself paints for glazing without any special problems arising. Do-it-yourself paints are faster drying as a rule, which one might expect to cause problems in keeping a wet edge going. But in practice I haven't found this happening. If anything the difficulty seems to be to keep the glaze from running together, blurring dragged stripes and sponge prints. This is probably due to a self-levelling ingredient in the paint; if it happens, leave the wet glaze to harden for a moment or two before dragging, sponging or whatever. Try the glaze out in a dark corner before launching off round the room.

Applying a glaze

Washes

Washes of colour diluted in water are trickier to apply and handle than oil-based glazes, just as watercolour is a more difficult medium to excel in than oil painting, but they give such luminous colour and airy transparency that some decorators find them irresistible. Walls washed over with clear pale colours have something of the ethereal freshness of old fresco painting.

A wash can vary in consistency, all the way from emulsion [latex] paint thinned to milkiness, to a mixture that is little more than tinted water, with a dollop of emulsion for 'body'. Thinned and tinted emulsion paint can be dragged, rag-rolled, sponged or slapped on every whichway for a dappled look. The effect is never going to be as delicately modulated and controlled as if you were working with an oil glaze, but it gives a streaky homespun effect and powdery texture that you might prefer. Use the ultra-thin colour washes for loose brushing on only, not distressing, as they dry too quickly to manipulate. Besides, colour applied like this has its own built-in distressing, a brushy quality, especially when the colours are at all strong. If you dislike this effect stick to pale colours – yellows, pinks, pale blues and greens.

Decorators invariably use the purest colours for making washes, favouring gouache colour especially for its vividness. I find powder colours, either artists' quality or the poster colours sold for children's use, make effective washes too, a bit cruder looking perhaps, but nicely reminiscent of those casually coloured old interiors one sees in France and Italy. Acrylics, also soluble in water, are another possibility, but more expensive.

Ground A wash must be applied over an emulsion [latex] base paint; it will simply trickle off an oil-based ground. The flatter the emulsion base is, in my experience, the more absorbent, and therefore the easier it is to apply an emulsion wash over it. On a mid-sheen finish a thin wash may run together in droplets or streaks, so that a beautifully dragged section of wall runs into broad blurry stripes after a few minutes. Where walls already have a mid-sheen emulsion finish, best forget about colour washes and choose a thinned paint glaze instead.

Thinning An emulsion [latex] wash suitable for such techniques as dragging, rag-rolling and sponging should be thinned about 1 part paint to 3 or 4 parts water. Use a much thinner version for colourwashing: 1 part paint to 8 or 9 parts water.

For the 'tinted water' washes, the proportions of colour to water will obviously depend on how vibrant you want the effect to be. A rough guide for a wash of this kind is to use 1 small tube of gouache to $\frac{1}{2}$ litre [1 US pint] water, plus a tablespoon of emulsion paint.

Tinting washes Tint thinned emulsion [latex] washes with gouache colours, acrylic colours, powder colours, or with universal stainers [tinting colours]. Dissolve the colours in water, then mix with full-strength emulsion paint before thinning as required. The critical part of mixing your own colours is to mix *thoroughly* – undissolved specks of pure colour will emerge as huge streaks on a wall.

Applying a wash The most important thing when applying a decorative finish over or with emulsion [latex] paints is to make sure the surface beneath is well cleaned of grease and grime. Water-thinned colours simply won't stick over greasy patches. Use a weak solution of a proprietary paint cleaner, or, if you feel the finish might rub off, wipe over with warm water plus something to cut the grease – ammonia, washing soda, vinegar. Rinse afterwards, and leave to dry out completely before putting on a wash.

The most likely problem in applying a wash, especially in hot weather, is that the wet edge will dry, leaving hard lines of colour that are difficult to disguise. If this happens, adding a spoonful of glycerine – bought from

228

a chemist or druggist – to the wash can help keep the paint 'open' and workable longer. Start with a teaspoon per $\frac{1}{2}$ litre [1 US pint], adding a little more if needed.

When you apply two washes on top of each other for richer colour, leave the first wash to dry for at least 24 hours before painting on the second, or the top colour may lift off the one beneath leaving bald patches of base coat showing through, which are not easy to touch up afterwards. If you do have this problem, try sponging on the second wash, using quick pecky movements so as not to disturb the wash below. If the second wash runs and drips too much, add a little more emulsion to make it thicker. You can drag one wash on top of another, but again brush it on quickly and lightly and try not to go over the same place too much or the wash beneath will soften and begin to lift.

When a glaze or wash doesn't behave quite as you expected, don't panic. Check through various possible explanations – is it too thin, too thick, is the base coat too slippery or greasy, is the weather exceptionally hot or are the walls damp? If it doesn't brush out evenly and looks messy, try sponging or ragging the wet glaze to even it up – use a sponge dampened with solvent if a glaze has hardened. Really patchy effects can be rescued by sponging a darker or lighter colour on over the top, glazing overall with a creamy colour, dragging with a darker colour, or adding a stencilled border. But before resorting to any of these measures, try hanging a few pictures and putting back some furniture – it is amazing how re-populating the space relegates the wall finish to second place. All decorators agree that some of their happiest effects have been part accidental – some unforeseen reaction that they had the wit to take advantage of.

Don't panic

Brushes

A brush consists of a handle, bound at the stock [block] to a filling previously 'set' in resin or vulcanized rubber. The filling is usually referred to as the 'bristles', although in fact bristle is only one of the available fillings, which also include hoghair, badgerhair, oxhair and synthetic filaments. The indications of quality in a brush are a thick, silky, flexible filling, well bonded to a handle that is nicely balanced and pleasant to hold. If you compare an expensive brush with a cheap one, you will find that the latter usually has a wider stock running between the bristles, giving the illusion of a generous clump.

There is no doubt that working with well-made equipment, scaled to the job in hand, is pleasurable and fast. If you can, go to a trade supplier, rather than a do-it-yourself centre, and ask the experts which brushes they recommend. It pays to buy the best brushes and look after them well – a good brush will last twice as long as a cheap one and always do the job more efficiently.

It is worth investing in a proprietary cleaner, too, to keep brushes in shape. Since these cleaners contain stronger solvents than white spirit [mineral spirits] they clean the bristles faster. Amateurs invariably skimp the tedious soaking and rinsing ritual, so the use of a brand cleaner will counteract any laziness here. Keep plenty of well-washed glass jars for the purpose – with the lid screwed on tightly to prevent evaporation, the same jar of cleaner can be used over and over again. Brushes used in emulsion [latex] paint must be cleaned immediately after use – either in soap and warm water or in proprietary cleaner. Never leave a brush standing in solution for days on end – this bends the bristles and weakens them. One professional dodge is to drill a hole through the handle, and slot a wire or pencil through, laying it across the top of the jar so that the bristles are suspended in the cleaner without touching the sides of the container, which will bend them. It is worthwhile drilling holes anyway, since hanging brushes from nails is a good way to store them when not in use. When you finally complete your painting, wrap the brushes in brown paper, newspaper or foil and lay them away flat for longterm storage.

To extract loose hairs from a new brush, bang it hard a few times on the edge of a horizontal surface, such as a table, or spin it between the palms of your hands. The hairs will soon work their way into sight, so you can easily pick them out of the brush.

STANDARD DECORATORS' BRUSHES All you need for large-scale decorative painting, at least to begin with, are three or four standard house-painting brushes in various sizes. Start with the minimum and buy more as special needs arise. A really wide, thickly bristled brush (1) is essential for walls – 100 or even 125 mm [4 or 5 in] wide, depending on how large your hands are. For painting woodwork, use a medium-sized brush (2), between 50 and 75 mm [2 and 3 in] wide.

For fiddly 'cutting in' on such surfaces as window frames and door panels, a small brush (3) – 25 mm [1 in] or narrower – is easier to control and you can use it for painting furniture and any other precision work, too. Brushes cut on the diagonal (4) are also available for cutting in.

BRUSHES FOR VARNISHING Varnishing requires scrupulous cleanliness in the brushes used, so buy and keep particular ones for that purpose only. It needs only a small amount of old paint to work itself down into the bristles to wreck any varnishing job undertaken with the same brush. You can use a standard decorators' brush, or try one of the specialized oval varnish brushes (5) that come in five widths between 25 and 75 mm [1 and 3 in] across. Professional painters often prefer these because the luxuriant crop of bristles holds more varnish and brushes it out more smoothly.

Most varnishes, whether synthetic or natural-resin based, should be cleaned off with white spirit [mineral spirits] or a proprietary cleaner, but check the instructions printed on the varnish tin to make sure. After thoroughly cleaning your brush, wrap a paper cover, held in place by a rubber band, round the bristles to keep them trim – splayed-out bristles make varnishing harder.

ARTISTS' BRUSHES The type of brushes sold for painting in oils, watercolour and so on are essential for fine decorative work, and can be found at any good artists' suppliers. The handiest are the soft-bristled type (sable, camel hair, squirrel) with a tapering point (6 and 7), although for *impasto* effects you may need blunt-ended brushes in the coarser hoghair (8). Faced with a watercolour and an oil brush with bristles of the same type and shape, I prefer the former because the handle is shorter, making it easier to use for painting designs on furniture – a long handle keeps tripping you up. As you gain experience you will discover the inbuilt strokes of a particular brush – many of the leaf- or comma-shaped strokes used in folk decoration are shaped by the brush itself. Thus, a fine, tapering brush will make thin leaf shapes, and a fatter brush, broad, juicy ones.

Buy three or four artists' brushes in sizes ranging from pencil fine (No 2A), to around half the girth of a shaving brush (about No 10). Sable is the softest, richest bristle, but it is expensive, so you could get one or two small sable brushes, and use cheaper bristle like camel or squirrel for the larger sizes. Store artists' brushes like kitchen spoons, standing them handle down in a jar.

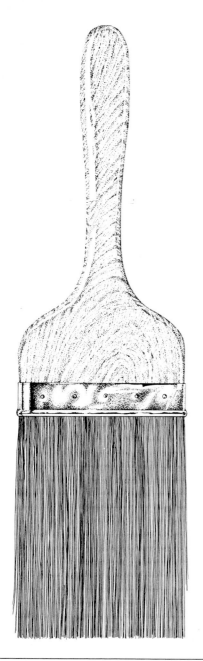

GRAINING BRUSH As the name suggests, this brush is used in woodgraining, the spaced bristles breaking up a glaze into finely spaced stripes, as in dragging. It does save time, although some painters still prefer to use a standard paintbrush, applying stronger pressure to make controlled brushmarks. It is only available from specialist suppliers, but a homemade version can be made by cutting out spaced

DUSTING BRUSH A very useful and versatile brush, and not expensive. It has soft, medium-length bristles set in a wooden handle. Decorators use it for stippling work on a small scale – furniture, woodwork – but it is not large enough to use for stippling walls, unless you are very patient and determined. You can also use it for softening and smoothing out glazes and washes, although it won't give as soft a bloom of colour as the badger. It should be cleaned very carefully – never immerse the stock [block] in cleaner, since the brush is designed to be used dry and solvent will dissolve the resin, causing the bristles to drop out.

clumps of bristle from a long-haired and not too thick decorators' brush.

DRAGGING BRUSH The brush most often used to produce a dragged finish is known, rather alarmingly, as a flogger. In the United States – where, however, it is very difficult to obtain – it goes under the name of a walnut stippler. It works best with transparent oil glaze, which its evenly spaced bristles control to a remarkable degree, producing crisp, fine 'tram lines' almost effortlessly. The flogger, which is stocked only by specialist paint dealers, comes in various sizes, from 75 to 150 mm [3 to 6 in] wide. It is expensive, because it is handmade from top-quality bristles with carefully selected split ends that help to produce the dragged effect, and

since the bristles are also unusually long and flexible, one can keep up an evenly light but firm pressure down the length of a wall. Many professional decorators prefer the softer effect given by using a wide standard bristle paintbrush with a tinted flat-paint glaze, and dispense with a special dragging brush, but I do feel that it is decidedly helpful to less skilled operators, since it makes a slick, expert-looking finish much easier to achieve. Anyone planning to drag a large wall area – a staircase or several rooms – would find buying the largest flogger a good investment: the wider the strip of wet glaze you can drag at a time, the faster you can go, and there is

also less likelihood of the 'wet edge' of glaze hardening unworkably as you move down the wall. Smaller standard brushes or floggers are convenient for dragging woodwork or furniture.

Like all aristocratic brushes the flogger needs careful upkeep. Rinse it out after use in a flat tray with lots of cleaner or white spirit [mineral spirits], changing the fluid if necessary, and wipe it on a soft clean cloth. Then wash it out again in warm water with pure soap (detergent is considered drying to high-class bristles – treat them like your own hair). Shake it out and dry it flat on newspaper in a warm room, never on a radiator.

OVERGRAINER This little tool, which comes in sizes between 25 and 100 mm [1 to 4 in], with pencil-like clumps of soft bristle, is used to put in darker grain and other fine detail on a dry, previously grained surface. Unlike the larger brushes, it is used to brush colour on rather than drag it off, and it gives precise, fine lines. The stock [block] acts as a handle so that the fingers grasp it close to the bristles to give greater control.

MOTTLER A small brush similar to the overgrainer, but bushier, used to distress and mottle graining glazes, and flirt in highlights. It, too, comes in 25 to 100 mm [1 to 4 in] sizes.

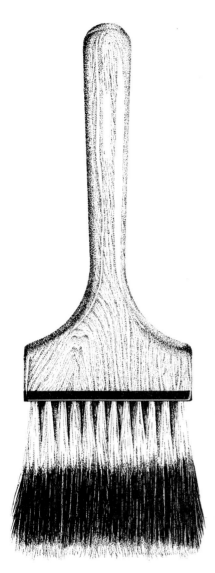

BADGER SOFTENER OR BLENDER Made of the finest, softest badgerhair – and as a result very expensive – this brush should be used only with watercolour paints. It is required only for the subtler decorative finishes, but anyone lucky enough to have one will probably want to use it in a variety of ways, because it is a superb brush to handle. Traditionally used in woodgraining, to spread a wash very thinly and evenly, or to produce woody striations of colour, it is also useful in other decorative work, giving washes a particularly soft, transparent effect. Try it for going over them to soften brushmarks, blotches and hard edges into a gauzy veil of colour. After use, rub it dry on a clean cloth, wash it out in tepid water with pure soap, rinse it thoroughly, shake it well and dry it flat at room temperature.

STIPPLING BRUSH This rectangular brush comes with alternative detachable handles: a long one for stippling walls, and a grip that fixes across the back for work on ceilings. No longer obtainable in the United States, elsewhere it is available in sizes between 100 by 75 mm [4 by 3 in] and 175 by 125 mm [7 by 5 in]. It is used to lift off fine flecks of paint or glaze to produce the typical freckle of stippled colour, and although expensive, nothing else does the job quite so well. But you can improvise

fairly successfully with an old, worn clothesbrush, a man's soft-bristled hairbrush or a roller. In some countries you can obtain stippling brushes with coarser bristles, which produce stronger markings – mottled rather than freckled. Rubber stipplers used to be sold in Britain, but are hard to track down today; they give a slightly bland effect, since they tend to beat the colour back into the surface.

Rinse your stippling brush out in cleaner, and dry and store it bristle-side up.

LINING BRUSH A number of brushes can be used for painting thin decorative lines. I frequently use a fine sable artists' brush, which does the job adequately provided you have a steady hand. A signwriter's lining fitch (11), with bristles cut diagonally, has the advantage that you can use it in conjunction with a straight-edge – no trained painter does, but never mind that.

More exotic is the sword liner (10), with the bristles tapering to a point like a Japanese beard. This is considered to be the best brush for making fine, straight lines freehand but you need a lot of practice to do this with confidence. After the usual cleaning routine, its scimitar-like bristles require a little extra maintenance to prevent them from drying with a kink. With damp fingers, stroke the hairs to a curving point (professional painters spit on them) and apply a trace of soap to act as a setting agent. Store the sword liner flat.

FITCH A round brush with fairly stiff bristles, the fitch (12) comes in sizes ranging from 4.5 mm [$\frac{1}{5}$ in] to about 30 mm [$1\frac{1}{4}$ in] wide. Traditionally used to paint fiddly detail, it is also suitable for spattering, stippling decorative details or painting small-scale stencils. Since it is not expensive, it is a useful brush to have on hand.

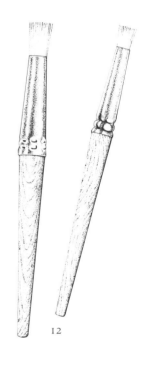

10

11

12

9

STENCILLING BRUSH (9) This looks like a man's shaving brush – short and fat, with stiff hoghair bristles, blunt cut at the end. It comes in various sizes, between 6 and 50 mm [$\frac{1}{4}$ and 2 in] across. You can use an ordinary paintbrush, which is perfectly adequate for simply brushing on colour, but a proper stencilling brush gives an extra delicacy and richness. What it does in

effect is to stipple colour through the stencil-holes, giving the pattern a softer, bloomier texture, and, because the colour is jabbed on, it is less likely to creep underneath the stencil, so the design comes out with a crisper edge. Stencilling brushes need thorough cleaning after use, to prevent yesterday's colour leaking into today's stencil.

If you have difficulty tracking down a *bona fide* stencil brush, a hoghair artists' brush, which also comes in a wide variety of sizes, is the best substitute. Choose one with bristle ends cut as straight as possible – a very slight dome at the end will not matter. Buy it from a good artists' suppliers. You can also use a fitch, see above.

234

List of suppliers

If you cannot find paints and painting sundries at your local dealer, the dealers and manufacturers on this list will be able to help you. All of them offer a mail order service. Artists' suppliers appear in italics.

Reading list

The following list combines books of inspirational photographs – particularly Scandinavian ones – with practical guides to a few of the techniques, as well as a couple of out-of-print decorating books that I have found especially useful. Old-fashioned books of this kind are always worth a look since they often carry helpful and out-of-the-way technical information about paint finishes.

Bishop, A. and Lord, C. *The Art of Decorative Stencilling* (Viking Press, New York, and Thames & Hudson, London, 1976)

Fales, D.A., Jr. *American Painted Furniture 1660–1880* (E.P. Dutton, New York, 1979)

Friis, L. *Gemmemøbler* (The National Museum of Denmark, Copenhagen, 1976)

Lipman, J. *American Folk Decoration*, reissued as *Techniques in American Folk Decoration* (Dover Publications, New York, and Constable, London, 1972)

Lipman, J. and Winchester, A. *The Flowering of American Folk Art* (Viking Press, New York, 1974, and Penguin, Harmondsworth, 1977)

Michelsen, P. *Frilands Museet: The Danish Museum Village at Sorgenfri* (The National Museum of Denmark, Copenhagen, and Humanities Press, Atlantic Highlands, 1973)

Mickelsson, H. and Svensson, I. *Friargåvor – och annat grant* (LTs Förlag, Stockholm, 1977)

O'Neil, I. *The Art of the Painted Finish* (Morrow, New York, 1971)

Pearce, W.J. revised by Hurst, A.E. *Painting and Decorating* (Charles Griffin, London, 8th edition, 1963)

The Practical Home Decorating and Repairs Illustrated (Odhams, London, 1952)

Schlee, E. *Volkskunst in Deutschland*, translated as *German Folk Art* (Kodansha International, Tokyo, New York and San Francisco, 1980)

Stalker, J. and Parker, G. *A Treatise of Japanning and Varnishing* (London 1688; new edition, Academy Editions, London, 1971; new edition in 3 vols, Transatlantic Arts, Levittown, 1968)

Steensberg, A. *Danske Bondemøbler* (Nyt Nordisk Forlag Arnold Busck, Copenhagen, revised 1977)

Waring, J. *Early American Stencils on Walls and Furniture* (Dover Publications, New York, and Constable, London 1968)

Index

Index prepared by Eleanor van Zandt.

Page numbers in *italic* refer to illustrations. Where illustration and caption appear on different pages, the reference is to the page bearing the caption.

Author's acknowledgments

Writing this book has been an unusually rewarding, if hectic, experience, largely because of the generous involvement of so many people along the way. Their lively interest did more than anything else to keep the initial excitement of the project fizzing away from first to last. Heartfelt thanks, in the first place, to that talented decorator, good friend and patient mentor, Graham Carr, who somehow always found time to elucidate, demonstrate or advise, and whose painterly use of colour and adventurous taste remained a mark for us to aim at. Likewise many thanks to Stewart Walton, whose loyal collaboration made lighter work of experiment and research alike, and whose meticulous craftsmanship brought all aspects of paint magic not only down to earth but within reach. Thanks, too, to my sister Miranda, whose decorative gifts found new expression in some charming original stencil designs. Among the many busy people who helped with problems and queries, often of an arcane sort, I would particularly like to thank the staff of Ploton for their time and assistance. To the many friends who helped in one way or another – Sandy, Buffo, Douglas, Alison, Barney, Steve Trundle and Pat Gallagher – thanks all round. Joan Shorter gets my special order of merit for allowing her bathroom to play guinea pig. I must not forget to thank Les and Tim from across the way, who have risen to the occasion magnificently, passing on messages, sorting out problems and acting as an unofficial answering service. On the production side, I must thank Frances for thinking up the idea, Felicity and Karen who kept my unruly text in firm but enlightened control, and Marianne and Roger who provided the magic ingredient of colour by way of pictures; and a special thank you to Antonia Gaunt whose flair as a stylist is matched by a talent for turning fantasy into fact.

Lastly, I should like to thank all my children, who have been so forbearing.

Publishers' acknowledgments

The Publishers would like to thank Berger Paints, Freshwater Road, Dagenham, Essex RM8 1RU for their help and support; Graham Carr for all his advice; Colefax & Fowler Designs Ltd, 39 Brook Street, London W1; The Department of Furniture and Woodwork, Victoria and Albert Museum; John Dinkel of the Royal Pavilion, Brighton; E. P. Dutton Publishers for permission to reproduce photographs from *American Painted Furniture 1660–1880* by Dean A. Fales Jr; Elizabeth Macfarlane and Felicity Binyon Hand Painted Stencils, 6 Polstead Road, Oxford; Ina Brosseau Marx; George Old; Isabel O'Neil; John Wilson Jr of Floorcloths Inc., P.O. Box 912, Severna Park, Maryland 21146; Stephen L. Wolf; and everyone who allowed them to photograph their houses.

(FLP = Frances Lincoln Publishers, d = designed by, p = painted by, t = top, b = bottom, l = left, r = right, c = centre)

PHOTOGRAPHS

6, 10–11, 14–15 Photo Bay Hippisley/ © FLP/d&p Jocasta Innes and Stewart Walton, stylist Antonia Gaunt
18–19 Photo James Mortimer/ © FLP/d&p Graham Carr
26 Photo Bay Hippisley/ © FLP/d&p Graham Carr
30–1 Photo Bay Hippisley/ © FLP/p Marianne Dormsjö
34–5 Photo Bay Hippisley/ © FLP/d&p A. and M. Turner
38–9 Photos Bay Hippisley/ © FLP/p Peter Farlow
43 Photo James Mortimer/ © FLP
46–7 Photos Bay Hippisley/ © FLP/d Angela Huth, p Hutchins & Green, Oxford
50–1, 54 Photos James Mortimer/ © FLP/d&p Graham Carr
59 Photos reproduced by permission of The American Museum in Britain, Bath
70–1 Photos James Mortimer/ © FLP/d&p Elizabeth Macfarlane and Felicity Binyon
74–5 Photo courtesy The Henry Francis du Pont Winterthur Museum
78–9 Photo James Mortimer/ © FLP/d&p Lincoln Seligman
79 Photo Bay Hippisley/ © FLP/d&p Lincoln Seligman
82–3 Photo Bay Hippisley/ © FLP/p Stewart Walton
86 Photo Bay Hippisley/ © FLP/d Prue Lane Fox, p John Cox and Martin Lane Fox
91 Photo James Mortimer/ © FLP/d Stanley

Falconer, p Graham Carr and Jean Hornak
94 (tl) Photo James Mortimer/ © FLP/d&p Lincoln Seligman (tr) Photo James Mortimer/ © FLP/d Stanley Falconer, p Graham Carr and Jean Hornak (bl) Photo James Mortimer/ © FLP/d Judith Gardiner, p Graham Carr and James Smart (br) Photo James Mortimer/ © FLP/d&p Graham Carr
95 (tl) and (tr) Photo Bay Hippisley/ © FLP/d Prue Lane Fox, p Martin Lane Fox (bl) and (bc) Photo courtesy The Royal Pavilion, Art Gallery and Museums, Brighton (br) Photo Bay Hippisley/ © FLP/d&p Ian Grant
98 Photo James Mortimer/ © FLP/d Stanley Falconer, p Graham Carr, trompe l'oeil by George Oakes of Colefax & Fowler Designs Ltd
101 Photos Bay Hippisley/ © FLP/p Stewart Walton
102–3, 106–7 Photos Bay Hippisley/ © FLP/p Graham Carr
110–11 Photo James Mortimer/ © FLP/d Colefax & Fowler Designs Ltd, p Graham Carr
114 (t) Photo Herbert Wise, from *Rooms with a View*, published by Quick Fox (b) Photo Elizabeth Whiting & Associates
115 (t) Photo Herbert Wise, from *Rooms with a View*, published by Quick Fox (b) Photo James Mortimer/ © FLP/d Stanley Falconer, p Jean Hornak
118 Photo Michael Boys/Susan Griggs
122 Photo James Mortimer/ © FLP/p Graham Carr
126 (t) Photo James Mortimer/ © FLP/d&p Elizabeth Macfarlane and Felicity Binyon (b) Photo Syndication International/d&p Lyn le Grice
127 Photo Charles Wiesehahn

130 (l) Photo James Mortimer/ © FLP/d&p Elizabeth Macfarlane and Felicity Binyon (r) Photo Syndication International/d&p Lyn le Grice
131 (l) Photo James Mortimer/ © FLP/d&p Judith Gardiner (r) Photo James Mortimer/ © FLP/d&p Graham Carr
134–5 Photos Bay Hippisley/ © FLP/p Stewart Walton
138 Photos Bay Hippisley/ © FLP/p Graham Carr and Stewart Walton
139 Photo James Mortimer/ © FLP/d Colefax & Fowler Designs Ltd, p Graham Carr
140–1 Photo Bay Hippisley/ © FLP/p Stewart Walton
143 Photos Richard Lowell Neas
146–7 Photos Ron Solomon/ © FLP/floorcloths by Floorcloths Inc.
150–1 Photo Bay Hippisley/ © FLP/d&p Jocasta Innes and Stewart Walton
154–5, 158–9 Photos © E. P. Dutton
162 Photo Hilding Mickelsson
163 (tl) and (r) Schöner Wohnen/Camera Press (b) © E. P. Dutton
166 Photo Karl-Erik Granath
171 Photo Tim Street-Porter/Elizabeth Whiting & Associates
174 Photo Herbert Wise, from *Rooms with a View*, published by Quick Fox
179 Photos Bay Hippisley/ © FLP/p Graham Carr
183 (t) Photo Bay Hippisley/ © FLP/p Graham Carr (l) Photo Bay Hippisley/ © FLP/p Jill Saunders (r) Photo Bay Hippisley/ © FLP/p John Fowler and Graham Carr
186 (t) Photo Bay Hippisley/ © FLP/p Salvatore Titian (bl) Photo Bay Hippisley/ © FLP/p Jocasta Innes (br) Photo Bay Hippisley/ © FLP/p Colefax & Fowler Designs Ltd
187 (tl) Photo Bay Hippisley/ © FLP/p Colefax & Fowler Designs Ltd (tr) Photo Bay Hippisley/ © FLP/p Graham Carr (bl) © E. P. Dutton (br) Photo Bay Hippisley/ © FLP/p Graham Carr
194 Photo Bay Hippisley/ © FLP/p Jocasta Innes and Stewart Walton
199 (tl), (cl) and (r) Photo Bay Hippisley/ © FLP/p Graham Carr (bl) Photo Bay Hippisley/ © FLP/p Stewart Walton
202–3 Photo Bay Hippisley/ © FLP/p Stewart Walton
206 Photo Bay Hippisley/ © FLP/p Jocasta Innes and Stewart Walton
207 © E. P. Dutton
210–11 Photo Bay Hippisley/ © FLP/p 1 and 5 Stewart Walton, 2 Judith Gardiner, 3 Graham Carr, 4 Nicholas Herbert, 6 and 7 Brenda Hodgson
222–3 Photo Bay Hippisley/ © FLP/d Roger Walton p Stewart Walton

ARTWORK

1, 2–3, 4–5, 29, 41, 44, 48 Alicia Durdos
60–1 Jennie Smith
62 (t) Miranda Innes (cl), (cr) and (b) Stewart Walton
63, 64–5 Miranda Innes
66–7 (l) and (r) Jennie Smith (c) Miranda Innes
70–1 Jennie Smith, after a design by Elizabeth Macfarlane and Felicity Binyon
73, 80–1, 88–9, 92, 96 Jennie Smith
97 (t) Miranda Innes (b) Jennie Smith
105 Alicia Durdos
125 Tim Foster/Aardvark Design
128–9 Jennie Smith
132–3 Miranda Innes
145, 149, 150–1, 180 Tim Foster/Aardvark Design
185, 190–1 Alicia Durdos
195 Tim Foster/Aardvark Design